INSIDERS'GUIDE®

OFF THE BEATEN PATH® SERIES

Off the Beaten Path®

NINTH EDITION

indiana

A GUIDE TO UNIQUE PLACES

PHYLLIS THOMAS

INSIDERS'G

GUILFORD, CONNECT

AN IMPRINT OF THE GLOBE PEQUOT PRESS

D1119719

The prices, rates, and hours listed in this guidebook were confirmed at press time. We recommend, however, that you call establishments to obtain current information before traveling.

To buy books in quantity for corporate use or incentives, call **(800) 962–0973** or e-mail **premiums@GlobePequot.com.**

INSIDERS' GUIDE®

Text design by Linda R. Loiewski
Maps by Equator Graphics © Morris Book Publishing, LLC
Drawing on page 35 rendered from photograph by Helen K. Link
Illustrations by Carole Drong
Spot photography throughout © Visions of America, LLC / Alamy

ISSN 1539-459X
ISBN 978-0-7627-4414-5

Manufactured in the United States of America
Ninth Edition/First Printing

For Bill and Alan—
I was twice blessed.
For Luisa, Eva, Larry, and Ace—
thank you for adding four
more blessings to my life.
And now there's Jordan—
the blessings continue.

Contents

Acknowledgments

If I were to personally thank each person who has contributed in some way to the writing of this book, the list would be longer than the contents of the book itself. I talked to many people during my travels throughout Indiana. They were, without exception, warm, gracious, and kind. We met as strangers and parted as friends. I am grateful to each and every one of them.

Introduction

Ask almost anyone what images Indiana brings to mind, and—after a long pause—he or she is likely to mention the Indy 500, cornfields, and perhaps the steel mills of Gary. This book has been written to advise you that Indiana offers a lot more than auto racing, corn, and steel.

State highways and byways lead to some of the finest travel gems in the nation. There are natural wonders and man-made splendors, irreplaceable slices of Americana and futuristic marvels, places stately and sublime, others weird and wacky—a cornucopia of attractions, restaurants, and inns that for the most part lie off the well-trodden paths and are overlooked by major travel guides.

The most difficult part of writing this book was deciding not what to include but what, because of space limitations, to leave out. Therefore, what you will find within these pages is merely a sampling of all that Indiana has to offer. It is my sincere hope that this book will help awaken your sense of adventure and encourage you to seek out other such places on your own.

Indiana's geography is sometimes a bit puzzling to strangers. They are often surprised to learn that South Bend is one of the northernmost cities in the state, while North Vernon is not far from the Ohio River, which forms Indiana's southern boundary. Along the Ohio-Indiana border on the east lies West College Corner, while way down in the southwest corner, just across the Wabash River from Illinois, there's East Mt. Carmel. And the towns of Center, Center Square, and Centerville are about as off-center as you can get.

To further confuse the traveler, a look at the official state road map (available free from the Indiana Department of Transportation, Room N755, 100 North Senate Avenue, Indianapolis 46204; 317–232–5533) reveals four Buena Vistas, three Fairviews, three Georgetowns, three Jamestowns, two Klondykes and one Klondike, three Mechanicsburgs, four Millersburgs, five Mt. Pleasants, three Needmores, and four Salems. Pairs of towns with the same name are too numerous to mention, but would you believe two Pumpkin Centers? No wonder the U.S. Postal Service insists on zip codes!

But never mind—this book will at least put you in the right county. And if you do get lost, you're likely to meet such warm, friendly people along the way that you won't mind it a bit.

If all else fails, you can call the Indiana tourism hot line for help. Dial (800) 677–9800 or (800) 289–6646 to request free printed materials that will help you plan your itinerary. The toll-free numbers are answered twenty-four hours a day and are accessible from anywhere in the contiguous United States. You can also visit their Web site at www.visitindiana.com or write to the Indiana Office of Tourism Development, 1 North Capitol Street, Suite 100, Indianapolis 46204; (317) 232–8860.

Happy wandering!

Key to Lodging Prices (average double occupancy in season)

Inexpensive: Under $70

Moderate: $70–$130

Expensive: $131–$190

Very Expensive: More than $190

Key to Restaurant Prices (per average dinner entree)

Inexpensive: Under $10

Moderate: $10–$20

Expensive: More than $20

Central Indiana

Indianapolis, at the hub of central Indiana, is crisscrossed by more interstate highways than any other metropolitan area in the country. Interstate 65, Interstate 69, Interstate 70, and Interstate 74 run through the heart of the city, and Interstate 465 encircles it. More than 800,000 people live in Indianapolis (affectionately known to Hoosiers as Indy), making this the twelfth largest city in the country.

Leave Indy behind and head in any direction, and in minutes you will find yourself in the heart of rural Indiana—open fields that seem to stretch forever, patches of scenic woodland, and charming small towns rich with local color.

Central Indiana offers a mix of the best Indiana has to offer—big city excitement, pastoral serenity, and the friendly folks for which the Hoosier State is justly famous.

Boone County

The entire community has pitched in to help restore the glory of yesteryear to Zionsville's downtown business district, and its citizens have succeeded admirably. Now known as the **Zionsville Colonial Village,** it's filled with interesting shops to explore. At **Lilly's Boutique Gallery,** the selection of unusual

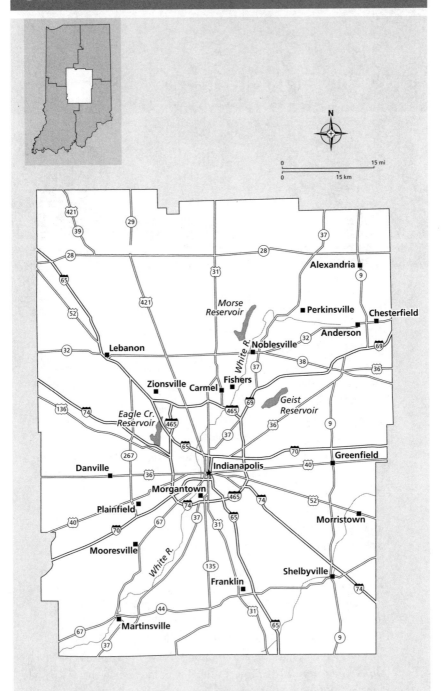

apparel and accessories includes many items by some 200 artists. Three vine-covered buildings filled with a variety of unusual items and nestled in a garden setting are known collectively as ***Brown's on Fifth.***

The Cedar Street Shoppes, a cluster of thirty-five individual shops under one roof, are located at the corner of Cedar and Main Streets; they feature a wide variety of arts and crafts. At 10 North Main Street, the ***Dragonfly Gallery*** sells Indonesian imports. The art of one of our nation's most famous and most successful artists can be seen at the ***Thomas Kinkade Gallery.*** At the ***Village Parfumerie,*** you can choose from among more than 130 essences to create your own personalized perfume or puchase fragrances and bath products imported from France.

Brick-paved Main Street, which runs through the heart of the village, is decorated with gas lamps and planters. For additional information contact the Greater Zionsville Chamber of Commerce, 135 South Elm Street, P.O. Box 148, Zionsville 46077; (317) 873–3836.

AUTHOR'S FAVORITE ATTRACTIONS/ EVENTS IN CENTRAL INDIANA

Camp Chesterfield
Chesterfield
(765) 378–0235
www.campchesterfield.net

Circle of Lights
Indianapolis; November
(317) 237–2222

Conner Prairie Pioneer Settlement
Fishers
(317) 776–6000 or (800) 966–1836
www.cornerprairie.org

**Eiteljorg Museum of
American Indians and Western Art**
Indianapolis
(317) 636–9378

Eiteljorg Museum Indian Market
Indianapolis; June
(317) 636–9378

The Giant
Pendleton
(765) 778–2757

Heartland Film Festival
Indianapolis; October
(317) 464–9405

Indianapolis Children's Museum
Indianapolis
(317) 334–3322 or (800) 208–5437
www.childrensmuseum.org

Indiana Medical History Museum
Indianapolis
(317) 635–7329

Indiana Transportation Museum
Noblesville
(317) 773–6000

Indy 500 Festival Parade
Indianapolis; May
(317) 614–6400

Memorial Day Ceremony
Crown Hill Cemetery
Indianapolis; May
(317) 925–8231 or (800) 809–3366

By Appointment Only

In the United States there are exactly three Rolls-Royce dealerships—one in Beverly Hills, California; one in New York City; and one in Zionsville, Indiana. Albers Rolls-Royce, which has been in business since 1963, is the oldest authorized Rolls-Royce dealership in the country. Herman Albers, the owner, also has a service shop that stocks thousands of Rolls-Royce and Bentley parts, including some for cars that were built more than seventy years ago. People from all over the country order parts from Albers or make the trip to Zionsville to have their Rolls-Royces serviced on the spot. Anyone thinking of dropping by Albers's dealership at 360 South First Street just to browse and dream, however, should be advised that prospective buyers are admitted only by prior appointment—and only very serious prospective buyers are given an appointment. If you happen to fall into that elite group, call (317) 873–2360 to set up a mutually agreeable time. If you just want to dream, check out www.albersrollsbentley.com

Zionsville is also home to the *SullivanMunce Cultural Center,* a small gem dedicated to assembling and preserving local history. The museum is named for Boone County's first white settler, Patrick Henry Sullivan, whose great-granddaughter, the late Iva Etta Sullivan, set up a trust fund to establish a historical foundation in Zionsville in his memory. Ms. Sullivan, a former librarian, had the financial wherewithal to set up the trust in part because she accepted the investment advice of her onetime employer, the late film director Cecil B. DeMille.

The museum, patterned after early-nineteenth-century architecture, rotates exhibits that feature period furnishings, antique clothing, farm tools, artwork, and quilts. A genealogical library houses a growing collection of family histories, diaries, letters, family Bibles, property deeds, maps, photos, and newspapers. Ms. Sullivan and her great-grandfather would be pleased. Admission is free, but donations are appreciated. Hours are 10:00 A.M. to 4:00 P.M. Tuesday through Saturday; open until 8:00 P.M. on Thursday. Closed major holidays. Visitors will find the museum at 225 West Hawthorne Street; call (317) 873–4900.

The *Boone County Courthouse* in *Lebanon,* built in the early 1900s, once drew sightseers from around the world. They came to marvel at the eight columns that adorn the north and south entrances, believed to be the largest one-piece limestone columns in the world. Each gigantic pillar—36 feet high, 4½ feet in diameter, and weighing about forty tons—is shaped from a single block of limestone. Inside, you can see the second largest stained-glass dome in the state.

Lebanon is also the home of Indiana's answer to Willie Wonka's chocolate factory. Any dyed-in-the-wool chocoholic will love a tour of *Donaldson's*

Finer Chocolates. Watch through glass doors as chocolates are cooked in copper kettles and fudge is kneaded on a marble slab. Donaldson's produces and sells seventy-five varieties of chocolates, including almond bark, chocolate-covered caramels, hand-dipped creams, and assorted nut clusters. Free guided tours are available by advance arrangement; by tour's end, just when you think you can't stand it another minute, you're given a free sample. The tours won't cost you a cent, and you're certainly under no obligation to buy, but if you don't, you have more willpower than most of us. You'll find Donaldson's at 600 South State Road 39, just south of where it intersects I–65 on the south side of Lebanon. The shop is open 9:00 A.M. to 5:00 P.M. Monday through Saturday. For more information call (765) 482–3334.

Hamilton County

Conner Prairie Pioneer Settlement, ranked as one of the nation's top five "living museums," remains suspended in the 1800s forever. A restored pioneer village breathes life into history, permitting visitors to wander at their leisure through the homes, shops, school, and other buildings that might have made up a pioneer community in 1836. "Residents" keep busy at tasks that must be performed to keep the settlement going; they also answer questions about the typical lifestyle of that era.

Ongoing meticulous research helps ensure the authenticity of the settlement. The orchard, for instance, was first planted in neat rows, but when it was learned that this was a twentieth-century method, fruit trees were scattered about at random. It was also discovered, much to everyone's surprise, that men did not wear beards in 1836, so all whiskers except muttonchops had to go. All lace trim had to be removed from the women's dresses—as it was not authentic either.

Conner Prairie

Also located on the 250-acre tract is a Federal-style mansion built in 1823 by Indiana statesman William Conner. Visitors can tour the main house and grounds, which feature a springhouse, a still, and a loom house where Conner Prairie staff members duplicate textiles used during the 1830s.

At the Prairie Adventure Center, trained craftspeople are on hand to assist visitors who want to learn pioneer skills firsthand. You can try your hand at such pastimes as weaving on an authentic loom, making candles, and whittling with period tools.

Nearby, a Delaware Indian camp and log trading post offer a glimpse of Indiana frontier life in 1816, the year in which Indiana became a state.

Another of Conner Prairie's historic areas is Liberty Corner, representative of an 1886 rural crossroads community. Visitors can explore a Quaker meeting house, a covered bridge, and a working farm. From February through November, visitors may spend an entire weekend on the farm, including sleeping in a Victorian farmhouse.

The Museum Center includes a shop that sells items handcrafted by Conner Prairie artisans, a restaurant that features a mix of modern and historical foods, and a bakery that offers nineteenth-century breads, pastries, and cookies.

Special events are also in keeping with the pioneer theme. Once a month the Methodist circuit rider arrives to preach his sermon. A presidential election is held in the fall, just as it was in 1836. Weddings, too, are authentic, and visitors are often surprised to learn that even in the mid-1800s women did not promise to "obey" their spouses. Brides agreed to "love, honor, and assist" their husbands, who in turn promised to "love, honor, and maintain" their wives.

On some weekends, a ninety-minute program entitled "Follow the North Star" allows visitors to realistically experience what life was like for runaway slaves. The role playing is so intense that many visitors must take time-outs along the way.

Conner Prairie is located in *Fishers,* 4 miles south of Noblesville. Open 9:30 A.M. to 5:00 P.M. Tuesday through Saturday and 11:00 A.M. to 5:00 P.M. Sunday. The Museum Center and indoor exhibits are open year-round; the outdoor exhibits are open from early April through late November; closed Monday, Tuesday in April and November, Easter, and major winter holidays. Special daytime and evening programs are presented throughout the year. Admission is charged. Contact Conner Prairie Pioneer Settlement, 13400 Allisonville Road, Fishers 46038–4499; call (317) 776–6006 or (800) 966–1836; or visit online at www.connerprairie.org.

At the *Indiana Transportation Museum* in *Noblesville,* you can follow the development of transportation in America, beginning with covered wagons. There are buggies, automobiles, trucks, fire engines, trains to sit in and climb onto, and a clanging trolley to ride along a 1-mile track. Each weekend a different special event takes place. The museum is in Forest Park, just north of Noblesville at 325 Cicero Road. It's open 10:00 A.M. to 5:00 P.M. Tuesday through Saturday and 10:00 A.M. to 4:00 P.M. Sunday, Memorial Day through Labor Day; 10:00 A.M. to 5:00 P.M. Saturday and 11:00 A.M. to 4:00 P.M. Sunday, April to Memorial Day and after Labor Day through October. There's a nominal admission fee; call (317) 773–6000.

Bundy Decoys in Noblesville produces duck decoys that are shipped to countries all over the world, including Japan, Italy, England, and Norway. Each decoy is a work of art—hand carved from solid white cedar, hand finished, and stained. Visitors can watch the entire process, except for the painting (a closely guarded secret), during a tour of the factory and showroom at 16506 Strawtown Avenue. Open 9:00 A.M. to 4:00 P.M. Monday through Friday and by appointment on weekends; admission is free. Call (765) 734–1148 or (800) 387–3831.

trivia

In 1923 Carmel, Indiana, installed what is believed to be the first electric traffic light in the United States. Because it had only red and green lights, motorists were unable to judge when the signal would change and were constantly running the red light.

If you appreciate cleanliness in the restaurant of your choice, try the **Classic Kitchen** in Noblesville. You can eat off the floor. Not only is the restaurant impeccably clean, it also serves some of the best food in central Indiana. Its herb bread draws raves from customers, who sometimes opt for additional portions of bread instead of dessert. Not to put down the desserts—discerning diners, who come from miles around, heap accolades on the white chocolate mousse, the chocolate gnocchi, the turtle sundae, and the homemade Key lime ice cream. One of those discerning diners is "Dave's Mom" (David Letterman's mother), a Hamilton County resident; the Classic Kitchen is one of her favorite restaurants. Prices are moderate to expensive. Open 11:00 A.M. to 2:00 P.M. for lunch Tuesday through Saturday; candlelight dinner 6:00 to 9:00 P.M. Friday and Saturday. Located at 610 Hannibal Street; (317) 773–7385. Reservations required.

trivia

Atkins Elegant Desserts in Noblesville makes cheesecakes that are served across the country in fine restaurants and above the country in *Air Force One*. President George H. Bush is said to have favored Triple Chocolate, while President Bill Clinton preferred St. Honore—a blend of buttery cookie crust, French cream filling, miniature pastry puffs, chocolate fudge sauce, whipped cream, and chopped pecans.

Dave's Mom

Her face and smile are known throughout the world—not bad for a woman the world at large had never seen until she was in her seventies and who has no appellation other than Dave's Mom.

The woman, of course, is the mother of Indianapolis native David Letterman; he, of course, is the late-night television host who popularized top ten lists and stupid pet tricks. Dave's mother, whose real name is Dorothy, first burst upon the world scene as the Letterman show's official Winter Olympics correspondent.

Neither Dorothy nor her son anticipated the way in which viewers would embrace her freshness and charm, nor could they have anticipated the endurance of her fame. Since her first assignment at the 1994 Olympics, Dorothy has been deluged with offers for appearances around the world. She was asked to fly to Iceland for a fashion show, to officiate at a World Wrestling Federation match, and to promote hams. All offers go through her son's agent, who has started considering only those that pay in excess of $1 million (he claims it weeds out the idiots).

Carmel is home to the charming *Museum of Miniature Houses,* filled with Lilliputian works of art. Visitors will see an amazing array of wee things faithfully replicated. Kitchens contain tiny canned goods, eating utensils, cookie cutters, and rolling pins. Elsewhere, a cat lays claim to a chair, a dog snoozes on a hearth, and a minuscule Monopoly board stands at the ready. One room box depicts a museum, wherein suits of armor, dinosaurs, and Oriental works of art await the scrutiny of visitors. An antique dollhouse, documented by its English builder, dates from 1861. Special collections that range from cars and cannons to dolls and teddy bears are exhibited on a rotating basis. The nonprofit museum also offers traveling exhibits and seasonal displays. Visitors may purchase such items as handcrafted miniatures, books, and periodicals in the museum's gift shop (small in size, of course). There's a nominal admission fee. The museum is located at 111 East Main Street; open 11:00 A.M. to 4:00 P.M. Wednesday through Saturday and 1:00 to 4:00 P.M. Sunday; closed major holidays and the first two school weeks of January. Special hours can be arranged in advance for large groups and out-of-town visitors; call (317) 575–9466 or go online at www.museumofminiatures.org.

A popular attraction for visitors and locals alike is the artesian well in *Flowing Well Park.* Discovered by accident in 1902, the free-flowing fountain provides mineral water free of charge to anyone who has an empty jug. You'll find the park on the northeast corner at the intersection of Gray Road and East 116th Street in Carmel. Don't be surprised if the well, housed in a small white gazebo, is surrounded by a thirsty crowd. For additional information contact the Carmel-Clay Chamber of Commerce, 37 East Main Street, Carmel 46032; (317) 846–1049.

Hancock County

Hancock County is James Whitcomb Riley country. He was born and raised and found the inspiration for many of his poems here, including such classics as "When the Frost Is on the Punkin," "Little Orphan Annie," "The Raggedy Man," and "The Old Swimmin' Hole."

Riley was born on October 7, 1849, in what is now the kitchen of a white frame house built by his father, who was an able carpenter as well as a lawyer noted for his oratory. Located at 250 West Main Street (U.S. Highway 40) in **Greenfield,** this house was immortalized in Riley's poems. It contains the rafter room where "the gobble-uns'll git you ef you don't watch out," the dining room "where they et on Sundays," and the side porch where Mary Alice Smith, who worked for the Riley family and is believed to have been the real-life "Little Orphan Annie," would "shoo the chickens off the porch." The **James Whitcomb Riley Birthplace and Museum,** complete with a collection of Riley memorabilia, is open to the public from 10:00 A.M. to 4:00 P.M. Monday through Saturday, April through mid-November. There's a nominal admission fee; call (317) 462–8539.

Although Riley was a lifelong bachelor and never had children of his own, he dearly loved them, and they returned his love. The statue of the famous Hoosier poet, seen today on the lawn of the Hancock County Courthouse (110 South State Street, Greenfield), was purchased entirely with funds contributed by the schoolchildren of Indiana.

Not far east of the Riley home, at the northwest corner of the intersection of US 40 and Apple Street, you'll find **Riley Memorial Park.** A boulder, into which are carved the words "Riley's Old Swimmin' Hole," stands on the banks of Brandywine Creek within the twenty-acre park and marks the exact spot where Riley and the friends of his youth once whiled away the hours on hot summer days. The youth of today frolic in a modern pool nearby. For additional information contact the Greenfield Chamber of Commerce, 1 Court House Plaza, Greenfield 46140; (317) 477–4188.

Although Riley eventually left Greenfield, he maintained his residence in Indiana until his death in 1916. You'll find his Indianapolis home and burial site described later in this section under Marion County.

Another place of interest in Riley Park is the two-story **Old Log Jail Museum.** Since log jails could hardly be called escapeproof, their builders resorted to various ingenious methods to keep prisoners incarcerated. This jail

ANNUAL EVENTS IN CENTRAL INDIANA

500 Festival Community Day
Indianapolis; May
(317) 614–6400

Indy Jazz Festival
Indianapolis; June
(317) 940–9945

Indiana Black Expo
Indianapolis; July
(317) 925–2707

Indiana State Fair
Indianapolis; August
(317) 927–7500

Indianapolis Greek Food Festival
Indianapolis; September
(317) 283–3816

Indy's Irish Festival
Indianapolis; September
(317) 713–7117

**Children's Museum Guild's
Haunted House**
Indianapolis; October
(317) 334–3322

Heartland Apple Festival
Danville; October
(317) 745–4876

Morgan County Fall Foliage Festival
Martinsville; October
(765) 342–0332

New Orleans Festival
Plainfield; October
(317) 837–9463 or (800) 761–WINE

Red Gold Chili Cook-Off
Elwood; October
(765) 552–0180

Small Town U.S.A. Festival
Alexandria; October
(765) 724–3514

International Festival
Indianapolis; November
(317) 225–5501

features an upstairs cell room and logs filled with nails to prevent prisoners from "sawing out." There's a nominal admission fee. For additional information contact the Hancock County Historical Society, 28 North Apple Street, Greenfield; (317) 462–7780.

Hendricks County

Rising from the cornfields of Hendricks County near Plainfield, the 124-acre complex of the *Islamic Society of North America* has served Muslims throughout the continent as a religious and educational center since 1982. The site, which is the national headquarters for several Islamic organizations, was selected for both its central location and its receptive environment. During the 1991 war with Iraq, the center's staff members were asked by the Pentagon to advise U.S. military leaders of the religious needs of the several thousand Muslims who serve in the military. The center also answers questions from non-Muslims who are interested in learning more about Islam. One item of interest is the fact that the society elected its first female president in August 2006. When former heavyweight boxing champion Mike Tyson was released from a nearby state correctional facility in 1995, after serving nearly four years on a rape conviction, this was the first place he came. Tyson converted to Islam while in prison. The public is welcome to tour the mosque, library, and teaching center; contact the center's public relations department at (317) 839–8157 to arrange a visit. You'll find the center, distinguished by its modern Middle Eastern design, approximately 3 miles south of Plainfield at 6555 South County Road 750 East.

Fans of *The Andy Griffith Show* from across the country have made the **Mayberry Cafe** in **Danville** a national destination. They come from all over, sometimes by the busload, to pay homage to those endearing folks who lived and worked in idyllic Mayberry, North Carolina, for eight television seasons, 249 episodes, and innumerable reruns. If you missed one, you may catch it here on one of the three television sets that run the shows nonstop. Photos of Sheriff Andy Taylor, son Opie, Aunt Bee, and Barney Fife adorn the walls. The cafe also sells such memorabilia as videos, books (including some of Aunt Bee's recipe books), and apparel. It will come as no surprise that the menu features such items as Barney's BBQ Ribs and Otis Stewed (Otis was the curmudgeonly town drunk). Framed newspaper and magazine articles from around the country sing the restaurant's praises. The food is good and reasonably priced. The Mayberry Cafe is open from 11:00 A.M. to 9:30 P.M. daily, and reservations are accepted; call (317) 745–4067. Located at 78 West Main Street, the restaurant is easy to find; just look for the Mayberry squad car (a 1962 Ford Galaxy restored to look like its television cousin) parked out front.

Johnson County

The **Johnson County Museum** is well worth the attention of history buffs. Housed in a former Masonic Temple, the museum displays more than 20,000 items, including antiques, Indian artifacts, guns, tools, and an interesting collection of nineteenth-century dresses. Four of its rooms have been furnished to depict the period between the Civil War and the early 1900s. But perhaps the most interesting (albeit a bit grisly) exhibit is the blood-spattered fan held by a woman who sat in Abraham Lincoln's box at Ford's Theatre in Washington, D.C., the night Lincoln was assassinated.

On the lawn outside the museum is an authentic log cabin built in 1835. It was discovered when an old house elsewhere in the county was being demolished—the house had been built around the cabin.

The museum, located at 135 North Main Street in **Franklin,** is open 9:00 A.M. to 8:00 P.M. Monday and Wednesday, 9:00 A.M. to 4:00 P.M. Thursday and Friday, and 10:00 A.M. to 3:00 P.M. the second Saturday of each month. Admission is free; (317) 736–4655.

When one happens upon **Morningside Gardens** in full bloom, it brings to mind a line from a poem by Edna St. Vincent Millay: "Lord, I do fear Thou'st made the world too beautiful this year." The daylilies of Debra and Walt Henricks are that stunning. Sprawling over eight acres at the Henricks' home south of Bargersville, daylilies of nearly 1,000 varieties bloom in multicolored splendor. Although the plants are for sale, visitors are also welcome to stop by just for the view. July is usually a good time to come for daylilies. The Henrickses sell other plants, too—daisies, gladioli, purple cornflowers, coralbells, and roses, to name a few.

The gardens are located on State Road 44 approximately 4½ miles west of State Road 135. There is a large sign in front of the gardens, which are open 10:00 A.M. to 5:00 P.M. Tuesday through Sunday. For additional information write the Henrickses at 7201 West State Road 44, Morgantown 46160; call (317) 422–9969.

The **grave of Nancy Kerlin Barnett** is a top contender for Indiana's most unusual burial site. Nancy, who died in 1831, often expressed her wish to be buried at a favorite spot overlooking Sugar Creek. Through the years Nancy's grave was joined by others. A footpath through the small cemetery eventually became a road. Increased traffic made it necessary to widen the road, and the graves had to be relocated—all, that is, but Nancy's. It's reported that one of Nancy's relatives greeted the road-wideners with a shotgun and threatened to shoot anyone who disturbed her resting place. That same relative persuaded county officials to give Nancy a special dispensation, and her grave can still be seen today, skirted on both sides by County Road 400 South (Camp Hill Road), near Amity. There's even a historical marker to honor Nancy's memory and, perhaps, to forestall questions from curious passersby. To see Nancy's grave, go to the intersection of U.S. Highway 31 and County Road 400 South at the south end of Amity; then turn east onto County Road 400 South and drive approximately 1.3 miles to the grave in the middle of the road.

Madison County

On the north side of the little country town of **Chesterfield,** two massive stone gateposts mark the entrance to the beautiful parklike grounds of **Camp Chesterfield.** They also mark the entrance to another world, for Camp Chesterfield is one of two major headquarters in this country for spiritualists. (For you curious types, the other is at Lily Dale, New York.)

Spiritualists, in case you don't have a dictionary handy, believe that mortals can communicate with the spirits of the dead through a medium. Using a variety of methods, the mediums at Camp Chesterfield attempt to do just that. They conduct séances, go into trances, evoke ectoplasms, cause spirits to materialize, and predict the future. The mediums are carefully screened before being selected to join the camp's staff, and each has his or her own specialty and sees clients by appointment in one of the cottages scattered about the forty-eight-acre grounds.

Visitors are welcome from 9:00 A.M. to 5:00 P.M. daily and at other times for special events. Fees, quite reasonable, are charged for private consultations with the staff member of your choice, but there is no charge to enter the camp, attend services at the Cathedral in the Woods, view various public demonstrations of psychic phenomena, or tour the fascinating art gallery and museum. The museum houses the memorabilia of the Fox sisters, who are credited with initiating the modern spiritualism movement.

If you'd like to read up on such subjects as reincarnation, astrology, and faith healing, you'll find books on these subjects and more in the camp's bookstore. A gourmet chef presides over a cafeteria that serves three meals a day, and several hotels offer overnight accommodations. There are even a few campsites for self-contained recreational vehicles. Occasionally, you can take courses in such subjects as the technique of spiritual healing, handwriting analysis, and trance development. All rates are reasonable.

Lest you scoff, remember that such notables as Sir Arthur Conan Doyle, creator of Sherlock Holmes, and Thomas Edison dabbled in spiritualism. Even Sigmund Freud expressed an interest in the movement and said, shortly before his death, that if he had his life to live over again he "would concern himself more with these matters." No matter what your beliefs, you will leave here with much food for thought. The camp has also been designated a U.S. Historic Place by the National Park Service, which recognizes cultural resources worthy of preservation. For a schedule of events and other information, write Camp Chesterfield, P.O. Box 132, Chesterfield 46017; call (765) 378–0235; or visit www.campchesterfield.net. To make hotel reservations, write the hotel manager at the same address or call (765) 378–0237. The camp is located at the north end of Washington Street.

Not far southwest of Chesterfield, atop limestone bluffs overlooking the White River, you can study the curious architecture of mound-building Indians. Of the eleven prehistoric earthworks preserved at **Mounds State Park,** the most exceptional is the circular Great Mound (circa 160 B.C.), nearly 1,200 feet in circumference and 9 feet high. Two other mounds are guitar-shaped, yet another is conical, and one is U-shaped. Excavations can be seen, and a naturalist is available to explain the cultures of the Adena and Hopewell Indians, who are believed to have built these mounds. The park, steeped in Indian legend, is reportedly home to the Puk-wud-ies, a peaceful tribe of little people who continue to inhabit the forest as they have for time immemorial. Some visitors have reported encountering the blue-gowned dwarves on park trails. In addition to historical tours, the park offers a swimming pool, hiking and cross-country ski trails, modern campsites, and canoeing on the White River. Canoes and ski equipment can be rented in the park. You can reach the park by taking Mounds Road (Highway 232) southwest from Chesterfield for about 2 miles. There's a nominal vehicle admission fee. Write to Mounds State Park, 4306 Mounds Road, Anderson 46017; call (765) 642–6627.

Gospel singer Sandi Patti, who was chosen Female Vocalist of the Year for eleven consecutive years by the Gospel Music Association, makes her home in Madison County. Her pure, clear voice is captured on albums and tapes at **Gaither Studios,** located at 1617 South Park Avenue in **Alexandria.** The state-of-the-art facility also produces the recordings of the Gaither Family and musical scores for television shows and feature-length movies. Bill Gaither, an Indiana native, is one of the best-known performers in Christian music; he has also, together with his wife, Gloria, written more than 500 songs. To make an appointment for a free tour, contact Gaither Family Resources at (765) 724–8405 or (800) 520–4664.

Elsewhere in Alexandria, house painter Mike Carmichael has spent his spare time working on his personal masterpiece. It all began with an accident in the mid-1960s, when Mike accidentally dropped a baseball in some paint. For some inexplicable reason, Mike decided to continue painting his baseball, and he's been at it ever since. Today, that baseball is hanging in a shed behind Mike's home, and virtually everyone in town, from the mayor on down, has added a layer or two of paint to it. At this writing, it weighs some 1,800 pounds, has a 123-inch circumference, and wears more than 19,600 layers of paint. Visitors are welcome to view Mike's big ball, and spectators from all over this country, as well as from Germany, Italy, Thailand, and Australia, have come to do just that.

Mike's project has been officially designated the **world's largest ball of paint** and is listed as such in the *Guinness Book of World Records.* His efforts have brought him fame and inspired Andy Cunningham, a young resident of Alexandria who has begun wrapping what he hopes will someday be the world's biggest ball of plastic wrap. A few years back, Alexandria was in the news when a 400-pound hairball was found in a town sewer. The *National Enquirer* ran a story about that event. The original hairball eventually dissolved, but local citizens created a replica and even gave it a place of honor in the town's annual Christmas parade. Now city officials hope Alexandria will gain fame as the town of balls.

If you would like to see Mike's ball of paint for yourself, give Mike a call at (765) 724–4088 to make an appointment. No appointment is needed if you drop by between 10:00 A.M. and 4:00 P.M. on Saturday. When you visit, he may ask you to paint a layer and add your name to the list of painters on his wall. Mike and his ball are located at 10696 North 200 West; admission is free.

The Church of God, with world headquarters at **Anderson,** has established **Anderson University** near the north edge of town. Here, you can visit the **Charles E. Wilson Library,** which contains the archives and personal papers of the man who served as Secretary of Defense under President Dwight D. Eisenhower. The **Wilson Art Gallery** houses a $250,000 porcelain bird collection donated by Wilson's daughter and a collection of 1,500 napkin rings that range in variety from a solid gold, jewel-encrusted ring once used by Louis XIV of France to rings made from toilet paper spools in a Japanese prison camp during World War II. More than 10,000 artifacts from the Holy Land are displayed in the **Bible Museum,** and **Reardon Auditorium** contains an unusual chandelier that holds some 10,000 light bulbs. For additional information contact the Anderson/Madison County Visitors and Convention Bureau (see address and phone numbers at the end of this chapter). The college is located at the corner of East Fifth Street and College Drive; (765) 649–9071.

One of the most extraordinary homes in the country belongs to Hoosier musician Vic Cook. Called **The Giant,** the 7,000-square-foot house overlooks Fall Creek near Pendleton. Its rustic design blends well with the patch of woodland that surrounds it, despite the fact that the house is 254 feet long and soars 38 feet high at its tallest point. Vic Cook is rightfully proud of the ingenious home he designed and built himself from fallen trees on his land, and he is happy to show visitors through it.

The Giant (a name excerpted from "one giant leap for mankind") reflects Cook's philosophy that it's time for people to return to a lifestyle that's in balance with nature. Unlike many others who have espoused a similar philosophy, however, Cook believes we can do so without giving up creature comforts.

Visitors will be amazed to learn that, although his fuel bill is $1.00 a day at the most, Cook's home contains a high-tech recording studio with a fantastic sound system, a big-screen television, two computers, and a washing machine. Perhaps the most interesting object in the house is the refrigerator Cook fashioned from a hollow beech tree. Lined with a special insulation, it is cooled by underground air and has a separate freezer section (further cooled by a microchip) that keeps even ice cream solid. Air-conditioning also is provided naturally by underground sources. Cook uses a few kerosene heaters in the winter, but he needs minimal fuel because his house is superinsulated. The house is powered by six storage batteries that are charged by solar panels, with a gasoline-powered generator on hand for alternative power when the weather stays cloudy for days. And yes, he does have an indoor toilet—a composting unit.

There's another bonus. Because Cook has no utility hookups, his real estate taxes are much lower.

Although The Giant took eight years to build, Cook believes it would be possible for a couple of reasonably fit people to build a similar structure in one summer for about $3,500.

To learn more about the man and The Giant, often described as being at the pinnacle of environmental science, make an appointment for a tour. An admission fee is charged, with proceeds going to a nonprofit environmental organization. Tours, which include an easy ½-mile hike through the woods, are available by reservation from May to mid-October. Contact The Giant, c/o EarthShip Corporation, P.O. Box 63, Pendleton 46064; (765) 778–2757.

Connoisseurs of the pork tenderloin sandwich, the beloved sandwich that has become a Hoosier icon, flock to tiny **Perkinsville** in droves. They're all headed for **Bonge's Tavern,** which has been honored time and again for serving the best pork tenderloin sandwich in the state. That's not to belittle the rest of the cuisine. This tiny restaurant in rural Indiana also serves gourmet food, featured on a constantly changing menu printed on a chalkboard over the bar. Because seating is limited and patrons are numerous, diners must sometimes wait for a table for up to two hours. If you bring a Sharpie, you can while away the waiting time by contributing to the restrooms' floor-to-ceiling graffiti—even the sinks and trash cans have been signed. Bonge's is open from 4:30 to 9:00 P.M. Tuesday through Thursday and 4:30 to 10:00 P.M. Friday and Saturday. Located at 9830 West 280 North; call (765) 734–1625.

Marion County

The **Indiana World War Memorial,** built as the centerpiece of a 5-block plaza in downtown **Indianapolis,** pays homage to Hoosiers killed during U.S. wars fought in the twentieth century. Patterned after the Tomb of King Mausolus at Halicarnassus, one of the seven wonders of the ancient world, the building is an architectural marvel. It is the Shrine Room, however, that is the glory of the memorial. Massive dark red marble columns surround a marble altar that commemorates fallen war heroes. A 17-by-30-foot American flag, supported by invisible wires, is suspended above the altar. Tiny blue lightbulbs that flicker off and on in the ceiling surround a huge Swedish-crystal light fixture in the shape of a star. Daylight filters through twenty-four deep blue glass windows. The memorial also houses a museum that contains such artifacts as a Korean War–era helicopter, a Navy Terrier missile, and some jeeps. On September 21, 2001, an exhibit honoring casualties from our country's latest war was officially dedicated. A display in the building's Grand Foyer will forever honor seven Hoosiers who lost their lives in the September 11, 2001, attacks on the World Trade Center and the Pentagon. Outside, on the south steps of the memorial, visitors will see a one-of-a-kind statue known as *Pro Patria*. The 24-foot-tall, seven-ton sculpture, cast in bronze in 1929 by a New York City artist, has stood here since the memorial was dedicated in 1930. In 1945 a B-25 crashed into the Empire State Building and sent flaming debris into the artist's nearby studio. The model for *Pro Patria* was destroyed, making the statue impossible to replace.

trivia

Elvis Presley gave his last public concert at Market Square Arena in Indianapolis on June 26, 1977. Less than two months later, on August 16, he died at his home in Memphis. He was forty-two years old.

Space has been reserved in the War Memorial Plaza to commemorate Hoosiers who lost their lives in the wars in Afghanistan and Iraq, but like most such memorials, it will be built when those conflicts are over. Until then, a modest but touching memorial to those lost in the war on terror has been established in the hall outside the office of the Indiana Department of Veterans' Affairs in the Indiana Government Center South at 302 West Washington Street. Known as the **Operation Enduring Freedom and Operation Iraqi Freedom Memorial Wall**, it consists of three panels of names, ages, hometowns, and photographs of the dead soldiers. New casualties will be honored as they occur. For hours and additional information, call the Department of Veterans' Affairs at (317) 232–3910.

Located at 431 North Meridian Street, the Indiana World War Memorial is open free of charge from 9:00 A.M. to 6:00 P.M. Wednesday through Sunday; call (317) 232–7615.

At 700 North Pennsylvania Street, the **American Legion National Headquarters** houses one of the world's most extensive collections of World Wars I and II posters—more than 800 from World War I and 1,200 from World War II. Approximately forty are on display throughout the American Legion Building, with the rest available for view on a slide collection. A museum on the top floor of the four-story building exhibits memorabilia from the wars our country fought in the twentieth century. You may tour the building free of charge at any time it's open; call (317) 630–1200 for specific hours and for an appoint-ment to view the slide collection.

If anyone ever compiles a list of national treasures, the **Indianapolis Chil-dren's Museum** should be on it. It is the largest children's museum in the world, and in this case, bigger *is* better. You can ride an early-twentieth-century carousel; explore the twisting passages of a limestone cave; visit a log cabin, an Indian tepee, an igloo, and an Egyptian tomb inhabited by the 3,000-year-old mummy of a princess; stand beside a fifty-five-ton, wood-burning locomotive; see a 30-foot-tall glass water clock, the tallest in the world; marvel at an 820-pound yo-yo that actually works (although it has to be lifted by a crane to do so); watch a spectacular collection of toy trains in motion (1,500 sets in total, but who's counting?); examine replicas of prehistoric creatures; and conduct scien-tific experiments. If you can coax the adults away from it, your child can sit behind the wheel of a 1940 Maserati that once competed in the Indy 500. Other exhibits, such as the computer center, provide a bridge to the future. Budding scientists can explore ScienceWorks. Outer space comes alive at the museum's planetarium, one of the few in the world equipped with a computerized star projector (properly known as Digistar) that simulates three-dimensional flight through space; your children will be even more impressed when they learn that it's the same projector used to create special effects in the *Star Trek* movies. Children are enthralled by the magic of live theater productions at the Lilly The-ater. In the innovative Center for Exploration, designed by teens for teens, young people can develop projects of their own choosing. Playscape offers learning through play for preschoolers, while Babyscape provides activities

Indianapolis Children's Museum

designed especially for children under three. Walk among animated dinosaurs in Dinosphere; see, hear, and smell them in the sixty-five-million-year-old environment in which they thrived; and view one of the world's largest collections of authentic dinosaur fossils.

In 2006 the museum added the sixty-six-million-year-old skull of a new, drag-onlike species of dinosaur to its collection. The name given to this first-of-its-kind dinosaur is *Dracorex hog-wartsia*; the name is a combination of the Latin words *draco* (meaning dragon), *rex* (meaning king), and *hogwartsia* (after the fictional Hogwarts School for Witch-craft and Wizardry created by author J. K. Rowling in the popular Harry Potter books).

trivia

Hockey great Wayne Gretzky began his professional career in 1978 with the Indianapolis Racers. The then-sixteen-year-old Gretzky played his first eight games with the Racers, scoring three goals and three assists.

Also added in 2006 was a magnificent 43-foot-tall, 3,200-piece tower of brilliantly colored glass, known as "Fireworks of Glass," that rises above a glass ceiling in the museum's central atrium. It is the largest permanent sculpture ever created by world-renowned artist Dale Chihuly. Visitors can sit on a revolving platform below the glass ceiling and look up at the more than 1,600 additional pieces of brightly colored glass embedded in the ceiling itself; it's an experience akin to looking at a kaleidoscope. Bathed in natural sunlight during the day and lit at night during special events, the tower and ceiling form the centerpiece of a hands-on exhibit that demonstrates how ordinary glass can be turned into extraordinary works of art.

Even the museum's restaurant offers a behind-the-scenes education—you can stand at a window and watch the bakers make such goodies as croissants and cookies. The Children's Museum store includes a cave stocked with glow-in-the-dark toys, a learning tree with built-in seating around its base for reading, and a 3-by-6-foot calculator that youngsters can use to total up the cost of their own merchandise.

trivia

Frank Sinatra's first appearance as a singer with the Tommy Dorsey Orchestra took place at the Lyric Theater in Indianapolis on February 2, 1940.

The five-level museum nourishes all those qualities we cherish in our children—a sense of wonder, curiosity, imagination, the desire to know and to create, and the ability to dream.

Even if you don't have children, come anyway; this is an enchanting place for everyone. It's easy to understand why the readers of *Child* magazine have voted this the best children's museum in the country.

There's a general admission fee; admission is free for families from 4:00 to 8:00 P.M. the first Thursday of each month, the museum's only evening hours. There are additional nominal fees for the Lilly Theater, the carousel, and the planetarium at all times. Museum and restaurant hours are 10:00 A.M. to 5:00 P.M. daily, mid-March through Labor Day; closed Monday the rest of the year; also closed on Easter, Thanksgiving, and Christmas. The carousel operates from 2:00 to 5:00 P.M. on school days and during regular museum hours other days. The museum is located directly north of downtown Indianapolis, at the corner of Thirtieth and Meridian Streets; the entrance is on Illinois Street (the first street west of Meridian Street). Look for the three dinosaurs escaping through a museum wall. Call (317) 334–3322 or (800) 208–KIDS (5437) or visit www .childrensmuseum.org.

The *Crispus Attucks Museum* showcases and celebrates the accomplishments of African Americans in Indianapolis, with a special focus on the graduates of Crispus Attucks High School. Back in the 1950s, when Attucks was a consolidated high school for the city's black youngsters, basketball great Oscar Robertson was a student here. Under his leadership the school's basketball team captured the state championship, the first black team and the first team from any Indianapolis high school ever to do so. (In 2006, the team was elected en masse to the Indiana Basketball Hall of Fame in New Castle.) Visitors can explore some thirty exhibits, including a basketball hall of fame, in four galleries. The museum is located at 1140 North Dr. Martin Luther King Jr. Drive on the campus of Crispus Attucks Medical Magnet High School. Named for a black man and former slave who was the first patriot to die in the American Revolution, Crispus Attucks High School was placed on the National Register of Historic Places in 1989. Browse the exhibits on your own any weekday from 10:00 A.M. to 2:00 P.M., or schedule an appointment for a guided tour; call (317) 226–2430. Admission is free, but donations are welcome.

A bit farther north, an outdoor garden of medicinal plants flourishes year-round on the campus of Butler University. The 40-by-150-foot *Apothecary Garden,* which lines a winding walkway between Robertson Hall and the Pharmacy Building, highlights the ancient medicinal herbs of North America, Europe, and China. Among the herbs that grow here are the narrowleaf coneflower, popular as an immune-system booster; Saint-John's-wort, believed to be a natural antidepressant; the weeping forsythia, used in China to treat sore throats and urinary-tract disorders; and elecampane, a Western European herb used to ease respiratory ailments. Each type of plant is labeled with its name and medicinal uses. The garden also includes many unusual landscape plantings that thrive in central Indiana and some native prairie plants and grasses. Butler University is located at 4600 Sunset Avenue in Indianapolis; call (317) 940–8000.

The **Royce Motors Museum** is one of Indianapolis's least known attractions. Located behind a retail racing shop called Stealth Motorsports, the museum houses eighty-five antique and classic vehicles collected since 1970 by the racing shop's owner, Louis E. Randle Jr. One of his most prized possessions is a car from the NASCAR circuit that was owned and driven by Dale Earnhardt. Randle bought the Earnhardt car one month before the legendary driver was killed in 2001 and has since turned down several six-figure offers for it. Among the other cars in Randle's collection are a 1948 Willys Jeepster, a 1911 Maxwell, a 1913 Stanley Steamer, a 1939 Graham that was built in Indiana, and a 1912 Detroit Electric (it tops out at about 20 miles per hour). Visitors are welcome at the museum from 8:00 A.M. to 5:00 P.M. Monday through Friday; admission is free. Located at 6565 Coffman Road; call (317) 290–3580.

The **Indianapolis Museum of Art,** situated on a bluff overlooking the White River, is far more than a museum. It's a 152-acre art park that includes a

A Woman of Distinction

The world remembers her today as Madame C. J. Walker, but she was born Sara Breedlove. Sara was born on December 23, 1867, the daughter of ex-slaves living in Louisiana. By the time she died in 1919 at the age of fifty-one, she was a self-made millionaire and believed to be the wealthiest black woman in the country.

Madame Walker's fascinating life story includes being orphaned at age seven, getting married at age fourteen, and becoming a widow with a two-year-old daughter at age twenty. When she and her daughter moved to Denver in 1905, she carried her entire life savings of $1.50. There she met and married a newspaper sales agent named Charles Joseph Walker and created the Walker line of hair care products for black women.

In 1910, Madame Walker moved her company to Indianapolis to take advantage of the city's eight railway systems as a means of distributing her products nationally, and she built a sales force of more than 2,000 women who generated annual revenues of $500,000. She also began developing the triangular-shaped Walker Building and Theatre, a project that was completed by her daughter after Madame Walker's death. Today, the Walker Theatre Center at 617 Indiana Avenue is a National Historic Landmark and a national model for African-American arts.

In recognition of her lifetime achievements, Madame Walker was elected to the National Business Hall of Fame in 1992. She was further honored on January 28, 1997, when the U.S. Postal Service issued a 32-cent commemorative stamp bearing her likeness. The stamp was dedicated in a special ceremony at the Walker Theatre.

For additional information about the many special events presented at the Walker Theatre and about tours of the building, call (317) 236–2099.

sculpture garden, botanical and formal gardens, patches of woodland, green-houses, a wildlife refuge, and a fine restaurant. Among its exhibits are the world's largest collection—outside the United Kingdom—of J. M. W. Turner watercolors and prints, a self-portrait of Rembrandt as a young man, and impor-tant collections of Asian, African, and neo-Impressionist art. An acquisition of screens and scrolls from the Edo period is the largest single purchase of Japan-ese art in U.S. history. The museum site was once the private estate of Mr. and Mrs. J. K. Lilly Jr. (of Lilly pharmaceutical fame), and there is also much of architectural interest here. Lilly Pavilion is the original Lilly mansion, formerly known as Oldfields; it's one of the few nineteenth-century American Country Place estates still in existence and the only one in this country to share the grounds of a major art museum. Many special events and programs are held here. Visitors can purchase a wide variety of flowering bulbs and plants at the greenhouses (open 10:00 A.M. to 5:00 P.M. Wednesday, Friday, and Saturday; 10:00 A.M. to 8:00 P.M. Thursday; and noon to 5:00 P.M. Sunday) and used art objects, clothing, and furniture at the Better-Than-New Shop (open noon to 4:00 P.M. Wednesday through Saturday). As part of an ongoing renovation proj-ect, world-famous chef Wolfgang Puck opened a restaurant for fine dining and a cafe for more casual fare on the premises. General admission to the museum is free, but fees are charged for special exhibitions. The main exhibition build-ings are open 11:00 A.M. to 5:00 P.M. Tuesday, Wednesday, and Saturday; 11:00 A.M. to 9:00 P.M. Thursday and Friday; and noon to 5:00 P.M. Sunday. The museum is located at 4000 Michigan Road; call (317) 923–1331 for up-to-date information or visit www.ima-art.org.

Indianapolis has gone wild over its state-of-the-art *Indianapolis Zoo*, a model for zoos of the future that opened to the public in June 1988. Stretching along the west bank of the White River, the innovative sixty-four-acre facility is the first zoo ever to be completely designed around the biome concept. Bio-mes are simulated natural environments in which animals are grouped by habitats rather than by the continents of their origins. Forest animals from around the world, for instance, share the forest biome, while other animals find appropriate homes in the desert, plains, and aquatic biomes.

Unlike most of its counterparts, the Indianapolis Zoo combines the best elements of a zoo and an aquarium, with particular emphasis on a marine exhibit that has been called the best of its kind outside of SeaWorld. After under-going a $10 million renovation, the 40,000-square-foot Dolphin Adventure Pavilion reopened in May 2005 to rave reviews. A 30-foot-diameter glass dome allows humans to walk under the water into the dolphins' large tank. A sea-horse exhibit featuring more than 300 seahorses and related species opened in March 2004; the seahorses, sea dragons, and pipefish live in ten tanks that hold

10,000 gallons of water. Only five zoos in the world are capable of accommodating walruses—this zoo is one of them. The zoo also made headlines around the world when two African elephants gave birth in captivity to two babies conceived through artificial insemination (sadly, one of those babies died in June 2003, at the age of three, but happily two more were born in 2006). Three rare South African white rhinos arrived at the zoo in 2003, and a mob (group) of meerkats came to live in the zoo's Desert Homes in 2006. Among the things you *won't* find here are cages and bars. Animals and people watch each other across such natural barriers as moats and boulders, and, where necessary, through meshwork that disappears as you look at it. One resident giraffe gave himself and his pals a room with a view by licking a hole through the wall of the giraffe barn—the barn is now equipped with windows 14 feet above the ground so that the lanky creatures can have a home with a view.

trivia

Union Station in Indianapolis, opened in 1888, was the nation's first union railway depot. A young Thomas Edison worked there as a Western Union telegraph operator.

Visitors will also find a behind-the-scenes train tour, a carousel, a family roller coaster, and a 4-D safari ride

The zoo is open 9:00 A.M. to 5:00 P.M. Monday through Thursday and 9:00 A.M. to 6:00 P.M. Friday and Saturday, Memorial Day through Labor Day; 9:00 A.M. to 4:00 P.M. Monday through Thursday and 9:00 A.M. to 5:00 P.M. Friday and Saturday from mid-March to the day before Memorial Day and on the day after Labor Day through October; 9:00 A.M. to 4:00 P.M. daily in November and December except Christmas Eve and Day; 9:00 A.M. to 4:00 P.M. Wednesday through Sunday in January and February. Hours and rates may vary, so it's best to contact them before going; call (317) 630-2001 or visit www.indyzoo.com.

The zoo is located just west of the downtown area at 1200 West Washington Street.

The **White River Gardens** adjacent to the zoo opened in June 1999 to accolades from the public. Included in the gardens' 3.3 acres are a glass-enclosed conservatory, water gardens, outdoor design gardens, and an outdoor wedding garden. From spring through Labor Day weekend, the conservatory is filled with more than 1,000 butterflies. Nearly fifty bronze sculptures of small animals are scattered over the grounds. Visitors enter the garden through a cylindrical rotunda that features a 360-degree mural depicting Indiana's changing seasons. Open year-round; 9:00 A.M. to 5:00 P.M. daily March through December and 9:00 A.M. to 5:00 P.M. Wednesday through Sunday the rest of the year, with extended hours from Thanksgiving through December 23.

A nominal admission fee is reduced slightly from November through February. Call (317) 630–2001 for specific and up-to-date information.

In addition to its reputation as the amateur sports capital of the world, Indianapolis is also noted for having the country's most impressive collection of American war memorials outside Washington, D.C. The newest—dedicated in May 1999—is the **_Congressional Medal of Honor Memorial,_** the only memorial in the United States that honors our nation's most highly decorated war heroes. Of the tens of millions of men and women who have served our country in the military, only some 3,400 have earned the Medal of Honor (76 are from Indiana); more than half were awarded posthumously. Covering one acre in White River State Park, the memorial comprises twenty-seven curved walls of glass that range from 8 to 10 feet in height. The name of each medal recipient is etched into the glass. As beautiful as the memorial is during the day, it is more spectacular at night, when the highlighted glass walls glow green. The outdoor memorial is open free of charge at all times; visitors who come at dusk will hear a recording, played over a public address system, of a Medal of Honor winner telling his own story.

Not far away, at 500 West Washington Street, the **_Eiteljorg Museum of American Indians and Western Art_** showcases the arts and crafts of the American West in a building reminiscent of an Indian pueblo, that's a work of art in itself. Opened in 1989 primarily to house the collection of the late Indianapolis businessman and philanthropist for whom it's named, the museum is one of only two of its type east of the Mississippi River. Its still-growing collection, currently valued at more than $45 million, includes sculptures by Charles Russell, bronzes by Frederic Remington, and paintings by Georgia O'Keeffe. A major 45,000-square-foot expansion that was opened to the public in 2005 doubled the museum's usable space. Special programs, some especially for children, breathe life into the exhibits; visitors may, for instance, see roping demonstrations or attend a lecture series that offers instructions on how to make a cowboy hat or a lariat. The gift shop features authentic arts and crafts from the southwestern United States, and a new on-site cafe offers inexpensive Southwestern cusine and a view of the city's skyline. There's a nominal admission fee. The museum is open 10:00 A.M. to 5:00 P.M. Tuesday through Saturday and noon to 5:00 P.M. Sunday; also open 10:00 A.M. to 5:00 P.M. Monday from Memorial Day through Labor Day; closed major winter holidays; (317) 636–9378.

When the Smithsonian National Museum of the American Indian (NMAI) opened in Washington, D.C., in September 2004, it selected the Eiteljorg as its first-ever alliance partner. The partnership allows the Eiteljorg to borrow and exhibit artifacts from NMAI's huge collection.

The zoo, the White River Gardens, the Medal of Honor Memorial, and the Eiteljorg Museum lie within the 250-acre **White River State Park,** which borders both sides of the waterway for which it is named. To view drawings and a model of future plans for White River State Park or to obtain up-to-date information about additional planned facilities, stop at the park's visitor center at 801 West Washington Street. The park includes **Victory Field** (home of the Indianapolis Indians, the city's AAA baseball team), **Military Park,** the state's only IMAX 3-D theater, the **NCAA Hall of Champions,** and the magnificent **Indiana State Museum.** The visitor center is open 8:30 A.M. to 5:00 P.M. Monday through Friday year-round; also noon to 5:00 P.M. Saturday and Sunday during warm-weather months; (317) 233–2434 or (800) 665–9056.

trivia

Hank Aaron, baseball's great home run hitter, made his professional debut with the Indianapolis Clowns as a teenage shortstop in 1951 and 1952. Aaron never played a game in Indianapolis, however. The Negro American League Clowns played all their games on the road.

During warm-weather months, you can ride an authentic Italian gondola on Indianapolis's Downtown Canal, complete with a serenade and a history lesson of gondolas in Venice. **Old World Gondoliers** operates from the Ohio Street Basin; cruises are offered in 15-minute increments from 3:00 to 9:00 P.M. Wednesday through Sunday from June through August. Call (317) 491–4835 for additional information and to make an advance reservation. If you prefer, you can walk along the paved, 5¼-mile-long towpath that borders the canal. The August 2005 issue of *Fitness Magazine* named the towpath the fifth-best metropolitan-area hiking trail in the country.

On August 2, 1995, a group of World War II veterans gathered in downtown Indianapolis to witness the realization of a long-cherished dream. They came to dedicate a memorial that would forever honor the memory of their fallen shipmates in one of the nation's greatest wartime tragedies, the sinking of the USS *Indianapolis.* When it was hit by a Japanese torpedo on July 30, 1945, the *Indianapolis* became the last U.S. Navy ship lost in World War II. The heavy cruiser was returning from a top-secret mission—delivering components of the atomic bomb that would be dropped on Hiroshima in early August. Because of the secrecy surrounding the mission, crew members spent five days in shark-infested waters 600 miles west of Guam before being spotted accidentally by a Navy seaplane. Only 316 of the 1,196 crew members survived. The loss of 880 men remains to this day the single largest loss of life in American naval warfare history.

Visitors can view the *USS* **Indianapolis** *Memorial* in the plaza along the east bank of the Central Canal in downtown Indianapolis, just behind the Navy EMPF Building at 714 North Senate Avenue. The south face of the black and gray granite monument is engraved with the names of the ship's crew and on the opposite face with a likeness of the USS *Indianapolis*. Engravings on the limestone base tell the story of the ill-fated vessel. Because this is an outdoor site, the memorial, impressive and sobering, can be viewed anytime. For additional information call (317) 232–7615.

A museum dedicated to the *Indianapolis* is being established on the ground floor of the Indiana World War Memorial; it's expected to be open by late July 2007. Highlights are expected to include stories of the ship's crew, artifacts from the ship, and information about the submarine that sank it. For up-to-date information write the USS *Indianapolis* Museum, Inc., Circle City Station, P.O. Box 441135, Indianapolis 46204; you can also visit www.INculture.org or www.ussindianapolis.org online.

One of the largest city parks in the United States, the 5,200-acre *Eagle Creek Park* is home to bald eagles, coyotes, and deer. An arboretum near the park's nature center boasts a 400-year-old Douglas fir log and a beech tree into which Daniel Boone carved his still-visible but fading initials. (If you wonder why the carving is so high up, naturalists surmise it's because Boone was on horseback when he left his mark there.) Much of the park's summertime appeal centers on the 1,300-acre Eagle Creek Reservoir, which features a three-acre swimming beach; pontoon boat cruises; the only internationally sanctioned canoe/kayak regatta course in the country (site of the 1988 U.S. Olympic trials and the 1994 World Rowing Championships); and a marina that rents boats, canoes, and sailboards. The park also offers hiking, bicycling, and cross-country ski trails; an eighteen-hole golf course; a joggers' outdoor exercise course; a world-class archery field; ice-skating ponds; and sled runs. The park is open dawn to dusk every day of the year; there's a nominal entrance fee, which is slightly higher on Saturday and Sunday. Enter the park at 7840 West Fifty-sixth Street; (317) 327–7110.

trivia

Marshal "Major" Taylor was once known as the fastest man on earth. In 1899, when bicycling was a major sport, he became the first black athlete to win the coveted title of world champion bicycle racer—and one of the first black athletes to hold a world champion title in any sport. In 1982, when bicycle racing was enjoying a resurgence in popularity, Indianapolis honored the memory of its native son by building one of the best bicycle racing tracks in the country and naming it the Major Taylor Velodrome. The Velodrome today hosts many world-class cycling events.

How to Move a Building

In 1930 the Indiana Bell Telephone Company in downtown Indianapolis badly needed additional space. The decision was made to move its eight-story building to an adjacent lot and erect a larger building at the original location. All this needed to be done, however, without an interruption in the company's around-the-clock service.

The move was begun by emptying the basement and attaching flexible hoses to water, sewage, and gas lines. The wires that carried electricity to the building were given some slack. Cables spliced into the telephone circuits added extra length.

A concrete slab foundation was poured on the adjacent site to accommodate the relocated building. The entrance to the building was connected to the sidewalk by a movable steel bridge. A system of jacks, I-beams, and rollers was placed next to each of the building's fifty-nine steel support columns.

With everything in place, the move was begun. The jacks raised the columns ¼ inch off their foundations, the columns were cut loose, and the weight of the building was transferred to 4,000 steel rollers. The jacks were then simultaneously given six pumps, resulting in a move of about ⅜ inch. Gradually, moving up to 8 feet a day, the building was turned until its east-facing doors faced north. The building was then inched westward to its new site, and there it stood until 1964, when it was finally torn down and replaced.

Throughout the move, phone company employees continued their work inside the building. They felt no movement but could observe the subtle shift of the view outside the windows. Outside, interested spectators were provided with a 300-seat grandstand built specifically for observation of the monumental occasion.

A new high-rise building was erected on the vacated site while workers continued to provide telephone service in the old building. The history-making move was done in this fashion because at the time it was the most cost-effective way to do it.

A marvelous getaway spot, especially in winter, is the serene world within the walls of the *Garfield Park Conservatory.* Outside, the world may be white with snow, but inside it is eternal summer. Vividly colored birds live among trees that shade giant ferns and lush vegetation. Tropical fish swim in a series of pools fed by a 15-foot waterfall. Walk beneath the falls and enter the environs of the desert, not barren at all but alive with cacti, succulents, and carnivorous plants. Outside, from May through October, the sunken gardens are brilliant with hundreds of blooms. The conservatory, located at 2505 Conservatory Drive in Garfield Park, is open 10:00 A.M. to 5:00 P.M. Tuesday through Saturday and noon to 5:00 P.M. Sunday, with special hours for seasonal shows. Admission is free except during special shows; call (317) 327–7184.

Holliday Park would certainly be a top contender for honors as Indianapolis's most unusual park. Located on the west bank of the White River at

6363 Spring Mill Road, the eighty-acre park was initially developed in 1936 as a botanical garden, and the grounds still contain more than 800 species of plants. Children love its nature center and its innovative playground, especially a rope-climbing contraption that resembles a giant spider web and some twisty tube slides.

The park is most famous however, for its "ruins." Three stone statues that formerly resided on the now-vanished St. Paul Building in New York City now perch on a ledge atop three Doric columns, dominating a setting that is the focal point of Holliday Park. Three times life-size, the kneeling figures represent white, black, and Asian males who have labored in unity. Just behind the statues is a grotto with a fountain and reflecting pool. Twenty-five 10-foot-tall columns obtained from a local convent when it was razed several years back surround the grotto and contribute to the ruins' effect. Nearby, four statues that once stood atop Marion County's old courthouse adorn the lawn. The collection of statuary is not only eye-catching but also an imaginative contribution to the recycling effort. The park is free and open to the public daily from dawn to dusk; the nature center's hours are 9:00 A.M. to 5:00 P.M. Monday through Saturday and 1:00 to 5:00 P.M. Sunday. Call (317) 327–7180 or visit www.hollidaypark.org.

In the midst of **Lockerbie Square,** a 6-block area of late nineteenth-century homes near downtown Indianapolis, stands an old brick house once occupied by poet James Whitcomb Riley (for information about Riley's birth-place, see Hancock County earlier in this chapter). Riley spent the last twenty-three years of his life here, and his memorabilia are everywhere. Built in 1872, the structure and its contents have been impeccably restored and preserved in keeping with the Victorian era. It is recognized as one of the two best Victorian preservations in the country. This is not a reinterpretation of history. Riley's pen is on his desk, his suits are in the closet, and his hat is on the bed. The carpets are slightly faded, and the upholstery shows signs of wear, just as it did when Riley lived here. A humble, unpretentious man, Riley would have been astounded to learn that his home is now a major tourist attraction. Located at 528 Lockerbie Street, the **James Whitcomb Riley House** is open 10:00 A.M. to 3:30 P.M. Tuesday through Saturday and noon to 3:30 P.M. Sunday; closed major holidays and the first three weeks in January. There's a nominal admission fee. For additional information write the James Whitcomb Riley Memorial Association, 50 South Meridian Street, Indianapolis 46204, or call (317) 631–5885.

When Riley died in 1916, he was interred in **Crown Hill Cemetery.** His grave, sheltered by an elegant but simple Greek temple, is at the crest of Strawberry Hill, the highest point in Indianapolis.

Among the other notables buried here are Benjamin Harrison, twenty-third president of the United States; three vice presidents; and the infamous John

James Whitcomb Riley House in Lockerbie Square

Dillinger. Ironically, it is Dillinger's grave that commands the most attention. His funeral in 1934 was the only occasion in Crown Hill's history that the cemetery had to close its gates and restrict attendance. Since then it has been necessary to replace his grave marker several times. Souvenir hunters chip away at them relentlessly, and one collector actually carried away an entire tombstone.

One of the newest and most touching monuments in the cemetery is the **Hearts Remembered Memorial,** a tribute to 699 children buried without headstones on what is known as Community Hill. The memorial, dedicated in June 2006, consists of three black granite monoliths. A 9-foot-tall center stone is flanked by two 5-foot-tall stones that are engraved with the names of the children. All the boys and girls buried here were abandoned and neglected orphans who died between 1892 and 1980, destined to be forgotten until a charitable foundation decided to remedy the situation. The center stone bears their poignant epitaph: EVERY LIFE TOUCHES SOMEONE, AND NO LIFE SHOULD EVER BE FORGOTTEN, ESPECIALLY THE LIFE OF A CHILD.

Also located here is **Crown Hill National Cemetery**—a cemetery-within-a-cemetery and the final resting place for nearly 2,000 soldiers, mostly Civil War veterans. The cemetery has set aside a four-acre tract of land on the north grounds to provide additional burial space for the military; it is also home to the Field of Valor Mausoleum for above-ground burials.

Each year on Memorial Day, the cemetery is the site of an impressive ceremony that honors fallen military heroes. Activities include a band concert, an artillery salute, the playing of "Taps," and a reading of the names of Hoosier soldiers who have died since the previous year's Memorial Day. There's also a Civil War Memorial Service, complete with a parade of Civil War reenactors and a salute with muskets. Both events are free.

A Remarkable Life

Indiana lost one of its most remarkable citizens on January 28, 1998, when John Morton-Finney of Indianapolis died at the age of 108.

The son of two slaves, Dr. Morton-Finney was born on June 25, 1889. During World War I he served in the Army unit of black soldiers known as the Buffalo Soldiers. He loved learning, believing that "when you stop learning, that's about the end of you." During his lifetime he earned fifteen college degrees, including degrees in law, mathematics, history, and French, and became fluent in five languages. He earned his last degree at age seventy-five.

Following World War I, he began a career in education, teaching languages in black colleges. The pay was low, however, so he accepted a position teaching languages in the Indianapolis Public School System. He was the first teacher hired for Crispus Attucks, an Indianapolis high school for black students that opened in 1927.

After retiring from teaching in 1947, he practiced law and actively participated in that profession until his death. He was admitted to practice before the U.S. Supreme Court in 1972 and was inducted into the National Bar Association's Hall of Fame in 1991.

When Dr. Morton-Finney turned 108, the federal government invited him to a special ceremony honoring him for his service to his country. He respectfully declined, saying that he was just too busy to attend.

At the time of his death, he was the last remaining survivor of the Buffalo Soldiers and was believed to be the oldest practicing attorney in the United States. He was laid to rest with full military honors in Crown Hill Cemetery.

It was once said of Winston Churchill that he lived a life, not an apology. The same could be said of John Morton-Finney.

The cemetery's main gate at 3402 Boulevard Place is open daily during daylight hours. Before entering, however, you should stop by the office at 700 West Thirty-eighth Street and ask for a map and/or directions to the various grave sites; the cemetery covers more than 500 acres and is crisscrossed by nearly 50 miles of roads. The office is open daily 8:00 A.M. to 6:00 P.M. April through September; 8:00 A.M. to 5:00 P.M. the rest of the year; (317) 925–8231 or (800) 809–3366. Several special guided tours are offered for a nominal fee; reservations should be made in advance.

Well-traveled deli connoisseurs will tell you that **Shapiro's Delicatessen** in southside Indianapolis can compete with the best New York and Chicago have to offer. Believe them! Shapiro's has been a much-loved family-operated business and local fixture since 1905, growing from a small grocery store with a few tables into a deli/restaurant that serves approximately 2,500 devotees each day. You'll find all the usual deli fare here and then some, generously served, moderately priced, and deliciously prepared. The corned beef, made from a family recipe that won a blue ribbon at the 1939 World's Fair in New York City, sells by the ton—about three tons a week, to be exact. *USA Today* called it "the best corned beef in America," and *Gourmet* magazine reported that "the corned beef sandwich is superb." Other highly rated treats include matzo ball and vegetable soups, pastrami sandwiches, potato pancakes, liver pâté, pickled herring, and, on Sundays only, *real* mashed potatoes. Don't forget the desserts—food critics and just plain eaters rank them with the best Indianapolis has to offer. The strawberry-topped and chocolate cheesecakes are without peer. Breakfast, lunch, and dinner are served every day of the week (eat in or carry out); open 6:30 A.M. to 8:00 P.M. Located at 808 South Meridian Street; (317) 631–4041; www.shapiros.com.

trivia

The summer of 1816 was the coldest Indiana summer on record. It began with ice, sleet, and snow in late April, then more snow in May and June. Temperatures dipped to the freezing mark in July, and August brought blizzards. With livestock frozen and food crops destroyed, Hoosiers ate such wilderness fare as raccoons and groundhogs to survive.

It began as one man's dream. That dream became a reality in March 1994 when the **Indiana State Police Historical Center** opened its doors to the public. One of only about a half dozen police museums in the country, it was funded entirely by private donations and is filled with exhibits that will fascinate visitors of all ages.

The museum collection features vintage police cars and motorcycles, an aluminum boat used by state police scuba divers, a copper moonshine still, some John Dillinger memorabilia, and handcuffs, firearms, and bulletproof vests. The Harger Drunkometer displayed here was developed in the 1920s; Indiana state troopers were the first in the nation to use it. Many of the exhibits are designed for hands-on inspection, and children especially love the two-headed police car (which is actually the front halves from two police cars welded together and facing in opposite directions). Kids can climb inside, turn on the lights and siren, and talk on the radio. There's also a tornado room where visitors can learn what to do when a tornado is approaching—the simulation is very realistic, complete with sound and fury.

The museum is the brainchild of Ernie Alder, the former director of youth services for the Indiana State Police. Located at 8500 East Twenty-first Street, the museum is open 8:30 A.M. to 4:30 P.M. Monday through Friday. Admission

trivia

Richard Gatling, an Indianapolis physician, invented the world's first rapid-firing machine gun in 1862. An early model fired 250 shots a minute; by 1898, the Gatling gun could fire 3,000 rounds a minute. Dr. Gatling envisioned his gun as a weapon so terrible that it would end war forever. Its modern version is still being used by the military.

is free, but donations are appreciated. Group tours and educational programs can be arranged by appointment. Call (317) 899–8293 or (888) 477–9688.

The Curtis Management Group (CMG) Worldwide protects the rights of some of the most famous people of the twentieth and twenty-first centuries, both living and dead. Such luminaries as Sophia Loren, Michael Jordan, and Garfield the Cat, as well as the estates of James Dean, Marilyn Monroe, Humphrey Bogart, Jackie Robinson, and Diana, Princess of Wales, are just a few of the clients who depend on CMG to make sure that their names and images are not exploited.

Mark Roesler, who founded CMG in 1981, is also a collector of artifacts related to his famous clients' lives. Visitors may view his collection of several hundred items in a museum in CMG's headquarters building. Known as the **Legends Museum,** it includes such memorabilia as the wig Marilyn Monroe wore in her last movie, *The Misfits;* James Dean's Indian motorcycle and a replica of the Porsche he was driving when he was killed; a dress Sophia Loren wore when she won an Oscar; an Ingrid Bergman outfit from *Casablanca;* a baseball signed by Babe Ruth; Hank Williams Sr.'s guitar; and one of Ella Fitzgerald's Grammy awards.

Roesler sometimes lends pieces to other museums, so displays may vary. The museum is open from 9:00 A.M. to 5:00 P.M. Monday through Friday; nominal admission charge. CMG is located at 10500 Crosspoint Boulevard in Indianapolis; call (317) 570–5000 for additional information or visit www.cmgww.com.

Just west of Indianapolis is the **Indianapolis Motor Speedway,** where each May the world-famous Indy 500 auto race is held. When the course is not being used for competition or test purposes, you can see the track as professional racers see it by taking a bus tour around the 2½-mile asphalt oval. Your pace, of course, will be much more leisurely, and you'll learn many interesting facts along the way.

In addition to hosting the Indy 500, the track also hosts the U.S. Grand Prix in June and the Brickyard 400 each August. The inaugural U.S. Grand Prix race in 2000 marked the return of Formula One racing to this country after a nine-year hiatus.

A **Hall of Fame Museum** inside the track houses a vast collection of racing, classic, and antique passenger cars—including more than thirty past winners of the Indy 500—and some valuable, jewel-encrusted trophies. Perhaps the best-known artifact is the unusual Borg-Warner Trophy, which displays the sculpted, three-dimensional faces of every 500 winner since 1936. You'll also see film clips of old races, a stock car, and the Brickyard 400 trophy. This National Historic Landmark attracts visitors from around the world.

The museum and track, located at 4790 West Sixteenth Street in the suburb of Speedway, are open 9:00 A.M. to 5:00 P.M. daily, year-round, except Christmas. Closing time is extended to 6:00 P.M. during May. A nominal fee is charged for both the museum and the track tour. Tour information and tickets are available at the museum; call (317) 492–6784 or visit www.brickyard.com.

Ever dreamed of jumping into a race car and speeding around that oval? Well, now you can! The *Track Attack Racing School* will put you in the driver's seat of a real race car on a real race track. You'll use a Le Mans racer that will accelerate to 120 miles per hour. Professional instructors show you the ropes and allow you to increase speed as your confidence level builds. Eventually, if you choose, you'll be allowed to race other students. A variety of programs are offered; students must be at least eighteen years old and must have a valid driver's license. Contact the school at 2525 North Shadeland Avenue, or call (317) 890–1519 or (888) 722– 3879, or visit www.trackattack.com for rates and details.

The state's first medical center is also the nation's oldest surviving pathology laboratory. Housed in the Old Pathology Building on the grounds of the now-closed Central State Hospital, it remains virtually untouched by time. Known as the *Indiana Medical History Museum,* it features a fascinating collection of some 15,000 medical artifacts, including "quack" devices used in the nineteenth and early twentieth centuries, and an impressive display of brains in jars. The forty-nine brains were taken from mental patients at the hospital. *Medical Landmarks USA,* a travel guide published by McGraw-Hill in 1990, describes it as a "marvelous museum quite simply without peer in the entire country." Nominal admission fee; open 10:00 A.M. to 3:00 P.M. Thursday through Saturday, other days and times by appointment. The museum is located at 3045 West Vermont Street in Indianapolis; (317) 635–7329.

In a small park on Indianapolis's north side, the *Landmark for Peace Memorial* recalls the deaths of Martin Luther King Jr. and Robert Kennedy.

trivia

The late Bernard Vonnegut, an Indianapolis native, was an internationally renowned atmospheric scientist who discovered how to make it snow or rain by seeding clouds with silver iodide. His younger brother, the late novelist Kurt Vonnegut Jr., once said that Bernard knew "more about tornadoes than any man alive."

Robert Kennedy came to this predominantly black neighborhood during his Presidential campaign in 1968 to deliver a scheduled speech. When he arrived in Indianapolis on April 4, he learned that Dr. King had been assassinated earlier that day. The crowd that awaited Kennedy's appearance had not yet heard of Dr. King's death, so in lieu of his prepared speech, Kennedy delivered the news and asked them to look beyond their grief to continue their quest for the goals of their beloved spiritual leader. Two months later Kennedy was dead, also the victim of an assassin.

More than one hundred communities across the country experienced some form of violence as the news of Dr. King's death spread, but there was not one incident of violence in Indianapolis. To preserve the memory of what happened to two remarkable men, the city erected the *Landmark for Peace Memorial* in the **Dr. Martin Luther King Jr. Park** at 1702 Broadway Street. The outdoor sculpture, which depicts the two men reaching toward each other with outstretched hands, was created from guns that had been turned in during a gun amnesty program and then melted down. A plaque at the site bears the words of Kennedy's speech. The memorial was formally dedicated by then-President Bill Clinton in 1994. Open daily from dawn to dusk; call (317) 327–7461.

Morgan County

Indiana limestone has been used on a grand scale to build some of the world's most durable and majestic buildings. Since 1970 it has also been used by **Martinsville** sculptor **Charles Schiefer** to create some much smaller but equally memorable works of art. Schiefer saws, shapes, sands, and polishes his abstract sculptures in a shop adjacent to his country home at 5270 Low Gap Road. Outside, the approximately 180 sculptures that populate his ten-acre yard and surround his lake startle passersby and, as the sculptor's fame grows, lure visitors from all over. Most days they find the artist at work in his shop, cutting and shaping his latest creation amid the stone dust that constantly swirls through the air. Schiefer's customers, like his statues, come in all shapes and sizes; they range from municipalities and corporations to homeowners and a group of schoolchildren who raised enough money to purchase a stone rhinoceros they cherished. Each October Schiefer presents a special sculpture garden show that features additional new sculptures; the garden is open for tours at other times by appointment. For additional information call (765) 342–6211.

If you're the type whose curiosity is piqued by life's mysteries, head for **Mooresville** and nearby **Gravity Hill.** Legend has it that an Indian witch doctor was buried long ago at the foot of this low hill, and the great energy and power he possessed in life still emanate from the good doctor's grave. Anyone who stops his car at the bottom of the hill and puts it in neutral will find himself coasting backward up the slope for nearly ¼ mile. Don't scoff until you've tried it—witch doctor or no, it really works! Gravity Hill is located on Keller Hill Road, which runs west off State Road 42 on the south side of Mooresville; after turning onto Keller Hill Road, proceed for about 1 mile over a few small hills. When you come to a big hill, you've arrived. For exact directions ask local residents or contact the Mooresville Chamber of Commerce, 4 East Harrison Street, Mooresville 46158; (317) 831–6509.

Amateur astronomers can visit the ***Goethe Link Observatory*** near Mooresville to keep an eye on happenings in the universe. On Saturday nights when the weather is clear, the general public can view the heavens free of charge through the observatory's 36-inch reflector and 10-inch refractor telescopes. The observatory is owned by Indiana University, which rarely uses it because these days professional astronomers use computers instead. In 1986 the university granted sole use of the observatory to the Indiana Astronomical Society, which holds several events here each year between May and October. The society generally schedules events five to eight times a month, weather permitting, and the public is welcome to attend any of them free of charge. For a schedule of events, call the society at (317) 882–8805 or www.iasindy.org.

Sharing the one-hundred-acre grounds of the Link estate with the observatory are the fifteen-acre ***Link Daffodil Gardens,*** resplendent with an estimated 250,000 blooms for about two weeks in April. The gardens are open daily, free of charge, during daylight hours. The late Mrs. Helen Link, a nationally recognized authority on the daffodil, raised an array of different types here.

Goethe Link Observatory and Link Daffodil Gardens

She personally bred more than forty named varieties, and several of her creations are on exhibit at the National Arboretum in Washington, D.C. To check blooming times, contact the Indiana Astronomical Society (see above) or the Morgan County Chamber of Commerce, 109 East Morgan Street, P.O. Box 1378, Martinsville 46151; (765) 342–8110. The Link estate, which is on Observatory Road, lies 1½ miles west of State Road 67, about 5 miles south of Mooresville near the tiny community of Brooklyn; follow observatory signs.

The **Rock House Inn,** an eye-catching house in **Morgantown,** has for many years been luring architects, geologists, and just plain folks from across the nation. Built between 1894 and 1896 as a private residence, the house is adorned with the turrets, gables, and cones that were popular in the Victorian era, but any similarity to other houses of its time ends there. The walls are constructed of concrete blocks, embedded on the exterior with rocks and geodes of all shapes and sizes, bits of colored glass, seashells, Indian relics, jewelry, marbles, dolls' heads, keys, a boar's skull, and even a picture of two puppies under glass. Since the original owner kept enlarging the house to accommodate a family that eventually included twenty-two children, many of the items on the walls depict segments of family history. There are no regular hours, but you can stop by for a free tour when the house is open (generally daily). In the past the house operated as a bed-and-breakfast and may again in the future. For up-to-date information, contact the Rock House Inn, 380 West Washington Street, Morgantown; (812) 597–5100 or (888) 818–0001.

trivia

At one time it was illegal in Indiana to take a bath in the wintertime.

Shelby County

An extraordinary dining experience awaits you in **Morristown.** Nestled amid lovely gardens, the **Kopper Kettle** is as much a museum as a restaurant. It occupies a picturesque, nineteenth-century manor house accented with stained-glass windows and filled with antiques and art objects from around the world. All this beauty should be regarded as a bonus, because the meal awaiting you inside would be unforgettable served in any surroundings.

The wide range of entrees changes somewhat from day to day, but you can't go wrong with fried chicken, steak, or seafood. You won't find anything really fancy here—just plain food distinguished by perfect preparation, moderate prices, and an elegant atmosphere. Such luminaries as Henry Ford, Herbert Hoover, and Charles Lindbergh have dined here.

OTHER ATTRACTIONS WORTH SEEING IN CENTRAL INDIANA

ANDERSON

Gruenewald Historic House
626 Main Street
(765) 648–6875

Historical Military Armor Museum
2330 Crystal Street
(765) 649–8265

Paramount Theatre and Ballroom Tour
1124 Meridian Plaza
(765) 642–1234 or (800) 523–4658

ELWOOD

House of Glass
7900 State Road 28 East
(765) 552–6841

INDIANAPOLIS

Colonel Eli Lilly Civil War Museum
Indiana Soldiers' and Sailors' Monument
1 Monument Circle
(317) 232–7615

Firefighter Museum and Memorial
748 Massachusetts Avenue
(317) 327–6094

Fort Harrison State Park
5753 Glenn Road
Post Road at Fifty-ninth Street
(317) 591–0904

Morris-Butler House Museum
1204 North Park Avenue
(317) 636–5409

National Art Museum of Sport
University Place Conference Center
850 West Michigan Street
(317) 274–3627

President Benjamin Harrison Home
1230 North Delaware Street
(317) 631–1888

Scottish Rite Cathedral
650 North Meridian Street
(317) 262–3100

Located at 135 West Main Street (U.S. Highway 52), the Kopper Kettle offers a lunch menu from 11:00 A.M. to 4:00 P.M. Tuesday through Saturday. The dinner menu is available from 11:00 A.M. to 8:30 P.M. (last seating) Tuesday through Saturday, and 11:30 A.M. to 6:30 P.M. (last seating) Sunday; closed Monday; winter hours vary. Reservations are recommended, especially on Easter, Mother's Day, Thanksgiving, and during December. Call (765) 763–6767, or visit www.kopperkettle.com.

Tiny Boggstown may seem like just another rural Indiana community—a pleasant place to be but in no way distinctive. But since July 1984, when the **Boggstown Cabaret** opened for business, the "joint has been jumping." From its beginnings as a venue for ragtime music, the cabaret has evolved into a lunch and dinner theater that re-creates a 1920s and 1930s supper club featuring live music and comedy. At last count, folks from every state and from more than twenty-five countries (including Russia, Spain, Germany, Thailand, and Australia) have trekked to the Boggstown Inn for a dose of nostalgia. Lunch and dinner are served seven days a week February through December. Special lunch and dinner packages include live musical shows; all lunch guests are served the same meal, but dinner guests may choose any entree on the menu. Show tickets are purchased separately. Reservations are a must and should be made at least two to three weeks ahead of your visit. Since few of the roads leading to Boggstown are marked on any map, you'll be sent directions for getting there when you make your reservation. Write the inn at 6895 Boggstown Road, Boggstown 46110; call (317) 835–2020 for general information and a show schedule or (800) 672–2656 for reservations for fewer than twenty people. For group reservations of twenty or more, call (317) 835–4239 or (800) 820–1313. You can also visit the cabaret online at www.boggstown.com.

The excellent ***Grover Museum of the Shelby County Historical Society*** contains exhibits that depict the history of the local area. In this respect, it is not

A Woman to Look Up To

When Sandy Allen of Shelbyville was born on June 18, 1955, she weighed six and a half pounds and gave no indication of the extraordinary life that awaited her. Today she stands 7 feet, 7¼ inches tall and is the tallest living woman in the world. (The world's tallest living man is believed to be Leonid Stadnik of Ukraine, who is currently 8 feet, 4 inches tall and still growing.)

The excessive growth hormone at work in Sandy's body was triggered by a tumor on her pituitary gland. If she had not had surgery to help control her growth when she was a teen, she might have grown even taller.

Sandy sews most of her own clothes, wears size 22 hand-me-down sneakers provided by players in the National Basketball Association, and sleeps in an 8-foot-long custom-made bed. She has also held a few jobs along the way, including one as a secretary in the office of a former mayor of Indianapolis and another as part of the staff at the Guinness Museum in Niagara Falls, New York.

Now in failing health, Sandy spends much of her time in a wheelchair. Although she can no longer work and make a living, her spirits remain high. She visits with schoolchildren as often as possible and delivers her message that "It's Okay to Be Different" with great wit and charm.

Upon meeting Sandy, it is impossible, of course, not to notice her physical stature, but after leaving her presence it is her enormous heart that one remembers. You can read the inspirational story of her life in a biography by John Kleiman entitled *Cast a Giant Shadow.* It can be ordered online from Amazon.com or by calling the publisher at (888) 519–5121.

unlike other county historical museums. One display, however, is unique. Visitors may view the underwear worn by our nineteenth-century ancestors. Among the many interesting tidbits of knowledge you'll glean from your visit is the fact that women's crotchless underpants did not originate with Victoria's Secret or Frederick's of Hollywood. They were worn for efficiency's sake (all those long skirts and outhouses to contend with, you know) by inventive females in the 1800s. The museum also houses a model railroad layout. Located at 57 West Broadway Street in downtown **Shelbyville,** the museum is open from 9:00 A.M. to 4:00 P.M. Tuesday through Saturday or by special arrangement. Admission is free; call (317) 392–4634.

Places to Stay in Central Indiana

ALEXANDRIA

Country Gazebo Inn
13867 North 100 West
(765) 754–8783
Moderate

DANVILLE

Country Comforts B&B
368 East County Road
450 North
(317) 745–0773
Expensive

FISHERS

Frederick-Talbott Inn at the Prairie
13805 Allisonville Road
(317) 578–3600
Moderate

FORTVILLE

Ivy House Bed and Breakfast
304 North Merrill Street
(317) 485–4800
Moderate

GREENWOOD

Persimmon Tree Bed and Breakfast
1 North Madison Avenue
(317) 889–0849
Moderate

INDIANAPOLIS

All Nations B&B
2164 North Capitol Avenue
(317) 923–2622
Moderate

Harrison House at Fort Harrison State Park
6002 North Post Road
(317) 543–9592 or
(877) 937–3678
Moderate

Nestle Inn Bed and Breakfast
637 North East Street
(317) 610–5200 or
(877) 339–5200
Moderate

Old Northside Bed and Breakfast
1340 North Alabama Street
(317) 635–9123
Moderate

Speedway Bed and Breakfast
1829 Cunningham Road
(317) 487–6531
Moderate

Stone Soup Inn
1304 North Central Avenue
(317) 639–9550 or
(866) 639–9550
Moderate

LAPEL

Kati-Scarlett B&B
1037 North Main Street
P.O. Box 756
(765) 534–4937
Inexpensive

McCORDSVILLE

Round Barn Inn Bed and Breakfast
6794 North County Road
600 West
(317) 335–7023 or
(888) 743–9819
Moderate

MARTINSVILLE

Tapestry Manor B&B
490 South Jefferson Street
(765) 342–6029
Moderate

SOURCES FOR ADDITIONAL INFORMATION ABOUT CENTRAL INDIANA

Anderson/Madison County Visitors and Convention Bureau
6335 Scatterfield Road
Anderson 46013
(765) 643–5633 or (800) 533–6569

Boone County Tourism Council
9381 West 450 North
Thorntown 46071
(765) 436–2909

Franklin (Johnson County) Chamber of Commerce
370 East Jefferson Street
Franklin 46131
(317) 736–6334

Greater Greenfield (Hancock County) Visitors Bureau
1 Courthouse Plaza
Greenfield 46140
(317) 477–8687 or (866) 384–8687

Greater Greenwood (Johnson County) Chamber of Commerce
550 South U.S. Highway 31
Greenwood 46142
(317) 888–4856

Greater Martinsville (Morgan County) Chamber of Commerce
109 East Morgan Street
P.O. Box 1378
Martinsville 46151
(765) 342–8110

Greater Zionsville (Boone County) Chamber of Commerce
135 South Elm Street
P.O. Box 148
Zionsville 46077
(317) 873–3836

Hamilton County Convention and Visitors Bureau
11601 Municipal Drive
Fishers 46038
(317) 598–4444 or
(800) 776–8687

Hendricks County Convention and Visitors Bureau
8 West Main Street
Danville 46122
(317) 718–8750 or (800) 321–9666

Indianapolis Convention and Visitors Association (Marion County)
1 RCA Dome, Suite 100
(317) 639–4282 or (800) 824–4639

Mooresville (Morgan County) Chamber of Commerce
4 East Harrison Street
Mooresville 46158
(317) 831–6509

Shelby County Chamber of Commerce
501 North Harrison Street
Shelbyville 46176
(317) 398–6647

PLAINFIELD

Wingate Inn
6300 Gateway Drive
(317) 279–2500
Moderate

ZIONSVILLE

Brick Street Inn
175 South Main Street
(317) 873–9177
Expensive

Places to Eat in Central Indiana

ALEXANDRIA

Hi Way Cafe
State Road 9 South
(765) 724–9969
Inexpensive
American

ANDERSON

The Lemon Drop
1701 Mounds Road
(765) 644–9055
Inexpensive
American

Lucy's Family Dining
2460 East County Road 67
(765) 643–3144
Inexpensive
American

Nile Restaurant
723 East Eighth Street
(765) 640–9028
Moderate
Greek/Turkish

ATLANTA

Fletcher's of Atlanta
185 West Main Street
(765) 292–2777
Expensive
American

BEECH GROVE

Napoli Villa Italian Restaurant
758 Main Street
(317) 783–4122
Moderate
Italian

CARMEL

Cancun Mexican Restaurant and Cantina
511 South Rangeline Road
(317) 580–0333
Moderate
Mexican

Woody's Library Restaurant
40 East Main Street
(317) 573–4444
Moderate
American

ELWOOD

Jim Dandy Family Restaurant
1803 South Anderson Street
(765) 552–5033
Inexpensive
American

Village Cafe
1424 Main Street
(765) 552–9007
Inexpensive
American

FISHERS

Nickel Plate Bar and Grill
8654 East 116th Street
(317) 841–2888
Moderate
American

Persimmons at Conner Prairie
13400 Allisonville Road
(317) 776–6008
Moderate
American

Peterson's
7690 East 96th Street
(317) 598–8863
Expensive
Steak/seafood

FRANKLIN

The Willard
99 North Main Street
(317) 738–9991
Moderate
American/pizza/Mexican

GREENFIELD

Carnegie's
100 West North Street
(317) 462–8480
Expensive
Italian

Dragon Palace
413 North State Street
(317) 462–4965
Inexpensive
Chinese

INDIANAPOLIS

Acapulco Joe's
365 North Illinois Street
(317) 637–5160
Inexpensive
Mexican

Arni's Restaurant
3443 West Eighty-sixth Street
(317) 875–7034
Inexpensive
American

Broad Ripple Steakhouse
929 East Westfield Boulevard
(317) 253–8101
Expensive
Steak/seafood

El Sol de Tala
2444 East Washington Street
(317) 635–8252
Inexpensive
Mexican

G.T. South's Rib House
5711 East Seventy-first
Street
(317) 849–6997
Inexpensive
Barbecue

Garam Masala
8553 Ditch Road
(317) 257–1213
Inexpensive
Indian

The Garrison Restaurant
6002 North Post Road
(317) 543–9592
Inexpensive
American

Hollyhock Hill
8110 North College Avenue
(317) 251–2294
Moderate
Home cooking

Iaria's Italian Restaurant
317 South College Avenue
(317) 638–7706
Moderate
Italian

The Iron Skillet
2489 West Thirtieth Street
(317) 923–6353
Moderate
Home cooking

Kona Jack's
9413 North Meridian Street
(317) 843–1609
Moderate
Seafood/sushi

Khoury's
1850 Broad Ripple Avenue
(317) 251–8610
Moderate
Greek/Middle Eastern

**Mama Carolla's Old
Italian Restaurant**
1031 East Fifty-fourth Street
(317) 259–9412
Moderate
Italian

Mix 5/Iraqi Shish Kebab
2989 West Seventy-First
Street, Suite 3
(317) 298–5355
Inexpensive
Iraqi

Old Spaghetti Factory
210 South Meridian Street
(317) 635–6325
Inexpensive
Italian

Plump's Last Shot
6416 Cornell Avenue
(317) 257–5867
Inexpensive
American

**Rathskeller at the
Athenaeum**
401 East Michigan Street
(317) 636–0396
Moderate
German/American

Rick's Cafe Boatyard
4050 Dandy Trail
(317) 290–9300
Expensive
Steak/seafood

**Scholar's Inn
Gourmet Cafe**
725 Massachusetts Avenue
(317) 536–0707
Moderate
American

Sky City Cafe
Eiteljorg Museum
500 West Washington Street
(317) 636–9378
Inexpensive
Southwestern

MOORESVILLE

Gray Brothers Cafeteria
555 South Indiana Street
(317) 831–3345
Inexpensive
Home cooking

NOBLESVILLE

Classic Kitchen
610 Hannibal Street
(317) 773–7385
Expensive
Eclectic/French-inspired

Lutz's
3100 Westfield Road
(317) 896–5002
Moderate
Steak house

**Sinclair's Gourmet
Pizza and Subs**
216 South Tenth Street
(317) 770–9099
Moderate
Pizza/subs

PENDLETON

Diner
609 East State Street
(765) 778–1974
Inexpensive
American

Jimmie's Dairy Bar
7065 State Road 67 South
(765) 778–3800
Inexpensive
American

PERKINSVILLE

Bonge's Tavern
9830 West 280 North
(765) 734–1625
Moderate
American

PITTSBORO

Frank and Mary's
21 East Main Street
(317) 892–3485
Moderate
American

SHELBYVILLE

Bavarian Haus Restaurant
2806 East Range Road
(317) 398–7174
Inexpensive
German

Fiddlers Three
1415 East Michigan Road
(317) 392–4371
Moderate
American

SHERIDAN

The Red Onion Restaurant and Lounge
406 South Main Street
(317) 758–0424
Moderate
American

SPEEDWAY

Union Jack Pub
6225 West Twenty-fifth Street
(317) 243–3300
Moderate
Variety

THORNTOWN

Stookey's Restaurant
125 East Main Street
(765) 436–7202
Moderate
American

TIPTON

Sherrill's Restaurant
U.S. Highway 31 South and State Road 28
(765) 675–3550
Inexpensive
American

WHITELAND

Whit's Inn
1020 North U.S. Highway 31
(317) 535–9511
Inexpensive
American

ZIONSVILLE

Il Villagio
40 South Main Street
(317) 733–3600
Moderate
Italian

Zorba's
30 North Main Street
(317) 733–0633
Inexpensive
Greek/Middle Eastern

Northeast Indiana

Perhaps best known as Amish country, northeast Indiana is home to one of the largest populations of Old Order Amish in the world. For the most part, it is a serene and pastoral world, sculpted long ago by the glaciers of the Ice Age. Beyond the scattering of towns and cities, the gentle hills sometimes seem to march on forever. Natural lakes are small but abundant; Steuben County alone is dotted with 101 of them.

Although travelers can hurry north and south on Interstate 69 or east and west on Interstate 80/90 (Indiana's only toll road), those who want to experience the simple charms of this part of the Hoosier State will set out on back roads and byways. It is there that they will discover the essence of this pocket of peace.

Adams County

Just south of Berne you can drive through a picturesque covered bridge across the Wabash River and leave the twentieth century behind. You are now in the land of the Amish, where windmills replace skyscrapers and horse-drawn buggies move sedately along dusty country roads. This is the home of *Amishville, U.S.A.,* a 120-acre Amish farm open to the public.

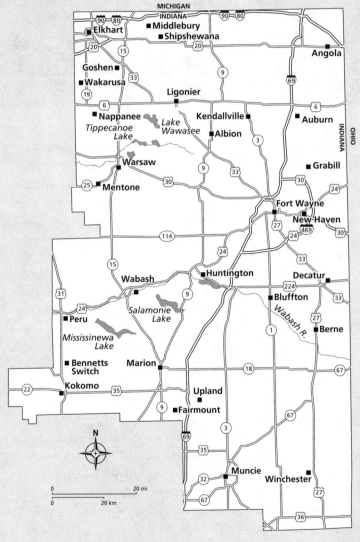

MICHIGAN
INDIANA

Middlebury
Elkhart
Shipshewana
Angola

Goshen
Wakarusa
Ligonier

Nappanee
Lake Wawasee
Kendallville
Auburn
Tippecanoe Lake
Albion

Warsaw
Grabill
Mentone

Fort Wayne
New-Haven

Wabash
Huntington
Decatur

Peru
Salamonie Lake
Bluffton

Mississinewa Lake
Wabash R.
Berne

Bennetts Switch
Marion

Kokomo
Upland
Fairmount

Muncie
Winchester

OHIO
INDIANA

N

0   20 mi

0   20 km

While members of the resident family go about their daily business of managing the farm, using the centuries-old methods of their ancestors, visitors stroll through the barn, milk house, smokehouse, washhouse, and old-fashioned garden. Modern conveniences have no place here; the Amish live their lives without motors, plumbing, refrigeration, radios, televisions, and automobiles. At Amishville you can learn all about the simple lifestyle these gentle people have chosen to embrace.

trivia

The Ceylon Covered Bridge, 2 miles northeast of Geneva in Adams County, is the last covered bridge on the fabled Wabash River.

Entrance is free, but nominal fees are charged for a guided tour of the authentic Amish house and outbuildings, and for buggy rides and hayrides in the summer and for sleigh rides in the winter. In deference to both Amish tradition and

AUTHOR'S FAVORITE ATTRACTIONS/ EVENTS IN NORTHEAST INDIANA

Aloha International Hawaiian Steel Guitar Convention
Winchester; July
(765) 584–3104, (765) 584–3266, or
(800) 905–0514

Auburn-Cord-Duesenberg Festival
Auburn; September
(Labor Day weekend)
(260) 925–3600

Auburn-Cord-Duesenberg Museum
Auburn
(260) 925–1444; www.acdmuseum.org

Circus City Festival
Peru; July
(765) 472–3918

Easter Pageant
Marion; Easter weekend
(765) 668–5435 or (800) 662–9474

Fairmount Museum Days/ Remembering James Dean
Fairmount; September
(765) 948–4555

Festival of Flight
Grissom Air Museum
Peru; October
(765) 689–8011

Grissom Air Museum
Peru
(765) 689–8011

International Circus Hall of Fame
Peru
(765) 472–7553
or (800) 771–0241

Lincoln Museum
Fort Wayne
(260) 455–3864
www.thelincolnmuseum.org

Menno-Hof Visitors Center
Shipshewana
(260) 768–4117

Midwest Museum of American Art
Elkhart
(574) 293–6660

Amishville, U.S.A.

the Swiss heritage of surrounding communities, ***Der Essen Platz*** (The Eating Place) at Amishville serves home-cooked foods that are favorites of both cultures. Two small lakes are available for fishing, swimming, and, in the winter, ice skating. For those who want to stay a spell and let the peace sink in, there's a large wooded campground.

You can reach Amishville by going south from Berne on U.S. Highway 27 for 3 miles; at County Road 950S, turn east and follow the signs. Open daily April through mid-December from 9:00 A.M. to 5:00 P.M. Monday through Sat-

Eight's Company

Decatur is home to one of Indiana's best-known families. Keith and Becki Dilley were catapulted into the national spotlight when Becki gave birth to sextuplets on May 25, 1993, in an Indianapolis hospital. For a while, the family resided in Indianapolis, with Keith and Becki working different shifts so they could take turns watching over their brood. When Keith accepted a job in Fort Wayne, about forty-five minutes from Berne, the Dilleys (Keith, Becki, four boys, two girls, and an assortment of pets) left their five-bedroom, four-bathroom home in Indianapolis to take up residence in a three-bedroom, one-bathroom home in Berne. The family recently moved a few miles up the road to Decatur.

People across the country have watched the six children grow through their regular appearances on the ABC-TV show *Primetime*. In May 1999 ABC also aired a made-for-TV movie about the sextuplets entitled *Half a Dozen Babies*.

Now teenagers, the sextuplets are good students with a diversity of interests—some as a group, some as individuals. On one point, though, they all agree: When asked what they were most looking forward to in their teen years, they replied in unison: "Driving!"

urday and 1:00 to 5:00 P.M. Sunday; guided tours available daily April through November. The campground is open April through October. Write Amishville, U.S.A., 844 East 900 South, Geneva 46740; (260) 589–3536.

In the Swiss village of **Berne,** you can visit the **First Mennonite Church.** Located at 566 West Main Street, the classic Gothic structure is one of the two largest Mennonite churches in North America. The main sanctuary can seat some 2,000 people. Of particular note is the Moeller organ with its 2,281 pipes, which have produced beautiful music since 1914. Visitors come from all over the United States, Canada, and Europe to tour the church and listen to the organ. The church is open to visitors daily from 9:00 A.M. to 4:30 P.M.; Sunday services are held at 10:00 A.M. Call (260) 589–3108.

At the **Swiss Heritage Village and Museum,** you can see fifteen restored structures that provide a glimpse of the lifestyle of the Swiss immigrants who settled in this area between 1860 and 1900. A **Swiss Heritage Festival** held each September features Swiss singing, stone throwing, historic crafts, and cider making on the world's largest cider press. Built during the Civil War, the gigantic press weighs about two tons. The village and museum are open 9:00 A.M. to 4:00 P.M. Monday through Saturday May through October, and at other times for special events; there's a nominal admission fee. Located at 1200 Swiss Way in Berne; (260) 589–8007; www.swissheritage.org.

For information about Berne's unusual shops and stores, many of which cater to the area's 4,000 Amish residents, contact the Berne Chamber of Commerce, 175 West Main Street, P.O. Box 85, Berne 46711; (260) 589–8080.

A turn-of-the-twentieth-century aura of a different sort is found in **Decatur.** The **Back 40 Junction Restaurant,** famous for both food and decor, is housed in a country railroad station. Outside, on remnant stretches of train track, you can view such railroad memorabilia as a 1920s-era club car, complete with original lighting fixtures, seats, and berths. The "little red caboose" is a gift shop. Inside the station is a fine restaurant decorated with hundreds of antiques and bits of Americana. Antique oil lamps that once belonged to actress Carole Lombard, an Indiana native, are here, as are a Tiffany chandelier, an old ox yoke, and a collection of the Burma Shave signs that once lined our nation's highways and provided many a laugh. Although the Back 40 Junction offers a regular lunch and dinner menu, it is best known for its moderately priced buffet. Open 11:00 A.M. to 8:00 P.M. Monday through Thursday, 11:00 A.M. to 9:00 P.M. Friday and Saturday, and 11:00 A.M. to 7:00 P.M. Sunday and holidays; closed Christmas. The restaurant is located at 1011 North Thirteenth Street (U.S. Highway 27/33) on the north side of Decatur. Reservations accepted; (260) 724–3355.

Allen County

John Chapman, better known as Johnny Appleseed, traveled on foot through much of the Midwest, planting seeds that would one day grow into vast apple orchards. In his own time he was much beloved, and he remains a folk hero to this day. What most folks don't realize is that Johnny didn't wander about in all those raggedy clothes because he had to. Johnny was a miser—kindly, but a miser nevertheless—who found free room and board with families along the routes he followed, planted some apple seeds in their fields, and eventually moved on. It was no surprise to those who knew him that his death on March 18, 1845, was due to exposure. He died near **Fort Wayne** and was buried there with honors. His gravesite, open at all times to the public, is located in the forty-three-acre **Johnny Appleseed Park,** which lies along East Coliseum Boulevard on the east side of the 4000 block of Parnell Avenue and just north of the St. Joseph River; (260) 427–6720.

The forty-two-acre **Fort Wayne Children's Zoo,** with more than 500 domestic and exotic animals, delights visitors of all ages. Although small, it has been internationally recognized for its landscaping and cleverly designed exhibits. *Travel America* says this is "simply the best children's zoo in the nation," the *New York Times* calls it one of the top five children's zoos in the country, and *Child* magazine calls it one of the "Ten Best Zoos for Kids." Children love to feed the animals, pet tame deer, and ride the miniature train. The whole family will love the safari through a re-created African veldt where all animals roam free. An exhibit devoted to Australian wildlife—the largest of its kind in North America—includes a 20,000-gallon Great Barrier Reef aquarium. The Indonesian Rain Forest features a Sumatran elephant skeleton, the world's only endangered-species carousel, and rare Sumatran tigers roaming in a half-acre re-creation of their outdoor habitat. Open 9:00 A.M. to 5:00 P.M. daily late April through mid-October. Nominal admission fee. Located at 3411 Sherman Boulevard in Fort Wayne's Franke Park; (260) 427–6800; www.kidszoo.org.

The world's largest private collection of Abraham Lincoln memorabilia, housed at the **Lincoln Museum,** includes some 18,000 books in twenty-six languages dealing exclusively with Lincoln; paintings, letters, and personal possessions of the family; and such curios as the flag that draped Lincoln's box at Ford's Theatre. The first item in the collection was the photograph of Lincoln that was used on the $5.00 bill; it was contributed by Lincoln's son, Robert Todd Lincoln, in 1928. A more recent acquisition is the inkwell Lincoln used to sign the Emancipation Proclamation. A remarkable collection of some 400 pictures of the sixteenth president and his descendants—the existence of these pictures was known only to family members for many decades—was acquired by the museum after the death in 1985 of the president's great-grandson, Robert Beckwith, last of the Lincoln lineage. The crown jewel of the collection, though, was acquired in 2005—a rare copy of the slavery-abolishing 13th Amendment to the Constitution signed by Lincoln and the senators who passed it. One of three known copies in existence, the sheepskin document is valued at about $1.5 million. The museum also features computerized exhibits, film clips about Lincoln's life as depicted in the movies and on television, and one of the largest museum stores in the state. Open 10:00 A.M. to 5:00 P.M. Tuesday through Saturday and 1:00 to 5:00 P.M. Sunday; there's a nominal admission fee. The 30,000-square-foot state-of-the-art facility is located at 200 East Berry Street; (260) 455–3864; www.thelincolnmuseum.org.

One of Fort Wayne's newest museums will delight car buffs. For a nominal admission fee you can see fifty-one of the finest restored Corvettes of every decade from the 1950s through the 1990s. The aptly named **Corvette Classics** is located at 6702 Point Inverness Way. Open 10:00 A.M. to 5:00 P.M. Monday through Saturday and noon to 5:00 P.M. Sunday; (260) 436–3444.

One of the most breathtaking sights in downtown Fort Wayne is the **Foellinger-Freimann Botanical Conservatory,** a series of three buildings connected by tunnels and one of the largest passive solar structures in the United States. Some 1,300 panels of insulating glass permit the sunshine to enter; moreover, the city passed special zoning laws to ensure that all available sunlight could reach the buildings unobstructed. Visitors will see displays of North American desert plants, rare tropical plants from around the world, a talking tree, a worm tunnel, and changing seasonal exhibits. Nominal admission fee. Open 10:00 A.M. to 5:00 P.M. Monday through Saturday and noon to 4:00 P.M. Sunday and holidays; closed Christmas. Located at 1100 South Calhoun Street; (260) 427–6440.

Lakeside Rose Garden, which covers more than three acres, is Indiana's only All-American Rose Selection Display Garden. Currently some 220 varieties flourish on nearly 2,500 labeled rosebushes against the backdrop of a lagoon, reflecting pools, and a Grecian-style pergola. The blooms are glorious from June to mid-October, but the scenic grounds are open daily throughout the year during daylight hours. Free admission; located in Lakeside City Park at the corner of East Lake Avenue and Forest Park Boulevard; (260) 427–6000.

Anyone interested in architecture will want to see the **Cathedral of the Immaculate Conception/Museum,** a Gothic-style church in the center of Fort Wayne. Its Bavarian stained-glass windows are recognized as the finest in the Western Hemisphere, and its hand-carved wood altar is considered one of the

ANNUAL EVENTS IN NORTHEAST INDIANA

James Dean Birthday Celebration
Fairmount; early February
(765) 948–4555

Wakarusa Maple Syrup Festival
Wakarusa; April
(574) 862–4344

Cole Porter Festival
Peru; June
(765) 472–1923 or (765) 473–9183

Windmill Festival
Kendallville; June
(260) 347–2334

Haynes-Apperson Festival
Kokomo; July 4th weekend
(765) 854–1234

Quilters Hall of Fame Celebration
Marion; July
(765) 664–9333

Swiss Days Festival
Berne; July
(260) 589–8080

Three Rivers Festival
Fort Wayne; July
(260) 426–5556

Pickle Festival
St. Joe; August
(260) 337–5461

Popcorn Festival
Van Buren; August
(765) 934–4888

Auburn-Cord-Duesenberg Festival
Auburn; Labor Day weekend
(260) 925–3600

Apple Festival
Nappanee; September
(574) 773–7812 or (800) 517–9739

Forks of the Wabash Pioneer Festival
Huntington; September
(260) 359–8687 or (800) 848–4282

Grabill Country Fair
Grabill; September
(260) 424–3700 or (800) 767–7752

Johnny Appleseed Festival
Fort Wayne; September
(260) 483–5638

The Christmas City Walkway of Lights
Marion; late November–late December
(765) 668–4453

finest woodcarvings in the country. Maps are available for self-guided tours of the church, which is open 7:00 A.M. to 4:00 P.M. daily. Located on Cathedral Square at 1100 South Calhoun Street; (260) 424–1485.

Other notable architectural sights in Fort Wayne are the **Concordia Theological Seminary** campus buildings designed by Eero Saarinen to resemble an early northern European village. They have won numerous national and worldwide awards for both design and landscaping. For a free tour contact the Seminary at 6600 North Clinton Street in Fort Wayne; (260) 452–2100.

The campus of the **University of St. Francis** boasts a college library housed in a mansion that in the early 1900s was a residential showplace. A stairway that spirals to the third floor of the thirty-three-room Romanesque structure is truly magnificent. A map and self-guided cassette tour describe the lavish wall hangings, hand-painted murals, and period rooms. Located at 2701 Spring Street in Fort Wayne; admission is free, but donations are welcome. Open for self-guided tours 8:00 A.M. to 9:00 P.M. Monday through Thursday, 8:00 A.M. to 4:30 P.M. Friday, noon to 5:00 P.M. Saturday, and noon to 8:00 P.M. Sunday during the academic year, but hours vary during the summer; (260) 434–7455 or (260) 434–3100.

Fort Wayne is also home to one of the finest genealogical research facilities in the country. The collection, second in size only to the one in Salt Lake City that's owned by the Mormon Church, is housed in the *Allen County Public Library,* at 200 East Berry Street. In 2002, *Family Tree Magazine* named this library the best public library in the nation for genealogy research. Included in the materials found here are more than 325,000 printed volumes, some 350,000 items of microtext, and an extensive computer database. Each month about 1,500 new items are added to the collection. More than 100,000 visitors use the resources of the genealogy department each year, free of charge. The library is open 9:00 A.M. to 9:00 P.M. Monday through Thursday, 9:00 A.M. to 6:00 P.M. Friday and Saturday, and 1:00 to 6:00 P.M. Sunday; closed Sundays from Memorial Day weekend through Labor Day weekend. For additional information write the library at P.O. Box 2270, Fort Wayne 46802; call (260) 421–1200, or visit www.acpb.lib.us.

DeBrand Chocolatier of Fort Wayne has gained a reputation as one of the world's elite makers of fine chocolates. Donald Trump is a customer; he contracted with DeBrand to stock the luxury suite used by *The Apprentice* candidates with about 3,000 gold-foil-covered chocolate coins stamped with a large T. For a nominal fee, you can see and taste why during a tour that includes a video presentation, a tour of the company's three kitchens, and a sampling of the wares. If you like what you taste, you can purchase more at an on-site shop to take with you. You can also purchase various desserts and drinks. Located at 10105 Auburn Park Drive; call (260) 969–8335 for tour information or visit www.debrand.com. Open 7:00 A.M. to 9:00 P.M. Monday through Thursday, 7:00 A.M. to 10:30 P.M. Friday, 10:00 A.M. to 10:30 P.M. Saturday, and noon to 6:00 P.M. Sunday. Although tours are offered every day, it's best to schedule one between 8:00 A.M. and 6:00 P.M. Monday through Friday in order to view an active chocolate-making process.

For a get-away-from-it-all experience, travel southwest from downtown Fort Wayne to *Fox Island County Park.* There, in a 270-acre state nature preserve, you'll see a 40-foot sand dune and an unusual (for Indiana) quaking bog whose surface ripples when you stamp your feet. You may also want to check out the nature center at the park. Located at 7324 Yohne Road; (260) 449–3180 or (260) 427–6000.

The peaceful little town of *Grabill,* located in the center of an Amish farming community northeast of Fort Wayne, is a lovely place to explore crafts and antiques shops. Each year in September, the *Grabill Country Fair* lures more than 100,000 people from throughout the Midwest. The fun includes contests for seed spitting, frog jumping, chicken flying, and wife calling. Go north from Fort Wayne onto State Road 1 to Hosler Road in the town of Leo, then turn east onto Hosler Road. For additional information contact the Grabill Chamber of Commerce, P.O. Box 254, Grabill 46741; (260) 627–5227 or (800) 939–3216. Information is also available at the Fort Wayne/Allen County Convention and Visitor Bureau, 1021 South Calhoun Street, Fort Wayne 46802; (800) 767–7752.

Railroad buffs will enjoy a visit to *TrainTown,* located at 15808 Edgerton Road in *New Haven,* where some part of railroad history is almost always being taken apart or put back together in a restoration shop by members of the Fort Wayne Railroad Historical Society. One of the most recent projects was the restoration of the old Nickel Plate 765 steam locomotive, restored piece by piece between 1993 and 2005.

Shop projects are ongoing. Visitors are welcome to lend a hand with whatever restoration program might be under way at the time of their visit. For a fee, a volunteer will show anyone eighteen or older how to operate a forty-four-ton working diesel engine built in 1953. Participants receive instruction on general locomotive operation on the society's trackage. The society also offers excursions on trains they've made roadworthy. Plans call for the now fully operational 765 to be on the road in 2007.

Plans in the works include building a working replica of Fort Wayne's former Nickel Plate Depot on TrainTown grounds and the restoration of the Lake Erie and Fort Wayne six-coupled steam locomotive No. 1. The workshops and a museum on the grounds are open free of charge from 10:00 A.M. to 4:00 P.M. on Saturday and 1:00 to 4:00 P.M. on Sunday. Everything here is done by volunteers, so call before visiting to make sure someone will be on hand to show you around. For additional information write the Fort Wayne Railroad Historical Society, P.O. Box 11017, Fort Wayne 46855; call (260) 493–0765; or visit www.765.org.

DeKalb County

A rare treat awaits old-car buffs in the town of *Auburn.* Housed in the administration building of the old Auburn Automobile Company is one of the country's finest collections of cars.

The *Auburn-Cord-Duesenberg Museum* and its contents complement each other perfectly. Constructed in 1930, the building is an architectural masterpiece of the art deco style. The automobiles within it are among the most beautiful ever produced—products of a golden age when luxury and power were the gods of the road. Some 140 classic, antique, special-interest, and one-of-a-kind cars dating from 1898 to the present are on permanent display here.

Indiana was once the automobile capital of the world, and Auburn was its heart, the birthplace of twenty-one of America's early motorcars. The Duesenbergs designed and produced here were the costliest domestic automobiles of the 1920s and 1930s—commanding prices of $15,000 to $20,000 even in the midst of the Great Depression. Greta Garbo owned one, as did Gary Cooper, Clark Gable, and many of the crowned heads of Europe. The cars were not only symbols of extravagant wealth but were also supremely engineered machines that could hurtle down the highway at speeds up to 130 miles per hour. Today Duesenbergs are worth hundreds of thousands of dollars as collector cars.

Various models of the Cord, more modest than the Duesenberg but still a cut above the rest, and the Auburn are displayed, along with more obscure cars, such as the Locomotive, Rauch-Lang, and McIntyre. The collection includes a flamboyant 1956 Bentley owned by John Lennon in the 1960s. Visitors will also see a 1948 Tucker and a 1981 DeLorean.

The museum, designated a National Historic Landmark in 2005, is open daily year-round, except for major winter holidays, from 9:00 A.M. to 5:00 P.M. There is an admission fee. Contact the Auburn-Cord-Duesenberg Museum, 1600 South Wayne Street, P.O. Box 271, Auburn 46706; (260) 925–1444; www.acd museum.org.

Each year on Labor Day weekend Auburns, Cords, and Duesenbergs from all over the United States return to the city of their creation for an annual festival. A highlight of the event is the collector-car auction, which has produced many world-record prices. Even for spectators it's an exciting show, with some 5,000 cars going up for auction each day.

One of the highlights of the 2006 auction was a yellow 2005 Lamborghini covered with celebrity autographs. Signed by Bruce Willis, Will Ferrell, and Regis Philbin, among others, it fetched $500,000 for a charity that works to prevent child abuse. Other 2006 sales included a Batmobile used in the movie *Batman Forever* for $335,000, a 1941 Packard limousine used by Franklin Delano Roosevelt for $290,000, and a 1938 Cadillac Town Car used by Pope Pius XII for $250,000.

A prized offering in 2003 was a 1930 Duesenberg Model J once owned by publisher William Randolph Hearst; one of only two Duesenbergs ever built with an all-aluminum body and extra-long chassis, it sold for $535,000. The 2001 auction featured a 1965 Clint Brawner Hawk race car that was driven by

OTHER ATTRACTIONS WORTH SEEING IN NORTHEAST INDIANA

AUBURN

Hoosier Air Museum
DeKalb County Airport
2822 County Road 62
(260) 927–0443

DUNKIRK

Dunkirk Glass Museum
309 South Franklin Street
(765) 768–6872

ELKHART

National New York Central
Railroad Museum
721 South Main Street
(574) 294–3001

Ruthmere Museum
302 East Beardsley Avenue
(574) 264–0330 or (888) 287–7696

FORT WAYNE

Science Central
1950 North Clinton Street
(260) 424–2400 or (800) 4–HANDS–ON

GREENTOWN

Greentown Glass Museum
112 North Meridian Street
(765) 628–6206

HUNTINGTON

Forks of the Wabash Historic Park
3011 West Park Drive
(260) 356–1903

KOKOMO

Seiberling Mansion
(Howard County Museum)
1200 West Sycamore Street
(765) 452–4314

MARION

The Quilter's Hall of Fame
926 South Washington Street
(765) 664–9333

MUNCIE

Minnetrista Cultural Center &
Oakhurst Gardens
1200 North Minnetrista Parkway
(765) 282–4848 or (800) 428–5887

WINONA LAKE

The Village at Winona
901 East Canal Street
(574) 268–9888

Mario Andretti in his first Indianapolis 500, Benito Mussolini's 1939 Lancia Astura, a 1948 custom Ford pickup owned by Wynonna Judd, and the El Camino used in the movie *The Mexican,* starring Julia Roberts and Brad Pitt. Among the cars sold in 1997, were the late Scott Brayton's two Indianapolis 500 pole cars, the Taco Bell *Star Wars* Hummer, Roy Orbison's 1985 Porsche 911, and a 1990 BMW 750IL that once belonged to singer John Mellencamp. Because of a tragic coincidence, an armor-plated Rolls-Royce used by Princess Diana during her visits to the United States fetched $100,000, more than three times the price auctioneers had anticipated. Diana was killed in an automobile accident the day before the auction. Write the Auburn-Cord-Duesenberg Festival at the museum's address, or call (260) 925–3600.

Complementing the Auburn-Cord-Duesenberg Museum is the **National Automotive and Truck Museum of the United States.** The museum, known locally as NATMUS, houses more than one hundred post–World War II cars and a truck collection that spans the entire motorized industry. A prize of the collection is the Endeavor, a truck built on a modified International Harvester chassis that set the world land speed record for trucks on the Bonneville Salt Flats of Utah. Thousands of toy model cars and trucks are also on display. NATMUS is located at 1000 Gordon M. Buehrig Place and is open 9:00 A.M. to 5:00 P.M. daily. Nominal admission fee. For additional information write NATMUS at P.O. Box 686, Auburn 46706-0686, or call (260) 925–9100.

Auburn also is home to four other museums. The **World War II Victory Museum** is the world's largest museum dedicated to that topic. Included in its collection are Adolf Hitler's parade car and vehicles used during the war by American generals Dwight D. Eisenhower, Douglas MacArthur, and George Patton. A recently acquired portrait of Adolf Hitler may be seen in the "Rising Tyrants" exhibit. Sharing the 200,000-square-foot structure is the **Kruse Automotive and Carriage Museum,** dedicated to the history of the automobile. Additionally, you can visit the **Northeast Baseball Association Museum,** which features baseball memorabilia dating from the early 1900s, and the **Philo T. Farnsworth Television Museum,** named for the inventor who began mass production of televisions in Fort Wayne. All together, they comprise a complex known as the **American Heritage Village,** an ongoing historical preservation project located at 5634 County Road 11A. One of the museums in the village will also soon house a collection of James Dean memorabilia, including a replica of the silver Porsche Spyder the actor was driving when he was killed in a car crash; the artifacts were donated by the owner of the recently closed James Dean Gallery in Gas City. A single admission fee admits you to all four museums. Open daily 9:00 A.M. to 5:00 P.M. Monday through Saturday and noon to 5:00 P.M. Sunday. Call (260) 927–9144.

In the tiny town of St. Joe, you can tour **Sechler's Pickle Factory,** where multitudes of midwestern cucumbers have been transformed into pickles since 1921. Along with the traditional types, the factory produces such unique varieties as candied orange strip, lemon strip, apple cinnamon, and raisin crispy pickles. Now a third-generation family operation, Sechler's is believed to be the only pickle manufacturer that makes an aged-in-wood genuine dill pickle (the same pickle made the same way by the first generation of Sechler pickle producers). Free tours are offered by appointment (drop-in visitors can sometimes be accommodated) from 9:00 to 11:00 A.M. and 12:30 to 2:00 P.M. Monday through Friday, May through October. Located at 5686 Highway 1; (260) 337–5461 or (800) 332–5461. A salesroom on the premises displays Sechler's plethora of pickles; you can also see them online at www.sechlerpickles.com. Mail orders are also accepted; the late Frank Sinatra ordered his favorites, the candied sweet dill strips, a case at a time.

Delaware County

In **Muncie** the winter winds can be fierce, the snows deep, and the temperatures subzero, but in two greenhouses on the campus of **Ball State University** a tropical garden of rare and exquisite orchids blooms all year long. The **Wheeler Orchid Collection** contains one of the most extensive collections of orchid species in the world. More than 7,000 plants thrive here in a simulated rain forest environment complete with rain, frogs, and a small waterfall, and the collection's species bank was the first such bank anywhere. Open free of charge 8:00 A.M. to 4:30 P.M. Monday through Saturday; (765) 285–8820.

The greenhouses are situated in seventeen-acre **Christy Woods,** where there's an arboretum, flower gardens, a demonstration wetland area, research facilities, and a nature center that serves as an outdoor laboratory for both Ball State students and the general public. Recorded messages guide visitors along trails that wind through the arboretum (tape recorders are available at the Orchid House). If you come in April or May, you'll also see a profusion of wildflowers. Free admission; open 8:00 A.M. to 4:30 P.M. Monday through Friday and 8:00 A.M. to 4:00 P.M. Saturday year-round; 1:00 to 5:00 P.M. Sunday, April through November. Call (765) 285–8820 or (765) 285–2641.

The **Ball State Museum of Art,** located in the Fine Arts Building, houses such treasures as paintings by Degas and Rembrandt, illuminated manuscripts, stone carvings from India, and wooden masks from Africa. Free admission; open 9:00 A.M. to 4:30 P.M. Monday through Friday and 1:30 to 4:30 P.M. Saturday and Sunday; hours may vary during spring and winter breaks and in the summer; (765) 285–5242.

The entryway to the Ball State Music Instruction Building is home to a stunning light painting by artist Stephen Knapp. Called **First Symphony,** it's a dazzling array of brilliant colors created with one hundred pieces of coated glass, polished steel brackets, and a few halogen light bulbs. The unique painting is highly visible, especially at night, through panes of glass, but it's colorful at all times. Its appearance changes depending on the time of day and the amount of light that filters through the windows. This is the only artwork of the Massachusetts-based artist in Indiana.

For information about other Ball State University attractions, contact the Campus Information Center in the Pittenger Student Center at 2000 West University Avenue; (765) 285–5000.

Nationally recognized for the hands-on experience it provides, the **Muncie Children's Museum** occupies a 2,000-square-foot exhibit center at 515 South High Street. Children can burrow through a human-size ant farm, learn how to escape from a building "on fire," join a railroad crew laying track across the country, and climb over, under, through, and on ten separate structures, including an eyeball. On Sunday afternoons visitors are treated to free "Garfield the Cat" movies. (Indiana-born Jim Davis, Garfield's creator, lives near Muncie.) Children may also participate as characters in a life-size Garfield cartoon that is videotaped and sent home with the young stars. Nominal admission fee; open 10:00 A.M. to 5:00 P.M. Tuesday through Saturday and 1:00 to 5:00 P.M. Sunday; closed July 4, Thanksgiving, December 25, and January 1; (765) 286–1660.

At a private museum in Muncie known as **Robinson's Jars,** you can see one of the most diverse collections of fruit jars in the country. This is a fascinating, mind-boggling display that will appeal to collectors as well as the merely curious. Ask to see the owner's favorite jar. The museum is located at the corner of Wheeling Avenue and West Cowing Drive. Admission is free, but donations are appreciated. Hours vary; call (765) 282–9707 for an appointment and/or additional information.

To see a fascinating fruit tree, stop by Davis Brothers' Greenhouse (765–282–5989) at 2105 Gharkey Street. Planted in the 1930s, this **ponderosa lemon tree** continues to bloom and bear fruit to this day. The greenhouse is open from 8:00 A.M. to 5:00 P.M. Monday through Friday and 8:00 A.M. to 11:00 A.M. Saturday and Sunday.

For five years, the 20-foot-tall wooden statue that stands outside the **Oasis Bar & Grill** on Muncie's southside was merely a curiosity—a fictitious basketball player named Barfly Cortez. Barfly wore a red uniform with the word *Oasis* printed across his chest. In 1994, however, the statue underwent a transformation. Barfly's uniform was repainted green and white. He was given a mustache, and his solid white tennis shoes were changed to black-and-white. No one really knew who Barfly was, but virtually everyone in Indiana knows his replacement on sight. **Larry Bird,** the former Boston Celtics star forward, former Indiana Pacers head coach, and current president of basketball operations for the Pacers, is a much-beloved Hoosier basketball legend. You can see this larger-than-life Larry at 1811 South Burlington Drive; (765) 282–8326.

Muncie became the world headquarters for model aviation in 1994, when the Academy of Model Aeronautics (AMA) moved here from Reston, Virginia. The 1,000-acre AMA complex consists of the **National Model Aviation**

Museum and a model-airplane flying field. Visitors to the museum will see the largest collection of model aircraft in the country. The craftsmanship and artistry of the master builders are astonishing. Academy members stage flying competitions on an almost continuous basis from mid-May until the end of September. The events include rocket launches, helicopter meets, jet power contests, air combat, soaring competitions, and a vintage radio control reunion. Museum hours are 8:00 A.M. to 4:30 P.M. Monday through Friday; weekend hours vary, so call before you visit. There's a nominal admission fee to the museum for non-AMA members. (Former astronaut Neil Armstrong can come for free because he's an AMA member.) Admission to the flying site is free to the public at all times. The complex is located at 5151 East Memorial Drive; (765) 287–1256 or (800) 435–9262.

Elkhart County

Some of the best farm cooking you'll ever treat your taste buds to is served up at the *Patchwork Quilt Country Inn* in *Middlebury.* Located on an eighteen-acre farm, the dining room is famous for the family-style, all-you-can-eat meals it serves Tuesday through Saturday (and the gourmet buffet it offers on Friday and Saturday).

The entree may be open-hearth-baked ham, beef pot roast, steak, seafood, or buttermilk pecan chicken (this dish once won a $5,000 first prize for the best chicken recipe in the United States). When the dessert tray arrives, you'll find it almost impossible to choose from the luscious-looking treats—almost. You'll be confronted with such unusual meal toppers as cheddar cheesecake, coffee toffee pie, charlotte russe, walnut torte, fruit parfait, grasshopper pie, and candied violet cake—delectable one and all. At least one dessert will probably feature strawberries—the inn's strawberry recipes have won national acclaim.

The Patchwork Quilt also offers overnight bed-and-breakfast accommodations Tuesday through Friday. Fifteen guest bedrooms are available, each with its own handmade patchwork quilt. A deluxe country breakfast is included in the room rate.

In 2002 *Arringtom's Bed&Breakfast Journal,* the most highly acclaimed trade publication for the bed-and-breakfast indus-

trivia

Alka-Seltzer was developed in the 1930s by Miles Laboratories of Elkhart. The famous "plop-plop-fizz-fizz" jingle used for years in Alka-Seltzer ads was written by the father of actress Julianna Margulies, best known for her role as Nurse Hathaway on the hit television show *ER.*

The Beast of 'Busco

In the long-ago spring of 1949, the small Whitley County town of Churubusco was consumed with the tale of the "Beast of 'Busco." Local farmer Gale Harris had reported seeing a turtle as large as a dining room table in a lake on his land, and the hunt was on.

Tales about a 400-pound turtle quickly spread far and wide. Newspaper reporters swarmed along the lake's shoreline, and small planes filled with photographers circled overhead. Divers suited up and plunged into the murky waters. In the course of one day, some 3,000 people tramped through Harris's fields to watch the goings-on. At the height of the search, some 400 cars an hour crept past the lake.

Traps were set but remained empty. Gale Harris tried to drain his lake but was unsuccessful. The huge turtle, dubbed Oscar, was never found, nor was he ever seen again. Experts who heard the story of Oscar speculated that, if the elusive reptile did indeed exist, he was probably a rare, unusually large alligator snapping turtle.

Whatever Oscar might or might not have been, he holds a very special place in the history of Churubusco. Recently, there has even been talk about setting up a museum memorializing him. A documentary film entitled *The Hunt for Oscar* premiered locally in November 1994. Signs in Churubusco still welcome visitors to "Turtle Town U.S.A.," and each June the community hosts a Turtle Days festival.

You can learn more about the festival that honors Oscar by contacting the Columbia City/Whitley County Chamber of Commerce at 201 North Line Street, P.O. Box 166, Columbia City 46725; (260) 248–8131.

try, named Patchwork Quilt one of the top fifteen bed-and-breakfasts in the country. Additionally, Patchwork Quilt was the only bed-and-breakfast in Indiana to earn the International Restaurant and Hospitality Rating Bureau's 5-Star Award of Excellence in 2003.

Middlebury is in the heart of one of the largest Amish settlements in the country, and the inn offers a guided tour that affords a look at the lifestyle of these people. It also hosts a quilts and crafts tour.

To reach the Patchwork Quilt Inn, go north from Middlebury on State Road 13 for 8 miles to County Road 2, then turn west for about 1 mile to the inn. Dinner is served from 4:00 to 8:00 P.M. Tuesday through Saturday. Closed all major holidays. Prices are moderate; reservations are recommended at all times and are required for tours and overnight accommodations. Smoking is not permitted anywhere on the premises. Write the Patchwork Quilt Inn, 11748 County Road 2, Middlebury 46540; Call (574) 825–2417; or visit www.patchwork quiltinn.com.

You can sample authentic Amish cuisine, as well as good country cooking, in Middlebury. The **Village Inn Restaurant** is a small lunchroom whose customers are as apt to ride up in horse-drawn buggies as in automobiles. All the food is hearty and good (not to mention loaded with calories), but the pies are splendid, the prices quite reasonable, and the people—both staff and guests—delightful. The Village Inn, located at 107 South Main Street, is open from 5:00 A.M. to 8:00 P.M. Monday through Thursday, until 8:30 P.M. Friday, and until 2:00 P.M. Saturday; (574) 825–2043.

Three miles east of Middlebury at 11275 West County Road 250N, you can tour the **Deutsch Kase Haus** and watch Amish cheesemakers at work. The free samples in the gift shop will help you choose your favorite flavor. You might want to try the colby longhorn; at the World Cheese Maker's Competition in 2000, it was awarded the title of best colby in the world. Open 8:00 A.M. to 5:00 P.M. Monday through Friday and 8:00 A.M. to 3:00 P.M. Saturday; call (574) 825–9511 for the cheese-making schedule.

One of the best ways to gain insight into the lifestyle of the Amish is through a visit to **Amish Acres,** an authentic eighty-acre restoration of a century-old farming community in **Nappanee.** Amish farmhouses dot the countryside, flat-topped black buggies wander the roads, farmers plow the fields, livestock graze behind split-rail fences, and women quilt, bake in an outdoor oven, and dip candles. You can see demonstrations of soap making, horseshoeing, and meat preserving; and visit a bakery, a meat and cheese shop, an antique soda fountain and fudgery, a cider mill, a smokehouse, a mint still, and a sawmill.

You may want to take a horse-drawn buggy ride or enjoy the excellent Amish cooking at the **Restaurant Barn.** The soup is always on in big iron kettles, and such typical dishes as noodles, spiced apples, and sweet-and-sour cabbage salad are on the menu. Be sure to try the shoofly pie; it was declared the best by the *Chicago Tribune* after a shoofly pie taste test in 139 towns around the country.

Amish Acres is located on U.S. Highway 6, 1 mile west of Nappanee. The restored farm is open daily 10:00 A.M. to 5:00 P.M. March through December. Admission fee; special package price for a guided tour. The restaurant is open 11:00 A.M. to 7:00 P.M. Monday through Saturday and 11:00 A.M. to 6:00 P.M. Sunday, March through December. Hours may vary, so check before you go. Write the Amish Acres Visitor Information Center, 1600 West Market Street, Nappanee 46550; or call (574) 773–4188 or (800) 800–4942. The information center also can assist you in making reservations for an overnight stay in an area farm home.

The area in and around Nappanee abounds with interesting shops and Amish businesses that can be toured. *Time* magazine honored the area in its December 8, 1997, issue by naming Nappanee as one of the top ten small-town success stories in the nation. The Nappanee Chamber of Commerce, at 451 North Main Street, Suite 100, Nappanee 46550, will be happy to provide you with additional information; (574) 773–7812.

Directly north of Nappanee via State Road 19 is the village of **Wakarusa,** where you can visit the unusual **Bird's-Eye View Museum.** Area buildings of distinctive architectural style are reconstructed from toothpicks, Popsicle sticks, and other pint-size materials—all built on the same scale (1 inch equals 5 feet). The project began when Devon Rose built a miniature feed mill for his son's electric-train layout and continued until the town of Wakarusa had been replicated in the most minute detail. Now one of the largest collections of miniatures in the world, it has won several awards. Not content to rest on his laurels, Mr. Rose has also re-created at least one building from every town or city in Elkhart County and plans to create a miniature reproduction of one signature building in each of Indiana's ninety-two counties (more than one-third of these have been completed). Located at 325 South Elkhart Street, the museum is open 8:00 A.M. to 5:00 P.M. Monday through Friday and 8:00 A.M. to noon Saturday. Nominal admission fee; (574) 862–2367.

The **Midwest Museum of American Art** would be a gem anywhere, but in the small municipality of **Elkhart** (population 43,000) it is a crown jewel. Noted for its extensive collection of Norman Rockwell lithographs (believed to be the largest collection anywhere) and photographs by such distinguished photographers as Ansel Adams, the museum has become one of Indiana's most important art institutions. Nominal admission fee; open 11:00 A.M. to 5:00 P.M. Tuesday through Friday and 1:00 to 4:00 P.M. Saturday and Sunday. Open free of charge 7:00 to 9:00 P.M. Thursday. Located at 429 South Main Street; (574) 293–6660.

Elkhart also is home to a museum that will warm the hearts of owners and wannabe owners of recreational vehicles. The **RV/MH Heritage Foundation Hall of Fame** showcases the growth, history, and accomplishments of the RV and manufactured-housing industries. Originally located in Washington, D.C., the Hall of Fame was moved to Elkhart, widely recognized as the RV Capital of the World, in 1991. Some twenty-five companies affiliated with the RV industry are headquartered here.

Among the exhibits are the first RV ever made (built in 1915), camping trailers of the 1930s, and the classic art deco Airstream. There's even a tiny pink trailer suitable for small pets and some scale models of trailer high-rises. Believe it or not, someone once envisioned building whole communities of vertical trailer parks with twenty stories of single-wide trailers stacked on top of one another. The more mundane RV Wall of Fame pays tribute to more than 170 people who are famous in the RV industry.

The museum is open 9:00 A.M. to 4:00 P.M. Monday through Friday year-round and from 10:00 A.M. to 3:00 P.M. Saturday in June, July, and August; nominal admission fee. Located at 801 Benham Avenue; (574) 293–2344 or (800) 378–8694. A new and larger Hall of Fame is under construction nearby. For up-to-date information, call the RV/MH Heritage Foundation, at the aforementioned phone numbers.

If you'd like to watch an RV being assembled, take a free plant tour at *Jayco, Inc.,* located at 903 South Main Street (State Road 13 South) in Middlebury. Tours are conducted at noon Monday through Friday; an additional 9:30 A.M. tour is added in June, July, and August. There's also a visitor center to explore during business hours; open 8:00 A.M. to 5:00 P.M. Monday through Friday. Call the factory at (574) 825–5861 for additional information.

trivia

The town of Goshen is home to a large population of black squirrels. Although their exact origin is unknown, they are rumored to have been brought here from England.

On the northwest corner of Main Street and Lincoln Avenue in **Goshen** stands an intriguing-looking **limestone booth.** The octagonal structure, complete with gun ports and bulletproof green glass, was erected in 1939 by the WPA (Works Progress Administration) to provide a lookout for local police. At that time, two banks stood at the intersection. A slew of recent robberies in surrounding communities had been widely publicized, and the local citizenry decided to take some precautionary measures. Their jitters apparently were not easily dispelled, because police continued to man the enclosure twenty-four hours a day until 1969. Since 1983 it has been owned by the Goshen Historical Society, 124 South Main Street; (574) 975–0033.

Grant County

The death of James Dean on September 30, 1955, catapulted the popular young actor to enduring fame as a cult hero. Although he made only three movies—*East of Eden, Rebel Without a Cause,* and *Giant*—Dean gave voice through his roles to the restlessness and discontent of his generation. He died at the age of twenty-four, the victim of an automobile accident on a lonely California highway. Dean was speeding along in his silver Porsche when he collided with a car making a left turn across the highway in front of him. Ironically, Dean had been given a speeding ticket a little over two hours before the accident that claimed his life. His family brought him home to Indiana to bury him. Today rarely a day goes by—no matter what the weather—that someone doesn't show up in **Park Cemetery** at **Fairmount,** where Dean grew up, to see his grave and mourn his passing.

For ten years after his death, Warner Brothers received as many as 7,000 letters a month addressed to Dean from devoted fans who refused to accept his death. His tombstone in Park Cemetery, defaced by souvenir seekers, was replaced in 1985. Within a few short months it, too, was defaced. A sign that read THIS WAY TO JAMES DEAN'S GRAVE lasted one afternoon, and handfuls of dirt regularly disappear from his burial site. People from as far away as Germany have wanted to purchase a plot here so that they can "be buried near Jimmy." To this day,

Everyone's Favorite Feline

Indiana's most beloved native is arguably Garfield the Cat. Although Garfield is lazy, fat, and selfish, he gets away with it precisely because he *is* a cat. It also helps that he is adorable.

Jim Davis, Garfield's creator, grew up in Fairmount, Indiana, where he and his family shared the family farm with about twenty-five cats. Today, Davis lives and works near the small town of Albany, which lies a few miles northeast of Muncie, Indiana. Davis's company, Paws Inc., is the licensing and merchandising firm for anything created in Garfield's image.

For the curious among you, here are some interesting facts about the cat and his creator:

Davis shares his tubby tabby's love for lasagna.

Garfield is Davis's grandfather's name (the two reportedly share a few traits).

More than sixty million Garfield books have been published worldwide, and Garfield has been the star of several CBS-TV specials. *Garfield,* a movie starring Bill Murray as the voice of Garfield, was released in 2004. Murray was again the voice of Garfield in *Garfield: A Tale of Two Kitties,* a movie that debuted in 2006.

The comic strip that features Garfield is the most widely syndicated strip in the world, read daily by some 200 million people in more than 2,700 newspapers in twenty-six different languages.

Davis and Garfield celebrated the fussy feline's twenty-fifth year in syndication in 2003.

books are still being written about Dean. When the U.S. Postal Service began issuing its "Legends of Hollywood" series, it was James Dean whose image was chosen for the second stamp in the series. (Marilyn Monroe's stamp, the first, was released in 1995; the Dean stamp was released in 1996.) Between 1986 and 1996, the estate of James Dean amassed more than $100 million from merchandising materials. In 2003 alone, his estate earned more than $5 million. At this writing, more than 200 companies worldwide market about 1,500 products that bear his name. In 2005, the editors of *Variety* magazine, a leading publication in the entertainment industry, asked show-business professionals and the public to choose the most influential entertainers of the past one hundred years; James Dean was seventh on the list, ahead of Marilyn Monroe, Mickey Mouse, and Elvis Presley. The phenomenon of James Dean shows no signs of letting up and can never be fully explained—a charisma that has not faded to this day. Park Cemetery, open daily dawn to dusk, is on County Road 150E; (765) 948–4040.

The *Fairmount Historical Museum* at 203 East Washington Street tells the story of Dean's life through a series of exhibits and a display of some of Dean's possessions from a family collection. Each September, near the date of Dean's death, the museum hosts the Fairmount Museum Days and the James Dean Film Festival. The museum also honors Fairmount's other favorite son— Jim Davis, creator of "Garfield the Cat." No admission fee, but donations are accepted. Open 10:00 A.M. to 5:00 P.M. Monday through Saturday and noon to 5:00 P.M. Sunday, March through November; also open on February 8 (Dean's birth date) and by appointment. Write Fairmount Historical Museum, P.O. Box 92, Fairmount 46928; or call (765) 948–4555.

The nearby town of *Marion,* where James Dean was born, is noted for its extraordinary *Easter pageant,* presented each Easter morning at 6:00 A.M.

Fairmount Historical Museum

True Love

Residents of Marion, Indiana, population 33,000 or thereabouts, suspected something big was afoot on June 27, 1993. They had their first clue when five tour buses and three stretch limousines pulled up near the county courthouse. Turns out singer Lyle Lovett and actress Julia Roberts had come to town to have a quiet wedding, sans media hype. Like all couples about to be married, they had stopped at the courthouse to pick up a marriage license.

Family and friends (actress Susan Sarandon and actor Tim Robbins among them) were on the scene for one of the surprise weddings of the year—in Marion or anywhere. Amazingly, the couple had managed to keep their romance a virtual secret. Only those closest to the couple knew about their whirlwind courtship.

Because the nuptials were planned only seventy-two hours in advance, the wedding attendants showed up in eclectic dress. No matter. All eyes were on the bride, who wore a simple white dress purchased for her by the bridegroom and walked down the aisle barefoot.

The couple chose Marion for their nuptials for two reasons: It was conveniently located between stops on the groom's summer concert tour, and it offered the privacy they desired. People in Indiana are known for giving celebrities their space.

Sadly, the marriage ended, but the town of Marion hasn't forgotten its happy beginning. Do residents consider the marriage the biggest thing that ever happened here? No. The very biggest thing happened in the mid-1970s. That was when the high school basketball team won back-to-back state championships.

Lauded as the equal of Oberammergau's famous passion play, the pageant draws spectators from all fifty states and from overseas. Free admission; for tickets and information contact the Marion/Grant County Convention and Visitors Bureau, 217 South Adams Street, Marion 46952; (765) 668–5435 or (800) 662–9474.

Ice cream lovers will want to journey to **Upland,** home of Taylor University, and visit **Ivanhoe's.** When they spy the menu here, they'll think they've died and gone to heaven. Sundae and shake flavors are arranged alphabetically—one hundred delicious flavors each, plus a special section for extras. If you manage to eat your way through all one hundred flavors in either category, your name is enshrined on a special plaque that hangs on the dining room wall. Hoe's, as it's known locally, also serves ice cream sodas, floats, and excellent sandwiches and salads. Located at 979 South Main Street, it's open from 10:00 A.M. to 10:00 P.M. Monday through Thursday, 10:00 A.M. to 11:00 P.M. Friday and Saturday, and 2:00 to 10:00 P.M. Sunday. Call (765) 998–7261.

Howard County

The world has stainless steel because **Kokomo** inventor Elwood Haynes wanted to please his wife. Well aware of her husband's ingenuity, Mrs. Haynes asked him to perfect some tarnish-free dinnerware for her. And in 1912, he did.

The remarkable Mr. Haynes also invented the first successful commercial automobile. On July 4, 1894, he put his gasoline-powered creation to the test on Pumpkinvine Pike east of Kokomo, speeding along at 7 miles per hour for a distance of about 6 miles. That same car is now on display at the Smithsonian Institution in Washington, D.C.

Another of Haynes's inventions is stellite, an alloy used today in spacecraft, jet engines, dental instruments, and nuclear power plants. New applications are still being found for it.

The **Elwood Haynes Museum,** housed in Haynes's former residence, contains a vast collection of Haynes's personal possessions and his many inventions. Visitors particularly enjoy the 1905 Haynes automobile, in which the driver sits in the backseat. Other exhibits reflect Howard County's history during and after the area's great gas boom.

The largest natural gas gusher ever brought into production in this country was struck in 1887 in what is now southeast Kokomo. Almost overnight the town was transformed into a center of industry. Kokomo's many contributions to the industrial growth of America, in addition to Haynes's inventions, have earned it the nickname "City of Firsts." Many of the items first produced here are among those featured in the upstairs rooms of the Elwood Haynes Museum, located at 1915 South Webster Street. Free of charge, it's open 8:00 A.M. to 4:00 P.M. Monday through Saturday and 1:00 to 5:00 P.M. Sunday; closed holidays. Call (765) 456–7500.

Just to the northwest of the Haynes Museum, at 902 West Deffenbaugh Street, enter **Highland Park** and view the city's most visited attraction, Kokomo's own **Old Ben.** Ben was a crossbred Hereford steer who at the time of his birth in 1902 was proclaimed to be the largest calf in the world, weighing in at 135 pounds. When you see Ben, you won't find it hard to believe. At four years of age the steer weighed 4,720 pounds, stood 6 feet 4 inches tall, measured 13 feet 6 inches in girth, and was an astonishing 16 feet 2 inches from his nose to the tip of his tail. For many years he was exhibited around the country in circuses and sideshows. He had to be destroyed in 1910 after breaking his leg, and shortly thereafter he was stuffed and mounted. Today he shares a place of honor with another of Kokomo's giant wonders—**the stump of a huge sycamore tree.** The stump—12 feet tall and 57 feet in circumference—is impressive enough, but it only hints at the mother magnificent tree. Originally

City of Firsts

Kokomo bills itself as the City of Firsts. Here are a few of the reasons why:

First commercially built auto (road tested locally on July 4, 1894)

First pneumatic rubber tire (1894)

First aluminum casting (1895)

First carburetor (1902)

First stellite cobalt-based alloy (1906)

First stainless steel (1912)

First American howitzer shell (1918)

First aerial bomb with fins (1918)

First mechanical corn picker (early 1920s)

First dirilyte golden-hued tableware (1926)

First canned tomato juice (1928)

First push-button car radio (1938)

First all-metal lifeboats (1941) and rafts (1943)

First signal-seeking car radio (1947)

First all-transistor car radio (1957)

The Kokomo/Howard County Convention and Visitors Bureau will be happy to elaborate (see Sources for Additional Information at the end of the chapter).

more than 100 feet in height, the tree grew to maturity on a farm west of Kokomo. Its hollow trunk once housed a telephone booth large enough to accommodate more than a dozen people at a time. When the tree was storm-damaged, around 1915, the enormous stump was pulled to the park by a house mover. Old Ben and the stump now occupy a building built specifically to display and protect them. Call (765) 456–7275 for more information.

The **Kokomo Opalescent Glass Company,** in operation since 1888, once supplied glass to Louis C. Tiffany. Today this small factory is known worldwide as a leading producer of fine art glass, and visitors can watch the glassmaking process from beginning to end. Free tours are offered at 10:00 A.M. on Wednesday and Friday, except on holidays and in December. Visitors must wear closed-toe shoes for safety. An adjoining retail shop is open 9:00 A.M. to 5:00 P.M. Monday through Friday; Saturday hours vary. Located at 1310 South Market Street; (765) 457–1829.

Huntington County

One of Indiana's most famous sons, J. Danforth Quayle (better known as Dan), is the fifth Hoosier to serve as our country's vice president. Quayle was born in Indianapolis in 1947, but his family moved to Huntington about a year later, and it is Huntington that Quayle calls home.

When George Bush and Quayle launched their campaign for the White House in 1988, they came to the Huntington County Courthouse to do it. When Quayle and his wife, Marilyn, received their law degrees from Indiana University in Bloomington, they came to Huntington to open a law office. When Quayle first ran for public office in 1976 (as a U.S. Representative), he ran as a resident of Huntington.

In June 1993, **Huntington** demonstrated its affection for Quayle by opening the **Dan Quayle Center and Museum** at 815 Warren Street. Visitors will see exhibits from every phase of Quayle's life, including a newspaper clipping announcing his birth, a baby footprint taken at the hospital in which he was born, and a photo of the newborn Quayle in a diaper. Of particular interest is Quayle's second-grade report card, boasting all As and Bs. A copy of Quayle's college diploma is missing a few pieces, thanks to a family dog (a photo of the offender, much loved nevertheless, is framed with the diploma). No museum honoring Dan Quayle would be complete without some golf memorabilia; an old golf bag and photos of a teenage Quayle holding trophies won in a junior tournament are among them.

You'll know when you get to Huntington. It would be hard to miss the sign at the city limits that proclaims this to be HUNTINGTON: HOME OF THE 44TH VICE PRESIDENT DAN QUAYLE.

Although the museum bears Dan Quayle's name, it pays tribute to all of our country's vice presidents—the only such museum in the country.

The museum is open 10:00 A.M. to 4:00 P.M. Tuesday through Saturday and 1:00 to 4:00 P.M. Sunday. Nomimal admission fee. Write the museum at P.O. Box 856, Huntington 46750, or call (260) 356–6356.

After you've toured Dan Quayle's museum, stop by and see **Hy Goldenberg's Outhouses.** You won't see any signs honoring Hy's outhouses, but the town is fond of them just the same.

Hy purchased his first two outhouses in the 1960s for strictly utilitarian reasons. He and his wife were building a home in a then-isolated spot on the banks of the Wabash River, and they needed a toilet the carpenters could use while working on the house. Because of that experience, Hy came to regard outhouses as an important segment of Americana and collected seventeen of them before his death several years ago.

Although most of the outhouses are variations of the typical square wooden ones, there is also an octagon-shaped concrete one. A three-seater model boasts a child-size seat in the middle for the family that enjoys togetherness. One of Hy's rarest outhouses is a round privy that sports a copper weather vane atop its roof. Hy paid a whopping $17 for that one. Although most of his outhouses cost $2.00 to $3.00 each, Hy had to bid against someone at an auction before he could call the cherished round privy his own.

Building outhouses was a source of employment for many men during the Great Depression. Although comfort and safety were certainly important considerations, aesthetics also played a role. Many were covered with roses and trellises to please the lady of the house.

After Hy's death, his widow, Lorry, donated part of her husband's collection to the **Huntington County Historical Museum.** The rest may be seen on what was once the Goldenberg's property but is now the **Tel-Hy Nature Preserve.**

trivia

On July 14, 1996, a crop circle was discovered in a farm field near Columbia City. Believed by many to be the result of alien spacecraft landings, these circles are characterized by bent (not broken) plant stalks, mutated plant DNA, odd magnetic readings, and abnormally high radiation levels. About 600 feet in circumference, the Columbia City circle consisted of an outer ring, three spiraled centers, and a radiation reading of two times the normal level.

For additional information contact the museum at 315 Court Street in Huntington; (260) 356–7264. The museum is open from 10:00 A.M. to 4:00 P.M. Tuesday through Friday and 1:00 to 4:00 P.M. Saturday. Admission is free, but donations are welcome.

Lest you doubt the current value of outhouses to our society, you should know they are still being built, albeit in more modern forms, in areas where it would be environmentally and economically impractical to install water and sewers. The most expensive outhouse in Indiana to date is a four-seat composting toilet in Charlestown State Park in Clark County that set the state back $87,000 when it was built in the mid-1990s. That one, however, is a piker compared to a four-seat outhouse in Glacier National Park in Montana, completed in 1998 at a cost of $1 million.

Kosciusko County

Some towns will do almost anything to get attention. **Mentone** grabbed its share of publicity by erecting a monument unique in the world. There it stands, right next to Main Street—a 12-foot-high, 3,000-pound **concrete egg.** If, when in Mentone, anyone should ask the perennial puzzler "Which came first, the chicken or the egg?" the answer would almost certainly have to be "the egg."

In 1946, when the monument was first "laid," every farmer in the area had a chicken house, and eggs were shipped all over the Midwest. That enterprise declined in the 1950s, but the lives of the town's 950 residents continue to be intertwined with eggs and chickens. Local businesses hatch eggs, provide chicken meat for soup companies, and separate egg whites from the yolks for bakeries. And each June the community celebrates industry, heritage, and monument with an Egg Festival. Food booths sell eggs most any way you like them, while some fun-loving residents dress up in chicken suits and strut about dancing and singing. (Don't knock it—Brad Pitt got his start wearing a chicken suit.) Contact the Kosciusko County Convention and Visitors Bureau, 111 Capital Drive, Warsaw 46582; (574) 269–6090 or (800) 800–6090.

Next to the city park on Oak Street, just south of State Road 25 West in downtown Mentone, you'll find the *Lawrence D. Bell Aircraft Museum.* It contains the memorabilia of Larry Bell, the Mentone native who forsook eggs and instead founded the Bell Aircraft Corporation. Bell produced twenty aviation firsts, including the world's first commercial helicopter, the nation's first jet-propelled fighter plane, the first jet vertical takeoff and landing airplane, and the first aircraft to shatter the sound barrier. Scale models of many Bell aircraft are on display, and a ten-minute video presentation describes Bell's life and career. The current museum is a work in progress; future plans include building a hangar that will display each aircraft ever manufactured by Bell. At this writing, the museum owns a "Huey," a type of medical rescue helicopter used in Vietnam (you'll see it sitting in the museum's yard), and a 47G helicopter like those used by MASH units in Korea. Guided tours are offered from 1:00 to 5:00 P.M. Sunday from Memorial Day weekend through October; other times by appointment. Nominal admission fee; write the museum at P.O. Box 411, Mentone 46539, or call (574) 353–7113, (574) 269–6090, or (800) 800–6090.

trivia

It was once against the law to read *The Stepford Wives* in Warsaw.

In honor of Kosciusko County's agricultural heritage, the Greater Warsaw Area Chamber of Commerce has put together two *drive-yourself farm tours.* Scenic country roads lead visitors past farms that produce chickens, buffalo, pigs, sheep, and cattle, as well as spearmint and various fruits and vegetables. Maple Leaf Farms is the largest producer of ducklings in the Western Hemisphere. Ault Stables trains harness horses. Many facilities, including one of the country's largest llama farms, offer guided tours by prearrangement. Free maps are available at the Kosciusko County Convention and Visitors Bureau, 111 Capital Drive, Warsaw 46582; (574) 269–6090 or (800) 800–6090.

The largest of only five such gardens in the United States, the **Warsaw Biblical Gardens** cover one acre in Center Lake Park in **Warsaw.** All plants mentioned in the Bible have been meticulously researched for this project, and thus far 115 identified varieties have been acquired.

An oasis of tranquility, the gardens are enclosed by a low fieldstone wall. Visitors can meander along stone paths that lead through six distinct plant environs: meadow, crop, orchard, forest, brook, and desert. A plaque for each of the species identifies the plant and its biblical reference. Water lilies, yellow iris, and sweet flag adorn a water garden that's shaded by an umbrella palm. A unique wooden arbor was designed by famous craftsman David Robinson, who served as the first coordinator for the restoration of New York City's Central Park before going into business for himself. Grape vines planted when the gardens were dedicated in June 1991 now nearly obscure the arbor, creating a cool, shaded retreat on hot summer days.

The gardens, located at the intersection of State Road 15 North and Canal Street, are open free of charge from dawn to dusk, April through October. For additional information call (574) 269–2136 or contact the Warsaw Community Development Corporation, 117 West Center Street, P.O. Box 1223, Warsaw 46580; (574) 267–6419.

Stop by the Party Shop in Warsaw and visit the **Hallmark Ornament Museum.** The first Hallmark ornament was created in 1973. That ornament and every Hallmark ornament created since then—more than 3,000 ornaments—are on display here. The Party Shop is the first and only place in the country to have a complete collection on public display. Admission is free; open 9:00 A.M. to 9:00 P.M. Monday through Saturday, noon to 5:00 P.M. Sunday. Located at 3418 Lake City Highway; (574) 267–8787.

LaGrange County

No place in this country has done better by its junk than the tiny hamlet of **Shipshewana.** Each Tuesday and Wednesday from May through October, it puts on what may be the biggest small-town sale in the country. Anything you've ever wanted has almost certainly, at one time or another, been available at the **Shipshewana** ("Shipshe" for short) **Auction and Flea Market.** The items available at one sale included old beer cans, garden tools, round oak tables, new hats and clothing at discount prices, doorknobs, bubble-gum machines, rare books, antique china, long-legged underwear, fenceposts, Aladdin lamps, fishing rods, parts for old wagons, extra pieces for a Lionel train

trivia

South Whitley is home to the Fox Products Corporation, the nation's largest producer of high-quality bassoons. The family-run operation, founded in 1949, ships its musical instruments to countries around the world.

set, hand and power tools, quilts, a worn-out butter churn, a half-full can of green house paint, baseball cards, homemade toy alligators, and—perhaps the most unusual item ever offered here—a used tombstone.

In addition to the flea market, a livestock sale and a miscellaneous auction take place. The vast array of sale items keeps about a dozen auctioneers busy from 7:00 A.M. to 5:00 P.M. on Tuesday and 7:00 A.M. to 3:00 P.M. on Wednesday, while in the livestock barn farmers do some hot-and-heavy bidding on 2,500 head of cattle, sheep, and pigs. Outside in the flea market yard, nearly 1,000 vendors display their wares. On average, $200,000 worth of livestock and goods changes hands, not including the several thousand dollars spent at the flea market. Although it would be a compliment to describe some of the merchandise as junk, there are also many valuable antiques and hard-to-find items.

The Shipshe Auction hosts as many as 30,000 visitors a day. License plates reveal they come from across the country and Canada. When winter comes the flea market closes down, but the auction simply moves under cover and continues throughout the year.

Each Friday the auction yard is the scene of a horse auction that draws buyers and sellers from all over North America to deal in Amish draft horses, reputed to be some of the finest in the land. (Shipshewana is in the heart of one of the largest Amish settlements in the United States.)

You'll have a grand time at the Shipshe Auction even if you don't buy a thing. It's one of the world's great spectator events. The auction yards are located at 345 South Van Buren Street (State Road 5) at the south edge of Shipshewana. For more details, exact hours, and information about special events, write to the Shipshewana Auction and Flea Market, P.O. Box 185, Shipshewana 46565; call (260) 768–4129 or (800) 254–8090; or visit www.shipshewanaflea market.com.

Since all the people who attend Shipshe's various auctions have to eat, a special *Auction Restaurant,* operated from one of the sale barns, is open three days a week in the summer. It dishes up delicious Amish food nonstop from 5:00 A.M. to 7:00 P.M. Tuesday and Wednesday and from 5:00 A.M. until the horse sales close for the day on Friday (open Wednesday and Friday only during winter months); (260) 768–4129.

To learn more about the Mennonite/Amish/Hutterite lifestyle and heritage, explore the fascinating exhibits at the *Menno-Hof Visitors Center,* located at

510 South Van Buren Street (State Road 5) opposite the Shipshewana Auction grounds. Of particular interest is a booth where visitors actually "feel, see, and hear" a simulated tornado. Nominal admission fee. Generally open 10:00 A.M. to 5:00 P.M. Monday through Saturday; hours may be seasonally adjusted. Call (260) 768–4117.

Stretching along the Pigeon River in northeastern LaGrange County and reaching eastward into Steuben County is the 11,500-acre **Pigeon River State Fish and Wildlife Area.** The hauntingly beautiful stream, edged by lush vegetation choked with hyacinths, flows through an outstanding variety of habitats—marshes, meadows, woods, swamps, and bogs. Bird-watchers love this area; more than 200 species of birds, many of them rare, have been sighted here. In the spring and early summer, wildflowers run rampant. It's all reminiscent of the Southland's fabled Suwannee River—a fine and private place in which to study nature; canoe; hunt mushrooms, nuts, and berries; hike; fish; pitch a tent; or ski cross-country.

The **Tamarack Bog State Nature Preserve** near the center of the wildlife area contains the largest tamarack swamp in Indiana and harbors such unique plants as the insectivorous pitcher plant and sundew. Contact the Pigeon River State Fish and Wildlife Area, 8310 East 300 North, Mongo; (260) 367–2164.

Miami County

The circus first came to Peru, Indiana, in the late 1800s, and it remains there to this day, the single most dominant force in the community.

It all began with native son Ben Wallace, who owned a livery stable in **Peru.** One winter a broken-down animal show limped into town and found shelter in Ben's stable. When spring came, Ben was left with all the animals in lieu of a fee. Using his Hoosier ingenuity, Ben spiffed things up a bit, started his own circus, and built it into one of the world's finest—the **Hagenbeck-Wallace Circus.** Winter quarters were set up on the vast farm fields just outside town, and other major circuses of the day, lured by the excellent facilities, also came to Peru in the off-season.

Among the show business greats who spent at least part of the year here were Clyde Beatty, the noted animal trainer (like Ben Wallace, a native son); Emmett Kelly, the renowned clown; Willi Wilno, "the human cannonball"; and Tom Mix, who later starred in Hollywood westerns. The late Red Skelton left his home in southern Indiana when he was just a boy to join the Hagenbeck-Wallace Circus and to launch one of the most famous and enduring careers in the entertainment business.

The circus—and Peru with it—flourished for many years before passing into near oblivion, but local folks, many of them direct descendants of stars who brightened the firmament of circus history, decided that their town's unique heritage should be preserved forever. And so each year in July, the circus once again comes to Peru. Called the *Circus City Festival*, the six-day event starts on the third Monday in July.

trivia

Dave Morecraft, a lifelong resident of Peru, Indiana, is the only steam calliope builder in the United States.

The performers, who must be residents of Miami County, range in age from six to twenty years old, and they are so skillful that you'll find it difficult to believe that this is not a professional show. Since many of the children of Peru begin their training in earliest childhood under the tutelage of some of the finest circus pros in the country, a constant supply of new talent is available. All the components of the old-time circus are here—aerialists, clowns, tightrope walkers, human pyramids, gymnasts, animal trainers, and much more. The whole thing is so authentic and entertaining that NBC-TV once filmed an hour-long documentary about it.

Some performers choose to turn their experiences into professional careers. Two notable examples are Brian and Tina Miser, who now work with the Ringling Brothers & Barnum and Bailey Circus as the world's only husband-and-wife human-cannonball team. Brian designed and built the double-barreled cannon that hurtles them through the air.

There are several performances during the annual festival, as well as a giant parade complete with calliopes, old circus wagons, and the rousing music of the Circus City Band. For additional information contact the Circus City Festival Office, 154 North Broadway, Peru; (765) 472–3918.

One of the finest collections of circus relics in the world is housed in Peru's *International Circus Hall of Fame.* One relic, an elaborately decorated circus wagon built in Peru in 1903, is the only one of its kind in the world. In 1995 the museum acquired the Italian-made tent of the Big Apple Circus, which plays at Lincoln Center in New York. Still under development, the museum currently occupies what used to be the Hagenbeck-Wallace Circus's wagon barn at the ten-acre Old Circus Winter Headquarters, a National Historic Landmark since 1988. The Hall of Fame is located just south of U.S. Highway 24 about 3 miles northeast of Peru; follow signs. Open 10:00 A.M. to 4:00 P.M. Monday through Saturday and 1:00 to 4:00 P.M. Sunday, May through October; open November through April by appointment. Nominal admission fee. For further information contact the Circus Hall of Fame, 3076 East Circus Lane, P.O. Box 700, Peru 46970; (765) 472–7553 or (800) 771–0241.

Even in death Ben Wallace chose to remain in Peru. He is buried in **Mount Hope Cemetery** on Twelfth Street, along with another well-known native son, **Cole Porter.** One of the few songwriters who wrote both words and music, Porter penned such classics as "Night and Day," "Begin the Beguine," "I've Got You Under My Skin," and "What Is This Thing Called Love?" Porter's life and music were depicted in the 2004 movie *De-lovely,* starring Kevin Kline as Porter and Ashley Judd as his wife, Linda.

The home in which Porter was born, located at the corner of Huntington and East Third Streets, is being renovated as a museum that will celebrate the songwriter's life. In his lifetime, Porter loved the chocolate fudge made at a local candy store and took goodly supplies with him wherever he went. The candy store closed a few years ago, but the museum plans to make Porter's much-loved fudge from the store's recipe and offer it for sale to museum visitors. For up-to-date information write the Ole Olsen Memorial Theatre, Inc., 154 South Broadway Street, Peru 46970, or call (765) 472–3680.

A few miles south of Peru along U.S. Highway 31, you'll come upon the **Grissom Air Museum State Historic Site,** where an outdoor museum displays historic military aircraft. A B-17 flying fortress; a massive B-47 Stratojet and its midair refueler, the KC-97; a tank-killing A-10 Warthog; and the celebrated EC-135 air command post of Desert Storm fame can all be seen here. A B-58 Hustler, a supersonic bomber, is one of only six remaining in the world. Grissom is also one of a handful of sites selected by the Navy to permanaently display a Navy F-14 fighter jet. It's okay to climb and sit on several of the planes, and visitors are welcome to climb into the cockpit of an F4 Phantom fighter. An indoor museum houses various types of military memorabilia, including bombs, missiles, and survival gear.

Visitors can climb to the top of a 40-foot-tall Cold War–era security tower to get a bird's-eye view of the museum's historic planes and gaze at sights up to 20 miles away. The museum is open from 10:00 A.M. to 4:00 P.M. Tuesday through Sunday; closed holidays and mid-December through mid-February; the outdoor exhibits are open daily from 7:00 A.M. to dusk. For additional information contact the Grissom Air Museum, 1000 Hoosier Boulevard, Peru; (765) 689–8011.

Near the intersection of US 31 and State Road 18, in the southwest corner of Miami County, is the once-upon-a-time hamlet of **Bennetts Switch.** The only commercial business in town (unless you count the United Methodist

Church) is **Miller's Police and Fire Equipment,** a fun place in which to browse. Browsing may be all you can do. Unless you have some identification proving you're an officer of the law or a firefighter, you'll not be allowed to buy much of anything—with the possible exception of a T-shirt and maybe a bumper sticker. Miller's is in business to sell its stock to police and firefighters. Such things as a T-shirt with DON'T FORGET YOUR RUBBERS imprinted on it and a bumper sticker that states COPS LIKE BIG BUSTS are popular items, but there are also more serious offerings like handcuffs and uniforms. Call (765) 457–7930 for hours.

Noble County

Fred Schultz of **Ligonier,** an aficionado of rare historical radios, has established the **Indiana Historic Radio Museum.** The building he chose is an old filling station that is itself historic. Fred thought his dream might be short-lived when a professional gave him an estimate of $100,000 to refurbish the filling station, but in the spirit of community the folks in Ligonier volunteered their labor to fix up the place. As a result, the building renovation cost about $10,000, and in 1995 Fred opened his museum. Thus far, some 20,000 visitors have dropped by to take a look at the more than 400 radios on display.

Among the exhibits, which emphasize radios from the 1920s and 1930s, are the first transistor radio, the Regency TR-1, a 1936 Scott ten-tube set, and a 1938 Emerson Mae West. If you're not too knowledgeable about radios, don't worry—each item bears an explanatory tag. One radio, you will learn, was carried on the back of a mule during World War I. There are also novelty radios in the improbable shapes of macaroni and cheese, french fries, and Elvis Presley.

trivia

Farmland claims that it is the only town in the world that bears its name. It was in large part because of the appeal of the town's name that *Elle* magazine brought an international staff here in spring 1999 for a fashion photo shoot. The photos, taken primarily at four rural locations, appeared in the September 1999 issue.

At this time, the Indiana Historic Radio Museum is one of only six museums of its kind known to exist in the country. It's sponsored by the Indiana Historical Radio Society, and many of the radios you'll see are owned by, on loan from, or donated by society members. Hours vary seasonally; admission is free. The museum building, located at 800 Lincolnway South, also houses the Ligonier Visitors Center. Call (260) 894–9000 or (888) 417–3562.

A few miles east of Ligonier, in **Kendallville,** is an even rarer museum. Opened in the summer of 1997, the **Mid-America Windmill Museum** is one of only two of its kind in the country. Currently, some fifty windmills have been restored and are on display on a 35-acre plot on Kendallville's southeast side. Plans call for the acquisition and restoration of about fifty more.

The gem of the collection is the Robertson Windmill, a replica of the first windmill built in what is now the United States (circa 1610). It was constructed from a set of blueprints on loan from the Colonial Williamsburg Foundation. Because it's built on a post, the entire structure can be turned to take advantage of the wind's direction.

Kendallville seems a logical place for such a museum because it's in the heart of an area that was once referred to as the windmill store of the nation. In the heyday of wind power, nearly eighty windmill manufacturers were located within a 150-mile radius of Kendallville, and the country's second-largest windmill maker was actually in Kendallville.

In the museum building are models and displays that show the advances in windmill technology around the globe and through the years, beginning with a wind-powered gristmill used in Persia that dates to about A.D. 200. All windmill restorations are done in this building, and visitors can view the process in various stages.

You'll find the museum at 732 South Allen Chapel Road (County Road 1000 East); a nominal admission fee is charged. Open 10:00 A.M. to 4:00 P.M. Tuesday through Friday, 10:00 A.M. to 5:00 P.M. Saturday, and 1:00 to 4:00 P.M. Sunday, May through October, and by appointment the rest of the year. A Windmill Festival is held here each June. For additional information call the museum at (260) 897–9918 or visit www.midamericanwindmillmuseum.com.

trivia

In 1988 *Sports Illustrated* labeled Don Lash the greatest distance runner our country has ever produced. Among his many achievements during a career that peaked in the 1920s and 1930s were seven consecutive national cross-country titles. Lash, a native of Bluffton, passed away in 1994 at the age of eighty-two.

Black Pine Animal Park in **Albion** is home to rescued, rehabilitated, and retired animals. What started out as a backyard menagerie has evolved into a full-time business, fed by people who enjoyed seeing and learning about the eighty-six animals that currently live here. At this writing, the park is temporarily closed while the lions, tigers, bears, chimpanzees, camels, leopard, and cougar are moved to a new and larger home at 1426 West 300 North. The new park is expected to open in summer 2007. For up-to-date information call (260) 636–7383 or visit www.blackpineanimalpark.com.

Gene Stratton-Porter, a native Hoosier who became a noted author, nature photographer, and environmentalist, lived among the swamps and wetlands that once covered much of northeastern Indiana. In 1913 she built a cabin on the south shore of Sylvan Lake near Rome City and spent the next six years of her life exploring, photographing, and writing about the natural setting in which she lived. Several of her books were made into movies, which she herself wrote and produced. One of her best-known books, *A Girl of the Limberlost,* was the first American book to be translated into Arabic. It is also one of the top five favorite children's books of J. K. Rowling, author of the popular Harry Potter books; Ms. Rowling says she rereads it all the time. Today the cabin and the 123 acres of fields, woods, and formal gardens surrounding it are preserved as the **Gene Stratton-Porter State Historic Site.** Ms. Porter, who died in 1924 at the age of sixty-one, is interred in a mausoleum near the orchard. The site is open from mid-March to mid-December; grounds are open dawn to dusk, and a visitor center is open 9:00 A.M. to 5:00 P.M. Tuesday through Saturday and 1:00 to 5:00 P.M. Sunday; closed Monday, Easter Sunday, and Thanksgiving. Guided cabin tours are offered on the hour when the visitor center is open. Admission is free, but a donation is appreciated. Located at 1205 Pleasant Point; call (260) 854–3790 for additional information.

Randolph County

At the **Silver Towne Coin Shop** in **Winchester,** all that glitters *is* gold—or silver—and the beautiful antique-decorated showrooms in which the collections are displayed are as dazzling as the shop's wares. Visitors will also see a stunning array of jewelry, sports memorabilia, and collectibles. Open 9:00 A.M. to 5:00 P.M. Monday through Friday and 9:00 A.M. to 4:00 P.M. Saturday; also open the six Sundays before Christmas (call for hours). Guided tours are available by appointment. Located at 120 East Union City Pike; (765) 584–7481 or (800) 788–7481.

People from all over the world flock to Winchester each July to attend the **Aloha International Hawaiian Steel Guitar Festival.** For three days the air is filled with music, and on Saturday night everyone's invited to a luau. Townsfolk celebrate the annual event with such decorative touches

trivia

The late Robert Wise, a Winchester native, achieved fame as a movie director. Two of the movies he directed, *West Side Story* (1961) and *The Sound of Music* (1965), received Academy Awards for Best Picture of the Year. He also worked as an assistant editor on *Citizen Kane,* considered by many to be the best film of all time.

as fake palm trees in a local cafe. Contact the Randolph County Visitor Information Center, 112 West Washington Street, Winchester 47394; (765) 584–3731. Or call Jack Fowler at (765) 584–7433.

Wick's Pies, Inc. bakes twelve million pies a year in huge ovens that hold hundreds of pies at once. Wick's is most famous for its sugar cream pies, but its pecan pies run a close second. If you come in March, April, May, September, or October, you can watch and smell the pies being made on a free tour. Don't

trivia

The Winchester Speedway, located in the town of the same name, is the fastest half-mile speedway in the world. Built in the early 1900s, it's the second oldest speedway still in use in the Hoosier State (after the Indianapolis Motor Speedway). ESPN, the sports cable network, comes to Winchester each year to broadcast sprint, midget, and stock car racing from the nationally known track.

just drop in, however; the tours usually fill up a year in advance, so reservations are essential. The bakery is located at 217 Greenville Avenue in Winchester; (765) 584–8401. If you'd like to sample the goods, head for **Mrs. Wick's Restaurant** near the bakery, where a large menu, daily specials, and more than twenty-five varieties of pies are featured daily. It's located at 100 North Cherry Street in Winchester. Open 6:00 A.M. to 7:00 P.M. Monday through Friday and 7:00 A.M. to 2:00 P.M. Saturday; (765) 584–7437.

Steuben County

Majestic **Potawatomi Inn,** the only state park inn in northern Indiana, is one of the finest in the system. Resembling an Old English lodge, it sits in a clearing on the shore of Lake James in 1,200-acre **Pokagon State Park** in **Angola.**

Winter is king here, and the main treat is a refrigerated twin toboggan slide, generally open on weekends from Thanksgiving Day through February, that whisks you over the hills and through the woods at speeds of up to 50 miles per hour. In this snowy park tucked into the northeastern corner of the Hoosier State, winter visitors will also find an ice-skating pond, a sledding hill, and cross-country ski trails. Toboggans and cross-country ski equipment can be rented in the park.

After frolicking in the chilly outdoors all day, you can retire to the inn for a sauna and whirlpool bath, do a few laps in the indoor pool, or bask in the warmth of the redbrick fireplace.

The inn features nearly 140 rooms and serves three meals daily in its highly rated dining room. The atmosphere is so down-homey that guests often come to eat in their stocking feet. Roast beef is a daily feature on a dinner menu that usually includes a choice of seafood, steak, and a chicken or ham dish. Rates range from $47 to $89 a night for a double room and from $5.00 to $12.00 for dinner, with lunch and breakfast prices even lower.

Although Pokagon State Park and its inn have gained a reputation as a winter resort, people also come here in other seasons, when the forests and the sweeping lawns of the inn are a lush green, park lakes are ice-free for swimmers and anglers, and park trails accommodate hikers instead of skiers. Horses can be rented at the saddle barn, and the tennis and basketball courts see heavy use.

The nature center is popular year-round, with naturalists always on hand to interpret each of nature's moods. Bison and elk reside in nearby pens. One park trail leads to the marshes, swamps, and forests of the **Potawatomi State Nature Preserve.** The largest known tamarack and yellow birch trees in the state, the only northern white cedars known to exist in Indiana, and several species of wild orchids grow within the preserve's 208 acres.

For information about either the park or the inn, write Pokagon State Park, 450 Lane 100 Lake James, Angola 46703. The park's phone number is (260) 833–2012; call the inn at (260) 833–1077 or (877) 768–2928. To reach the park, go west from Angola on U.S. Highway 20 to I–69. Turn north on I–69 and proceed to State Road 727; State Road 727 leads west from I–69 to the park entrance.

All of Steuben County is noted for its natural beauty. Its combination of 101 lakes and verdant forests have earned it the nickname "Switzerland of Indiana," and no less an impresario than P. T. Barnum once pronounced Lake James "the most beautiful body of water I have ever seen!" What's more, Steuben County contains more dedicated state nature preserves than any other county in the state; you can learn more about them by writing or calling the Department of Natural Resources, Division of Nature Preserves, 402 West Washington Street, Room W267, Indianapolis 46204; (317) 232–4052.

Wabash County

In the town of **Wabash, Modoc the Elephant** is the stuff of legend. The huge pachyderm came to town with the Great American Circus in 1942. Shortly after their arrival, she and two other elephants broke loose and headed downtown, perhaps enticed by the smell of peanuts roasting inside a local drugstore. Modoc's two companions were soon rounded up, but Modoc would not be deterred from getting to those peanuts. She squeezed through the front door, ate her fill, and exited through the back door. With her would-be captors hot on her trail, she traipsed around the county for a week, creating havoc and making headlines around the country in the process. A sweet-talking circus trainer with twenty-six loaves of bread finally managed to capture her (the fact that she had a cold and had lost some 800 pounds might have had a bit to do with it, too). Today, the drugstore is Modoc's Market, and statues of elephants saunter along the sidewalk outside its door. Visitors can see circus and elephant memorabilia inside the store and view a large mural painted on the wall of a downtown building that commemorates the day Modoc came to town. Modoc's Market is located at 205 South Miami Street; (260) 569–1281.

Although the folks in Wabash didn't realize it at the time, Modoc was a very famous elephant who is remembered today for much more than her long-ago jaunt through a small Indiana town. The story of her remarkable life may soon be told in a movie called *Modoc: The True Story of the Greatest Elephant That Ever Lived*, based on the book of the same name by Ralph Helfer.

Wells County

Bluffton native Charles C. Deam (1865–1953) was the Hoosier State's first state forester and an internationally recognized authority in the field of botany. Approximately 4 miles northwest of **Bluffton,** you can see the **Deam Oak,** a rare hybrid tree named in the forester's honor. The tree, discovered in 1904, is believed to be the first of its kind; its acorns have since been distributed across the country. A natural cross between white and chinquapin oaks, the tree stands at the center of a small tract of state-owned land at the junction of State Road 116 and County Road 250 North.

You can learn more about Deam and his oak tree at the **Wells County Historical Museum** in Bluffton. Also featured here are the memorabilia of Everett Scott, another Bluffton native, who played for the Boston Red Sox and the New York Yankees in the 1920s. A baseball autographed by Scott and his friend and sometimes roommate, Babe Ruth, is a highlight of the exhibit. Civil War buffs can read pages from the Civil War diary of William Bluffton Miller, the first child born in Bluffton. The museum is located at 420 West Market Street; open 1:00 to 4:00 P.M. Wednesday and Sunday, June through August. Donations are appreciated; call (260) 824–9956.

trivia

In 1890 a major oil strike was made on a farm in Wells County. By 1904 nearly 20,000 producing oil wells were scattered over a 400-square-mile area in Indiana that included Wells County, and Petroleum came into being as the state's newest boomtown. The oil is long gone, and Petroleum has nearly gone with it. Today the tiny town on State Road 1 is inhabited by approximately 150 people.

Places to Stay in Northeast Indiana

ANGOLA

Potawatomi Inn
Pokagon State Park
6 Lane 100 A Lake James
(260) 833–1077 or
(877) 768–2928
Moderate

**Tulip Tree Inn Bed
and Breakfast**
411 North Wayne Street
(260) 668–7000 or
(888) 401–0002
Moderate

AUBURN

**Whispering Pines Lodge
B&B**
3190 County Road 36
(260) 925–3666
Moderate

**Yawn to Dawn Bed
and Breakfast**
211 West Fifth Street
(260) 925–2583
Moderate

BERNE

Black Bear Inn and Suites
1335 U.S. Highway 27 North
(260) 589–8955
Inexpensive

FORT WAYNE

At the Herb Lady's Garden
8214 Maysville Road
(260) 493–8814
Moderate

Carole Lombard House
704 Rockhill Street
(260) 426–9896 or
(888) 426–9896
Inexpensive

Sleep Inn
2881 East Dupont Road
(260) 490–8989
Moderate

FREMONT

**Wild Winds Buffalo
Preserve B&B**
6975 North Ray Road
(260) 495–0137
Moderate

GOSHEN

Checkerberry Inn
62535 County Road 37
(574) 642–4445
Moderate

Eden Haus B&B
3545 South 1200 West
(574) 642–4276
Moderate

LAGRANGE

Brick House Inn
408 North Detroit Street
(260) 463–4981
Moderate

LEESBURG

Prairie House B&B
495 East 900 North
(574) 658–9211
Inexpensive

LIGONIER

**Solomon Mier Manor Bed
and Breakfast**
508 South Cavin Street
(260) 894–3668
Moderate

MIDDLEBURY

**Bee Hive Bed and
Breakfast**
51129 County Road 35
P.O. Box 1191
(574) 825–5023
Inexpensive

Country Victorian B&B
435 South Main Street
(574) 825–2568
Moderate

Essenhaus Inn
240 U.S. Highway 20
(574) 825–9447
Moderate

**Patchwork Quilt
Country Inn**
11748 County Road 2
(574) 825–2417
Moderate

NAPPANEE

The Inn at Amish Acres
1234 West Market Street
(574) 773–2011 or
(800) 800–4942
Moderate

**Olde Buffalo Inn Bed
and Breakfast**
1061 Parkwood Drive
(574) 773–2223 or
(888) 773–2223
Moderate

The Victorian Guest House
302 East Market Street
(574) 773–4383 or
(877) 773–4383
Moderate

NORTH MANCHESTER

Fruitt Basket Inn
116 West Main Street
(260) 982–2443
Moderate

PERU

Rosewood Mansion
54 North Hood Street
(765) 472–7151
Moderate

PORTLAND

Hilltop Farm B&B
3168 Boundary Pike
(260) 726–8029 or
(877) 455–3313
Moderate

SHIPSHEWANA

Morton Street Bed and Breakfast
120 Morton Street
(260) 768–4391 or
(800) 447–6475
Moderate

Old Carriage Inn Bed and Breakfast
140 East Farver Street
(260) 768–7217 or
(800) 435–0888
Moderate

SYRACUSE

Anchor Inn B&B
11007 North State Road 13
(574) 457–4714 or
(888) 347–7481
Moderate

UNION CITY

Mansion Bed and Breakfast
526 West Division Street
(765) 964–6805
Moderate

WARREN

Huggy Bear Motel
7588 South Warren Road
(260) 375–2503 or
(800) 523–5972
Inexpensive

WATERLOO

Maple Leaf Inn
425 West Maple Street
(260) 837–5323

Places to Eat in Northeast Indiana

ANGOLA

Lelli's Hatchery
118 South Elizabeth Street
(260) 665–9957
Moderate
American/Italian/wild game

BERNE

The Palmer House
Main and Fulton Streets
(260) 589–2306
Inexpensive
American/Amish

BLUFFTON

Snug Cafe
126 West Market Street
(260) 824–0718
Inexpensive
American

DECATUR

Decatur Gardens
1402 Winchester Road
(260) 724–9701
Moderate
American

ELKHART

Bulldog Restaurant
3763 East Jackson Boulevard
(574) 294–6000
Moderate
American

FORT WAYNE

Casa D'Angelo
3402 Fairfield Avenue
(260) 745–7200
Moderate
Italian

Cindy's Diner
830 South Harrison Street
(260) 422–1957
Inexpensive
American

Firehouse Cafe and Firefighters Museum
226 West Washington Boulevard
(260) 422–4850
Inexpensive
American

World Famous Coney Island Weiner Stand
131 West Main Street
(260) 424–2997
Inexpensive
Hot dogs

FREMONT

Clay's Family Restaurant
7815 North Old 27
(260) 833–1332
Moderate
American

Auburn/DeKalb County Visitors Bureau
204 North Jackson Street
P.O. Box 430
Auburn 46706
(260) 927–1499 or (877) 833–3282

Berne/Adams County Chamber of Commerce
175 West Main Street
P.O. Box 85
Berne 46711
(260) 589–8080

Bluffton/Wells County Chamber of Commerce
211 West Water Street
Bluffton 46714
(260) 824–0510

Elkhart County Convention and Visitors Bureau
219 Caravan Drive
Elkhart 46514
(574) 262–8161 or (800) 250–4827

Fort Wayne/Allen County Convention and Visitor Bureau
1021 South Calhoun Street
Fort Wayne 46802
(260) 424–3700 or (800) 767–7752

Huntington County Visitor and Convention Bureau
407 North Jefferson Street
Huntington 46750
(260) 359–8687 or (800) 848–4282

Kokomo/Howard County Convention and Visitors Bureau
1504 North Reed Road
(U.S. Highway 31)
Kokomo 46901
(765) 457–6802 or (800) 837–0971

Kosciusko County Convention and Visitors Bureau
111 Capital Drive
Warsaw 46582
(574) 269–6090 or (800) 800–6090

LaGrange County Convention and Visitors Bureau
440½ South Van Buren Street
(State Road 5 South)
Shipshewana 46565
(260) 768–4129 or (800) 254–8090

Ligonier Visitors Center
800 Lincolnway South
Ligonier 46767
(260) 894–9000 or (888) 417–3562

Marion/Grant County Convention and Visitors Bureau
217 South Adams Street
P.O. Box 745
Marion 46952
(765) 668–5435 or (800) 662–9474

Muncie/Delaware County Visitors Bureau
425 North High Street, Suite 5
Muncie 47305
(765) 284–2700 or (800) 568–6862

Noble County Convention and Visitors Bureau
2010 West North Street
(U.S. Highway 6)
P.O. Box 934
Kendallville 46755
(260) 599–0060 or (877) 202–5761

Peru/Miami County Chamber of Commerce
13 East Main Street
Peru 46970
(765) 472–1923

Randolph County Visitor Information Center
112 West Washington Street
Winchester 47394
(765) 584–3731

Steuben County Tourism Bureau
207 South Wayne Street
Angola 46703
(260) 665–5386 or (800) 525–3101

GARRETT

Railroad Inn
104 North Peters Street
(260) 357–5756
Moderate
American

GOSHEN

Citrus, An American Bistro
The Checkerberry Inn
62535 County Road 37
(574) 642–4445
Expensive
American

Old Mill Inn
49 State Road 15
(574) 533–4994
Moderate
American

South Side Soda Shop-Diner
1122 South Main Street
(574) 534–3790
Inexpensive
American

HUDSON

Dillinger's
302 North Main Street
(260) 587–3377
Moderate
American

HUNTINGTON

Nick's Kitchen
506 North Jefferson Street
(260) 356–6618
Inexpensive
American

LIGONIER

Fashion Farm Restaurant
1680 Lincolnway West
(260) 894–4498
Inexpensive
Home cooking

MARION

Good Time Charlie's
3448 South Adams Street
(765) 674–5984
Inexpensive
American

MIDDLEBURY

Das Dutchman Essenhaus
240 U.S. Highway 20
(574) 825–9471 or
(800) 455–9471
Moderate
Amish/American

Village Inn Restaurant
107 South Main Street
(574) 825–2043
Inexpensive
American

MONTPELIER

Frosty's
659 West Huntington Street
(765) 728–2257
Inexpensive
American

Grandma Jo's
619 West Huntington Street
(765) 728–5444
Inexpensive
Home cooking

NORTH MANCHESTER

Main View Inn
141 East Main Street
(260) 982–9900
Inexpensive
American

Mr. Dave's Restaurant
102 East Main Street
(260) 982–4769
Inexpensive
Sandwich shop

ROANOKE

Joseph Decius Restaurant
191 North Main Street
(260) 672–1715
Expensive
Contemporary/American

SHIPSHEWANA

Blue Gate Restaurant
105 East Middlebury Street
(260) 768–4725
Moderate
Amish

SWEETSER

The Cove
102 South Main Street
(765) 384–7820
Inexpensive
Home cooking

SYRACUSE

Oakwood Inn
702 East Lake View Road
(574) 457–5600
Moderate
American

TOPEKA

Tiffany's
414 East Lake Street
(260) 593–2988
Inexpensive
American

WABASH

Great Wall Restaurant
1439 North Cass Street
(260) 563–7987
Inexpensive
Chinese

WARSAW

Dig's Diner
114 North Buffalo Street
(574) 269–9696
Inexpensive
Home cooking

ViewPoint Restaurant
2519 East Center Street
(574) 269–2323
Moderate
Family dining

Northwest Indiana

Northwest Indiana is a land of contrasts. The most heavily industrialized region of the Hoosier State shares the Lake Michigan shoreline with the hauntingly wild and beautiful Indiana Dunes National Lakeshore. Lake County, which covers 501 square miles in Indiana's northwestern corner, is the state's second most populous county—some 475,000 people live within its borders. Not far south lie the rich farmlands of Benton County, whose 407 square miles are inhabited by about 9,000 people.

Two of Indiana's most fabled rivers wend their way through northwest Indiana. The Kankakee River, which flows southwest from South Bend to the Illinois border, and its adjacent wetlands evoke memories of the lush 500,000-acre Grand Kankakee marsh it once nourished. Indiana's longest waterway, the Wabash River, cuts a swath through four of this region's counties on its 475-mile journey west across the width of the state and then south to the Ohio River.

Visitors travel to and through northwest Indiana on Interstate 80/90, an east-west highway that is Indiana's only toll road; Interstate 65, a north-south route; and several excellent U.S. highways.

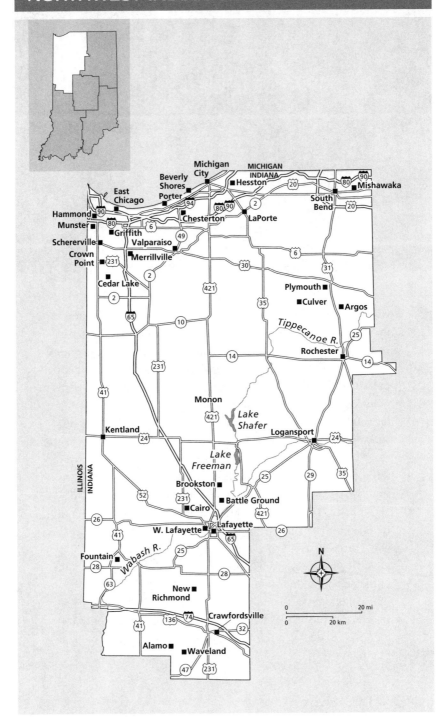

Cass County

The pride of **Logansport** is its turn-of-the-twentieth-century *carousel.* About a century old, it is one of only two all-wood, hand-carved merry-go-rounds still operating in Indiana. (The other is in the Indianapolis Children's Museum.) Delighted riders compete for a mount on the perimeter and the chance to snag the coveted brass ring as the carousel spins round and round. The brightly colored mounts—a mix of thirty-one horses, three goats, three reindeer, three giraffes, a lion, and a tiger—were produced in 1892 by the talented hands of German craftsman Gustav A. Dentzel, who moved to the United States in 1860 and became this country's chief carousel maker.

The carousel is owned by a nonprofit citizens' group; a small fee is charged for each ride to help offset maintenance costs. You'll find the merry-go-round in **Riverside City Park,** located along the south bank of Eel River at 1300 River-

AUTHOR'S FAVORITE ATTRACTIONS/EVENTS IN NORTHWEST INDIANA

Buckeye Powered Parachutes Fly-In
Argos; July (Fourth of July weekend)
(574) 892–5566

Chapel of the Resurrection
Valparaiso University
Valparaiso
(219) 464–5093 or (888) 468–2576

Feast of the Hunters' Moon
Lafayette; October
(765) 447–9999 or (800) 872–6648

General Lew Wallace Study and Museum
Crawfordsville
(765) 364–5175 or (800) 866–3973

Indiana Dunes National Lakeshore
Lake, Porter, and LaPorte Counties
(219) 926–7561

Indiana Fiddlers' Gathering
Battle Ground; June
(765) 742–1419

Kentland Dome
Kentland
(219) 474–5125

Marshall County Blueberry Festival
Plymouth
September
(574) 936–5020 or (888) 936–5020

Popcorn Festival
Valparaiso; September
(219) 464–8332

Shades State Park
Waveland
(765) 435–2810

Studebaker National Museum
South Bend
(574) 235–9714 or (888) 391–5600
www.studebakerrmuseum.org

Wolf Park
Battle Ground
(765) 567–2265
www.wolfpark.org

ANNUAL EVENTS IN NORTHWEST INDIANA

Maple Syrup Time
Hobart; March
(219) 947–1958 or (800) GRISTMILL

Redbud Trail Rendezvous
Rochester; April
(574) 223–4436

**Voyageur Rendezvous on the
Riviere de Teakiki**
Hebron; May
(219) 769–PARK (7275)

Grecian Festival
South Bend; June
(574) 277–4688

Mint Festival
North Judson; June
(574) 896–5481

Round Barn Festival
Rochester; June
(574) 223–4436

Canal Days
Delphi; July
(765) 564–6572

Pierogi Fest
Whiting; July
(219) 659–0292 or (877) 659–0292

**College Football Hall of Fame
Enshrinement**
South Bend; August
(574) 235–9999 or (800) 440–FAME

Kouts Porkfest
Kouts; August
(219) 766–2867

International Culture Festival
Hammond; September
(219) 554–0155

Scarecrow Festival
Wanatah; September
(219) 733–2183

Steam and Power Show
Hesston; September
(Every weekend from Memorial Day
through Labor Day)
(219) 872–5055

**Trail of Courage Living
History Festival**
Rochester; September
(574) 223–4436

Wizard of Oz Festival
Chesterton; September
(219) 926–5513, (219) 926–2255, or
(800) 283–8687

Elvis FANtasy Fest
Portage; October
(219) 926–2255

**Northwestern Indiana
Storytelling Festival**
Chesterton; October
(219) 926–1390

side Drive—just follow the sound of music. It operates 6:00 to 9:00 P.M. Monday through Friday and 1:00 to 9:00 P.M. Saturday and Sunday, Memorial Day through Labor Day. Contact the Logansport/Cass County Chamber of Commerce, 300 East Broadway Street, Suite 103, Logansport 46947; (574) 753–6388; www.logan-casschamber.org.

Four miles west of Logansport off U.S. Highway 24 you'll come upon *France Park* and its picturesque swimming hole. An abandoned limestone quarry, partly hemmed in by precipitous cliffs, is filled with clear, brisk water that's irresistible on a hot summer day. Scuba and cliff divers like it, too.

Patches of woodland and a mossy, 15-foot waterfall on Paw Paw Creek add touches of beauty to the 500-acre county park. Seven miles of hiking/biking trails include a towpath that follows the remains of the old Wabash and Erie Canal. Visitors will also find a water slide, miniature golf course, some 200 campsites, and, near the entrance, a century-old log cabin. Nominal admission fee. Beach open Memorial Day through Labor Day; park open daily year-round 9:00 A.M. to 11:00 P.M. Contact France Park, 4505 West US 24, Logansport; (574) 753–2928.

Fountain County

It will never give the folks in Utah anything to worry about, but Indiana does have a unique stone arch that's been declared both a National Natural Landmark and a state nature preserve. Through the years the meanderings of a tiny stream in northwestern Fountain County have carved a 30-by-12-foot opening through a massive sandstone formation and created a natural bridge known as **Portland Arch.** Nearby Bear Creek flows through a deep ravine edged by rugged sandstone cliffs. The rare bush honeysuckle grows here, and this is the only known site in the state where the Canada blueberry is found. At times a cover of mosses and lichens and several species of ferns growing in the crevices of the cliffs create a landscape of green velvet. A quaint pioneer cemetery on the 253-acre preserve contains eleven marked graves.

Portland Arch State Nature Preserve is located on the south side of the town of **Fountain.** Signs lead the way to the preserve and two parking lots, each adjoined by a self-guiding trail. The loop trail leading from the first and main parking lot follows a hilly route about 1 mile long to Portland Arch. For additional information write or call the Department of Natural Resources, Division of Nature Preserves, 402 West Washington Street, Room W267, Indianapolis 46204; (317) 232–4052.

Fulton County

Fulton County is peppered with round barns, the legacy of a turn-of-the-twentieth-century fad. At last count eight of the original barns, the newest of which was built in 1924, were still standing. They are kept in excellent repair and are both unusual and beautiful to behold. No two are alike. The main idea behind this flurry of round-barn building was to create one centralized feeding station for livestock, thus increasing the efficiency of the farm operation. The barns were billed as being easier, quicker, and less costly to build, but the idea was abandoned.

In 1988 the **_Fulton County Museum_** near **_Rochester_** opened its doors to the public. A round barn, rebuilt on the premises and opened in 1990, showcases historic farm tools and machinery. Together they offer a glimpse into the county's past and provide information about its unique heritage. Maps are available for a driving tour of the county's barns. Although the barns are not officially open to the public, many owners, if they're at home when you arrive, are happy to show you through their barns. Several barns are also open to the public for one weekend each June when the county celebrates a Round Barn Festival. Admission to the museum is free; open 9:00 A.M. to 5:00 P.M. Monday through Saturday. The museum is located at 37 East 375 North, Rochester; (574) 223–4436. The Fulton County Historical Society, which has its headquarters at the museum, founded the National Round Barn Center to keep track of and to help preserve all round barns in the country.

Jasper County

Each fall one of Indiana's most magnificent natural spectacles takes place at the 8,000-acre **_Jasper-Pulaski State Fish and Wildlife Area._** During the last week in October and the first week in November, some 15,000 to 20,000 greater sandhill cranes pause here to rest on their annual journey south for the winter. Jasper-Pulaski is believed to be the only place east of the Mississippi River where this unusual species stops en masse during migration.

These beautiful blue-gray birds, which stand about 3½ feet tall and have a wingspan of up to 7 feet, are as impressive to hear as they are to look at. The

Round Barn at Fulton County Museum

best times to view them are at dawn, when they rise up from the misty marshes and call to one another in noisy unison, and again at sunset, when they return to the marsh for the night.

You can pick up literature about the cranes and obtain a free observation permit at the area headquarters, then continue on to one of two observation towers.

The cranes also migrate through Jasper-Pulaski between late February and mid-April, but they are usually present in greater concentration in the fall.

Although the sandhills are the main attraction, other wildlife species are here as well. Canada geese, quail, woodcock, and deer live in the wild year-round, and elk and bison roam fenced-in pastures. Part of Jasper-Pulaski serves as a game farm where pheasant are reared as stock for wildlife areas throughout the state. Natural history and wildlife exhibits are maintained in one of the service buildings, and hiking trails wind through the area.

Located in the area's northwest corner is the 480-acre *Tefft Savanna State Nature Preserve,* home to many plants that are extremely rare in the Midwest. The entire fish and wildlife area actually occupies portions of three counties— Jasper, Pulaski, and Starke—but the majority of its 8,000 acres are in Jasper County. It's open daily year-round at all times, and entrance is free. The headquarters office is open 8:00 A.M. to 3:30 P.M. Monday through Friday, but hours may be extended in certain seasons.

To reach the refuge, go north from Medaryville (in Pulaski County) on U.S. Highway 421 and turn west onto State Road 143; proceed 1½ miles to the entrance on the right side of the road; follow the signs. Write or call Jasper-Pulaski State Fish and Wildlife Area, 5822 North Fish and Wildlife Lane, Medaryville 47957; (219) 843–4841.

Lake County

When the first white settlers came to Indiana, seven-eighths of the land was covered with a forest so dense that a squirrel could visit every tree in the state without ever once touching the ground. The far northwest corner, including what is now Lake County, was a sea of grass—grass so tall in places that a rider on horseback could not be seen above it. It was a long time before residents realized the value of saving some remnants of that original landscape, and by then most of it was irretrievably lost.

Two of the finest examples still in existence can be seen in Lake County. *German Methodist Cemetery Prairie* covers just one acre at the rear of the cemetery for which it's named, but more than eighty rare and vanishing plant species thrive in its rich black soil. In late summer, when most of them are in bloom, it is a place of incredible beauty.

This tiny preserve is probably the most botanically diverse acre in Indiana. You'll find it in the midst of farm fields on the east side of U.S. Highway 41, 1 mile south of the intersection of US 41 and 141st Street in **Cedar Lake.** The old cemetery is still there and should be respected. Behind it is the prairie, surrounded by a chain-link fence to protect the fragile plant life. For additional information write or call The Nature Conservancy, Indiana Field Office, 1505 North Delaware Street, Suite 200, Indianapolis 46202; (317) 951–8818.

Hoosier Prairie, the largest virgin prairie in Indiana, sprawls over 439 acres near **Griffith.** It contains some 300 species of native plants, including grasses that reach 12 feet in height. A trail about 2 miles long leads through some of the preserve's less sensitive areas and permits a look at the diverse habitats. You may even spot a deer along the way. Hoosier Prairie, a state nature preserve, is located west of Griffith on the south side of Main Street; a small parking lot is near the trailhead. Open daily year-round during daylight hours; admission is free. Write or call the Department of Natural Resources, Division of Nature Preserves, 402 West Washington Street, Room W267, Indianapolis 46204; (317) 232–4052.

The late Pastor Win Worley of the **Hegewisch Baptist Church** in Highland gained worldwide fame as an exorcist. He began casting out evil spirits in 1970, and within one year, with no publicity other than word of mouth, more than 1,000 first-time visitors were streaming into the small church annually. At an Exorcism Open House sponsored by the church in 1992, for instance, some 500 people from twenty-eight states and three foreign countries showed up. Now several Deliverance Workshops are held each year, and you are welcome to attend. For additional information write Pastor Michael Thierer, Hegewisch Baptist Church, 8711 Cottage Grove Avenue, P.O. Box 9327, Highland 46322; call (219) 838–9410; or visit www.hbcdelivers.org.

The **Carmelite Shrines** in **Munster** offer a haven of serenity. On the grounds are twenty shrines that display Italian sculptures in a grotto studded with crystals and unusual rocks. The overall effect is enhanced by special lighting. You'll also find an arboretum and, in the monastery, a replica of the Vatican's Private Audience Hall. The grounds are open free of charge 1:00 to 5:00 P.M. daily, weather permitting; building interiors can usually be seen on request. The shrines are located at 1628 Ridge Road, ½ mile west of US 41; (219) 838–7111.

When hunger pangs strike, head for **Teibel's Restaurant** in **Schererville.** Teibel's first opened its doors in 1929, the year the stock market crashed and launched the Great Depression. That the restaurant operated continuously through those lean years and still thrives today should tell you something. One reason for its longevity is that the old family recipe for fried chicken, which initially earned the restaurant its reputation, is a winner. The chicken (as well as fried perch) is served on an all-you-can-eat basis. Prices are moderate. Open

11:00 A.M. to 10:00 P.M. Monday through Saturday and 11:00 A.M. to 8:00 P.M. Sunday, April through December; 11:00 A.M. to 9:00 P.M. Monday through Saturday and 11:00 A.M. to 8:00 P.M. Sunday the rest of the year. Located at the corner of U.S. Highways 41 and 30; (219) 865–2000; www.teibels.com.

Crown Point is dominated by the "Grand Old Lady of Lake County," the magnificent *Old Lake County Court House,* which many regard as Indiana's most impressive. Built in 1878, it served as the seat of county government until 1974. Today it houses more than a dozen crafts and specialty shops, as well as the *Lake County Historical Museum.* Don't miss its arched brick ceilings and intriguing hallways. The courthouse is located at the corner of Joliet and Court Streets; its shops are generally open from 10:00 A.M. to 5:00 P.M. Monday through Saturday (until 7:00 P.M. on Friday); hours may vary. The museum is open 1:00 to 4:00 P.M. Thursday through Saturday May through October; other times by appointment. There's a nominal admission fee for the museum. For additional information call (219) 662–3975 or contact the Lake County Court House Foundation, 200 Court House Square, Crown Point 46307; (219) 663–0660; www.crownpoint.net.

In 1896 William Jennings Bryan stood on the courthouse steps and campaigned for the presidency. A then-unknown car designer, Louis Chevrolet, came here to accept the winner's cup for the first major auto race in the United States, a race held in 1909 that was the forerunner of the Indy 500. From 1916 to 1941 the courthouse became famous for its instant marriages; the usual blood test and three-day waiting period were not required here. Among the thousands married at the courthouse during that period were Joe DiMaggio, Red Grange, Colleen Moore, Tom Mix, Muhammad Ali, Ronald Reagan (to Jane Wyman), and, at the height of his career, Rudolph Valentino.

The magnificent *SS. Constantine and Helen Greek Orthodox Cathedral* rises from amid thirty-seven acres of grounds at 8000 Madison Street in *Merrillville.* The only such church in the state, it features twenty-five large stained-glass windows, Byzantine mosaic work, and a rotunda 100 feet in diameter and 50 feet in height. Open 9:00 A.M. to 5:00 P.M. Monday through Friday and 10:00 A.M. to 2:00 P.M. Saturday. Each year on the second weekend of July, a Greek festival takes place here; (219) 769–2481.

Visitors to *Hammond* can see the world's largest reproduction of Salvador Dali's famous painting *The Persistence of Memory.* The 20-foot-tall painting adorns the wall of one of the city's tallest buildings some 80 feet above the street. Plans call for the reproduction of eight to ten more famous paintings on the same wall, which is known as the *Midwest Wall of Classics.* The building is located at the intersection of Russell Street and Hohman Avenue; the wall bearing the Dali mural can be seen from Hohman Avenue. For additional information contact South Shore Arts, 435 Fayette Street, Hammond; (219) 933–0200.

Built in 1917 as a planned worker community for a steel company that has long since vanished, **Marktown** is a historic district that is home to some 650 residents. Marktown's two-story stucco homes, all in Tudor Revival style and painted in pastels for color and variety, line narrow streets that once were given mention in Robert Ripley's *Believe It or Not* column. Ripley, chronicler of the unique, noted that Marktown residents used the streets as walkways and parked their cars on the sidewalks. Although the town never reached completion, ninety-four homes were constructed, and all remain standing today. Marktown is bounded by Pine and 129th Streets and Dickey and Riley Roads in **East Chicago.** For information about walking and driving tours, write or call the Marktown Preservation Society at 405 Prospect Street, Marktown Historic District, East Chicago 46312; (219) 397–2239.

The frogs' legs served at **Phil Smidt's Restaurant** in Hammond have been celebrated since 1910, when the restaurant first opened for business. Once the frogs' legs were gathered from the shore of nearby Lake Michigan; today they come from Bangladesh. They are still delicious, however, and what's more, they're served in a stunning room. One side is open, two walls are a soft rose hue, and the third bears murals of gigantic roses done in high-gloss paint on a shiny black background. Soft light filters through blocks of aquarium glass. The white tablecloths are bordered in pink, and each place is set with rose-colored napkins and rose-embossed water glasses. Be sure to ask to be seated in the Rose Room; there are five other dining rooms as well.

Another specialty of the house is lake perch, served whole or boned and cooked to perfection. Top off your meal with warm gooseberry pie. Outside, freight trains rumble by, and smokestacks spew smoke—an incredible contrast to the beauty within.

You'll find Phil Smidt's Restaurant at 1205 North Calumet Avenue; it's open for lunch and dinner from 11:15 A.M. to 9:00 P.M. Tuesday through Thursday, 11:15 A.M. to 9:30 P.M. Friday, 1:00 to 9:30 P.M. Saturday, and 1:00 to 7:00 P.M. Sunday; closed Monday. Call (219) 659–0025 or visit www.philsmidts.com.

The building that has housed the **Lake County Convention and Visitors Bureau** since September 1, 1999, is a tourist attraction in itself. Built at a cost of $6 million, the structure is domed with blue glass and stainless steel that symbolize the waves of Lake Michigan crashing against the shore to the north. An undulating south wall represents the Kankakee River, which forms Lake County's southern border. Also along the southern portion of the building is a silo that pays tribute to the county's agricultural heritage. An exhibition hall displays artifacts from various Indiana attractions, including an Indianapolis 500 race car and an Amish buggy.

OTHER ATTRACTIONS WORTH SEEING IN NORTHWEST INDIANA

DELPHI

Wabash and Erie Canal Park and Interpretive Center
1030 North Washington Street
(765) 564–6572

LINDEN

Linden Railroad Museum
520 North Main Street
(765) 339–7245 or (800) 866–3973

MICHIGAN CITY

Great Lakes Museum of Military History
360 Dunes Plaza
1710 East U.S. Highway 20
(219) 872–2702 or (800) 726–5912

SOUTH BEND

College Football Hall of Fame
111 South St. Joseph Street
(574) 235–9999 or (800) 440–FAME

Copsaholm Mansion/Northern Indiana Center for History
808 West Washington Street
(574) 235–9664

VALPARAISO

Anderson's Orchard and Winery
430 East U.S. Highway 6
(219) 464–4936

Old Jail Museum
153 South Franklin Street
(219) 465–3595

WEST LAFAYETTE

Fort Ouiatenon Historical Park
3129 South River Road
(765) 743–3921

Located just south of the intersection of Kennedy Avenue and I–80/94 at 7770 Corinne Drive in Hammond, the visitors bureau is open 8:00 A.M. to 5:00 P.M. Monday through Friday and 9:00 A.M. to 5:00 P.M. Saturday and Sunday. Call (219) 989–7979 or (800) ALL–LAKE (255–5253).

LaPorte County

At the tiny town of **Hesston,** northeast of LaPorte, you can see the **Hesston Steam Museum.** Spread out over a 155-acre site is an assemblage of steam-powered equipment worth several million dollars—trains, cranes, buzz saws, and a boat among them. You can take a 2-mile ride on a steam train or watch a miniature train, authentic to the tiniest detail, whiz by on a 3½-inch track. Feel free to toot a horn or ring a bell—it's that type of place.

You can walk through the exhibits any day except Monday, but the equipment is only in operation noon to 5:00 P.M. on Saturday, Sunday, and holidays, Memorial Day weekend through Labor Day, and Sunday only from Labor Day through October. An especially exuberant celebration takes place during the Annual Labor Day Weekend Steam and Power Show. The outdoor museum is located at 1201 East County Road 1000 North, approximately 2½ miles east of State Road 39. Admission is free except on Labor Day weekend; a nominal fee is charged at all times for train rides. Contact the LaPorte County Historical Steam Society at 2940 Mt. Claire Way, Long Beach, Michigan City 46360; (219) 778–2783. You can also learn more about the museum on the Web at www .michigancity.com/Hesston/Hesston.htm.

In the town of *LaPorte* you can tour the *LaPorte County Museum,* which moved to new and roomier quarters in 2004. Among the more than 80,000 exhibits are a recently acquired auto collection that includes a Duesenberg, a Cord, a Tucker, a DeLorean stainless steel car, a Baker electric car, a 1903 Winton, and an Amphicar that runs on land and water, as well as several early airplanes. The W. A. Jones collection of antique firearms and weapons is recognized as the best collection of its kind in the United States and one of the three best in the world. There's also a display that tells the story of Belle Gunness, LaPorte's Madam Bluebeard, who in the early 1900s lured at least a dozen men to her farm north of town by promising to marry them; once there, the would-be husbands were promptly killed for their money and buried in the farmyard. When Belle's house burned to the ground in 1908, the skeletons of her three adopted children and a headless woman were found in the ashes. The woman's body was much too short to be Belle's, but it was never learned what really happened to her. The museum, located at 2405 Indiana Avenue, is open from 10:00 A.M. to 4:30 P.M. Tuesday through Saturday (closed holidays); (219) 326–6808. Nominal admission fee.

trivia

Dr. Scholl, friend to sore feet everywhere, was a real person and a real doctor. A native of LaPorte County, Dr. William Scholl graduated from medical school in 1904.

At the *Angelo Bernacchi Greenhouses,* you can treat your visual and olfactory senses to the thousands of growing green things that make this the largest grower and retailer of plants in the entire Midwest. There are acres to browse through all year long. The retail shop is open 8:30 A.M. to 5:00 P.M. Monday through Friday and 8:30 A.M. to 4:00 P.M. Saturday; special tours on May 1 and December 1. Located at 1010 Fox Street, LaPorte; (219) 362–6202 or (800) 759–0978.

To view some outdoor blooms, visit the ***International Friendship Gardens*** in ***Michigan City.*** Currently undergoing restoration, these gardens are representative of those found in major countries around the world. Plant specimens are arranged as they would be in each nation's homeland. The wooded trails that surround the gardens provide a cool and peaceful retreat on a hot summer day. Nominal admission fee. Open 10:00 A.M. to 4:00 P.M. Saturday and Sunday, May through October. Located at the junction of U.S. Highway 12 and Liberty Trail; (219) 878–9885.

The ***Barker Civic Center*** at 631 Washington Street in Michigan City exudes turn-of-the-twentieth-century elegance. Once the home of millionaire industrialist John H. Barker, it contains thirty-eight rooms; ten bathrooms; several fireplaces with hand-carved teak, walnut, or mahogany woodwork; and a mirrored ballroom. Adjacent to the library terrace is a sunken Italian garden. Tours at 10:00 A.M., 11:30 A.M., and 1:00 P.M. Monday through Friday; also at noon and 2:00 P.M. Saturday and Sunday, June through October; closed major holidays. Nominal admission fee; (219) 873–1520.

A meat market that's a tourist attraction? Yes, say its many visitors. Step through the door and into the past at ***Lange's Old-Fashioned Meat Market*** in Michigan City. Lange's specializes in homemade mettwurst, bratwurst, and Polish sausage, using recipes handed down from past generations of owners. The real treat, though, is the yesteryear atmosphere of the shop—complete with sawdust-strewn floors—and the character behind the counter. You'll also see a scale model of Michigan City's historic downtown. Located at 218 West Seventh Street; (219) 874–0071. Open 9:00 A.M. to 6:00 P.M. Tuesday through Saturday and 11:00 A.M. to 4:00 P.M. Sunday; closed January and February. Free thirty-minute tours are offered by advance arrangement; visitors are encouraged to ask questions as they learn how old-world sausage is made and how meats are smoked and cured.

Not far away, a fishing pier that extends into Lake Michigan offers a view of Indiana's only operating lighthouse. On a clear day you can also see the Chicago skyline.

The area's natural history is explored at the ***Old Lighthouse Museum*** in ***Washington Park,*** Michigan City's ninety-acre lakefront park. Situated on Heisman Harbor Road at the park's west entrance, the museum contains a rare fourth-order Fresnel lens, shipbuilding tools, and other maritime artifacts. Open 1:00 to 4:00 P.M. Tuesday through Sunday, March through December; closed Monday, January and February, and holidays. There's a nominal admission fee; (219) 872–6133.

The Washington Park Zoo at 115 Lake Shore Drive features more than 180 species of animals. An observation tower that provides views of Lake

Old Lighthouse Museum

Michigan has been perched atop a sand dune in the park since the 1930s. After undergoing a three-year renovation, the six-story building reopened in 2005; access to the tower is included in the zoo's nominal admission fee. The zoo is open daily 10:30 A.M. to 5:00 P.M. Memorial Day through Labor Day, and from 10:30 A.M. to 3:00 P.M. from April 1 to the day before Memorial Day and the day after Labor Day through October (closed November through March). Call (219) 873–1510.

Marshall County

If you visit the small town of **Argos,** you're likely to see a lot of people looking up. That's because they're scanning the skies for a glimpse of the powered parachutes manufactured at **Buckeye Industries,** the world's largest manufacturer of these colorful aircraft. The company, which has its national headquarters in Argos, gives demonstration rides to curious spectators, and the skies are almost constantly filled with action.

The powered parachute was originally developed at the University of Notre Dame (in South Bend, Indiana) in the late 1960s and early 1970s and has only been on the market since 1985. The popularity of the lightweight craft has soared since then, in part because it is one of the most inexpensive ways to fly and no previous flight experience is necessary. The pilot sits in an open-air machine that vaguely resembles a motorized go-kart attached to a huge, rectangular parachute. Most people can solo after approximately two hours of instruction.

Although people from all over the world flock in and fly in for Buckeye's annual Fourth of July Five-Day Fly-In, visitors are welcome at any time. The

The Trail of Death Regional Historic Trail

In 1838, the Potawatomi Indians of northern Indiana were rounded up by federal troops and led on foot to the land on which the government had decreed they should henceforth live. The tribe of Chief Alexis Menominee numbered more than 850 when it started its westward walk. During the 900-mile trek to Kansas, some 150 Potawatomis perished from disease, fatigue, and adverse weather conditions. That fateful journey is recorded in history as the Trail of Death.

From the north bank of Twin Lakes in Marshall County, where the long walk began, the trail leads south to Logansport before turning southwest to follow the banks of the Wabash River to the Indiana-Illinois border. Numerous markers and memorials have been established along the trail, but the most impressive of all is the granite statue of Chief Menominee that stands on the site his tribe once called home. Visitors will find it on South Peach Road a little southwest of the town of Plymouth.

Mas-saw, a Potawatomi Indian who survived the Trail of Death, was the great-grandmother of Jim Thorpe. Thorpe, an athlete who excelled at several sports, is generally recognized as the best male athlete of the first half of the twentieth century.

late John F. Kennedy Jr. came here in 1997 to trade in the single-passenger model he'd purchased in 1996 for a two-seater. His late wife, Carolyn, who accompanied him, said that her husband liked the solitude he experienced when piloting his parachute.

For additional information contact Buckeye Industries at 16095 Linden Road, Argos; (574) 892–5566.

Since the U.S. Army Cavalry was disbanded in 1950, the ***Black Horse Troop*** of Culver Military Academy (a college preparatory boarding school in the town of ***Culver***) has been the nation's largest remaining cavalry unit. The sixty-three young men who compose its ranks hone their skills in the academy's extensive horsemanship programs. Organized in 1897, the troop has taken part in thirteen presidential inaugurations, escorted kings and queens, and been featured in major horse shows throughout the country, but you can see it free, with all its pomp and pageantry, each Sunday afternoon from May through October. That's when the troopers don their military dress, mount their black steeds, and parade across the academy's well-kept grounds. While you're there, pick up a map at the administration office and tour the 1,500-acre campus, beautifully situated near the shoreline of Lake Maxinkuckee. Contact Culver Military Academy, CEF 129, Culver; (574) 842–3264.

For an informative one-hour tour, visit ***Pioneer Hybrid International*** in ***Plymouth.*** You'll learn firsthand how corn gets from the stalk back to seed again. Workers at the plant unload, dry, and shell the corn, then sort it according to the size of the kernel and package it for storing. The tour is free, but call in advance to schedule a time. Located at 7900 North Pine Road; (574) 936–3243.

Montgomery County

For sheer natural beauty it's hard to beat **Shades State Park** near **Waveland,** but to fully appreciate its magnificent scenery and outstanding geologic features you'll have to do some hiking. Only by taking to the trails can you see the primeval terrain for which the park is noted. Some first-time hikers do a double take when they see what awaits them—a landscape like this just isn't associated with Indiana.

About 470 acres of the 3,000-acre park have been set aside as the **Pine Hills State Nature Preserve.** Within its boundaries are four narrow rock ridges from 75 to 100 feet tall that are recognized as the finest example of incised meanders in the eastern United States. This observation was made by no less an authority than the National Park Service, which designated the preserve a National Natural Landmark.

Giant hemlock trees, not usually found this far south, rare Canada yews, and native white pine are relics of a long-ago past when this area was much cooler. The arrival of spring is first announced by the flowering of the rare snow trillium, and the coloring of the land continues through May, when the dogwoods and redbuds show off their blossoms. Through it all flows Sugar Creek, the most beautiful stream in the state.

When early European settlers first cast eyes on the lush forests and deep gorges along Sugar Creek, they referred to this place as "the Shades of Death." The long shadows cast by the heavy growth of trees initially appeared ominous to them, but as they became more familiar with the area the nickname was shortened to "the Shades." It remains appropriate to this day, since the land has remained virtually untouched by human hands.

trivia

In 1836 siltstone slabs covered with crinoid (sea lily) fossils were first discovered at the north edge of Crawfordsville. The location is now internationally famous, yielding some of the best crinoid fossils ever found. Crawfordsville crinoids can be seen in museums around the world.

Two other impressive features are Silver Cascade Falls, one of eleven waterfalls in the park, and Devil's Punchbowl, a large, circular grotto cut into the sandstone by two small streams.

Canoeists take to Sugar Creek in droves, and if you're into solitude you'll want to avoid a trip on summer weekends. Weekdays in May or June or any day in August or September when the water level is down promises quieter floats. The most scenic stretch, which lies between Shades State Park and Turkey Run State Park (located to the southwest in adjoining Parke County), can be seen in one day. Put in at Deer's Mill Covered Bridge, which spans Sugar Creek along State Road 234 on the eastern edge of Shades State Park. For an enjoyable two-day trip, put in at Elston Park in Crawfordsville. Both trips end at West Union Covered Bridge in Parke County. Always check water conditions at park headquarters before starting out, however; the creek can be dangerous at flood stage.

Although most of the park is undeveloped, visitors will find more than one hundred primitive campsites, special campgrounds for backpackers and canoeists, and several picnic areas, some with shelters. Bicycles can be rented in the park, and a naturalist is on duty in the summer.

Shades State Park is located along both banks of Sugar Creek in southwestern Montgomery County and spills over into Parke County. The entrance is on County Road 800S, just west of State Road 234; look for signs. It's open daily year-round; there's a nominal vehicle admission fee. Write or call the property manager at Shades State Park, 7751 South 890 West, Waveland 47989; (765) 435–2810.

Just north of Shades State Park, County Road 875W leads north off State Road 234 to the Hoosier State's own *Alamo,* which the town's fifty residents hope you'll remember. There, on the outside front of an old school gymnasium, a local artist has created a series of colorful murals that depict both Alamos—the one in Texas and the one in Indiana.

Another small town in the northwestern corner of the county achieved fame without even trying. When Hollywood came to Hoosierland looking for an idyllic rural area in which to film the principal exterior shots for the movie *Hoosiers,* it chose *New Richmond.* (For readers who missed it, *Hoosiers* is loosely based on the true story of a small-town high school basketball team that defied all odds to win the Indiana state championship.) Now tourists, enthralled with what they saw on the screen, travel here to see the real thing— the storefronts, the main street with its single traffic light, the farm fields bathed in sunset gold. The sign that identifies the community as New Richmond is now embellished with the words WELCOME TO HICKORY (the town's movie name), and the Hickory Festival, held in late September, features a basketball game and *Hoosiers* film clips.

For information about Alamo and New Richmond, contact the Montgomery County Visitors Bureau, 218 East Pike Street, Crawfordsville 47933; (765) 362–5200 or (800) 866–3973. For additional information about the making of *Hoosiers,* see Ripley County in the Southeast Indiana section.

The Old Montgomery County Jail at 225 North Washington Street in *Craw-fordsville* was the first of only seven rotary jails ever built worldwide and is the only one still operational. Completed in 1882, it remained in daily use until 1973. The cell blocks are arranged in a circle in such a way that the sheriff, with the turn of a crank, could rotate the cells around him and check on his prisoners without ever taking a step. Now known as the *Old Jail Museum,* it's open from 1:00 to 4:30 P.M. Wednesday through Saturday, April, May, September, and October; 10:00 A.M. to 4:30 P.M. Wednesday through Saturday, and 1:00 to 4:30 P.M. Tuesday and Sunday, June through August; also open 1:00 to 4:00 P.M. Sunday in March and November. Nominal admission charge; (765) 362–5222.

The campus of *Wabash College,* at the corner of West Wabash and Grant Avenues in Crawfordsville, is of interest because of the mid-1800s architecture of its buildings and its arboretum of native Indiana trees. Students apparently find the setting conducive to learning. Out of 1,500 colleges and universities in this country, Wabash ranks sixteenth in the percentage of graduates who go on to earn Ph.D.s. Perhaps it's the lack of distraction—Wabash is an all-male college. Call (765) 361–6100 or (800) 866–3973.

Also in Crawfordsville, on the corner of Wallace Avenue and East Pike Street, you'll find a four-acre park that contains the *General Lew Wallace Study and Museum.* One of Indiana's most fascinating native sons, Wallace was a soldier in the Mexican War, the Union Army's youngest major general during the Civil War, and a state senator. He served as prosecutor during the Lincoln assassination trial, signed Billy the Kid's death warrant, was U.S. Minister to Turkey, and made violins. Nevertheless, Wallace is probably best remembered as the author of the novel *Ben-Hur.* Published in 1880, it was one of the most popular novels of all time, becoming the first book ever to exceed the Bible in annual sales (more than one million copies were sold through the Sears catalog alone). A dramatic version was one of the longest-running plays in history. Hollywood twice made *Ben-Hur* into a movie, once as a silent picture in 1926 and again as a remake in 1959. The latter won eleven Academy Awards, including one for Best Picture. Wallace's eclectic study, designed by Wallace himself, is a mix of French, Byzantine, Romanesque, and Greek styles. The 20-foot-tall bronze statue of Wallace that stands nearby is a replica of one that was unveiled in Washington, D.C., in 1910. Each year in mid-October, a Circus Maximus is staged on these grounds, complete with a chariot race and Greek food. Open 10:00 A.M. to 5:00 P.M. Wednesday through Saturday and 1:00 to 5:00 P.M. Sunday, February to mid-December; nominal admission fee. Call (765) 364–5175 or (800) 866–3973, or visit www.ben-hur.com.

Fred Ropkey has been obsessed with military memorabilia ever since he was given his great-grandfather's Civil War pistol at the tender age of eight.

That obsession has resulted in the second-largest collection of armor in the country. (The largest is in California, and Ropkey helped get that one started.) His collection includes Stuart, Chaffee, Pershing, and Walker Bulldog tanks, as well as three Sherman tanks. Ropkey has driven some of them himself in such movies as *Tank, The Siege,* and *The Blues Brothers,* and he supplied the tank seen in the movie *Mars Attacks!* His tanks have also starred in documentaries seen on the Learning, History, and National Geographic television channels. Visitors to the **Ropkey Armor Museum** at 5649 East 150 North in Crawfordsville will also see exhibits of self-propelled artillery, military motorcycles, jeeps, trucks, and boats. Future plans include building an airfield so that his military aircraft can also be displayed here. Admission is free, but donations are appreciated. Open 10:30 A.M. to 4:30 P.M. Monday through Friday; call (765) 794–0238 or visit www.ropkeyarmormuseum.com.

At the **Magic Light Neon Sign Company** in Crawfordsville, owners Bill and Kathy Platipodis and eleven employees bend neon (as it's called in the vernacular of the craft) in a process that hasn't changed since the creation of the first neon lamp in 1902. The folks at Magic Light repair and replicate historic signs and make new ones. Weekday visitors who call ahead for an appointment are welcome to watch the neon benders at work. The company occupies a circa 1915 warehouse at 100 East North Street; (765) 361–1856.

Newton County

What is often described as a unique natural feature in Indiana is a peculiar layering of rock near **Kentland.** Elsewhere in the state, layers of rock are almost horizontal, but here many of the layers are vertical. The deformed rocks bear mute testimony to a force of nature so incredible that it folded and fractured layers of rock that lay in a horizontal position 1,800 feet below the surface of the earth and thrust them above the surface in a nearly vertical position.

Currently, two theories exist. One is that a huge meteorite hit here several million years ago and created the huge crater seen today. A second theory is that a sudden, violent explosion of trapped underground gases caused the faulting.

While geologists have been speculating about the cause of the disruption since the 1880s, when the strange formation was first discovered, no geologic evidence yet exists to explain the origin of what is now called the **Kentland Dome.** To this day, it remains a geologic enigma.

Although the formation is on private property, visitors may view it by advance appointment. For further information write or call the Newton County Quarry, Rogers Group, Inc., US 24 East, P.O. Box 147, Kentland 47951; (219) 474–5125.

The Governor's Bull

In a lonely field in Newton County, a fading stone monument marks the final resting place of Perfection Fairfax. The occupant of the grave is the grand champion of the 1907 International Livestock Exposition, a prize bull that brought fame and fortune to his owner.

Warren T. McCray brought his prize-winning perfect bull to his stock farm near Kentland, where the bull became the progenitor of many perfect little bulls and made a tidy sum of money for his owner. When Perfection Fairfax died in 1920, his owner buried him with much pomp and honor.

To see the stone that memorializes McCray's bull, go east from the intersection of County Roads 50E and 1300S for about ⅓ mile, then turn north for about ¼ mile. On a clear, sunny day, the stone can be seen from several miles away.

The fortune to which Perfection Fairfax had contributed so much helped propel McCray into Indiana's statehouse, where he served as governor from 1921 to 1924. During his tenure in office, McCray sponsored the amendment to the state constitution that gave women the right to vote, created the state gasoline tax to fund much-needed highway construction, and improved teachers' pensions. Unfortunately, he also earned the dubious distinction of being the only Indiana governor (to date) to go directly from the statehouse to the Big House. Tried and convicted of mail fraud and forgery, McCray was sent to the federal prison in Atlanta, where he resided until 1930, when President Herbert Hoover pardoned him. Some believe the governor was set up because he appointed the attorney who in 1925 successfully prosecuted D. C. Stephenson, grand dragon of the state's then-politically powerful Ku Klux Klan.

Porter County

Indiana does not have a Grand Canyon or a Yosemite, but it does have some of the largest sand dunes this side of the Sahara. Since 1972, most of them have been part of the 13,000-acre *Indiana Dunes National Lakeshore,* a miracle of survival in the midst of one of the most heavily industrialized regions in the country. Its lovely sand beaches along the southern shoreline of Lake Michigan are legendary for miles around, but they are only part of what can be seen and done here.

Mt. Baldy inches away from the lake each year; its name hints at why. Because it has not been stabilized by vegetation, the 135-foot-tall dune is kept in constant motion by wind and water, forcing the dune to take giant steps backward. Climb to the top for a sweeping view of Lake Michigan.

Not all of the landscape is sand and water. There are also grassy hills, patches of prairie, lush wetlands, and cool forests with a canopy so dense that sunlight barely filters through. Miller Woods, Cowles Bog, and Pinhook Bog would be exceptional natural areas anywhere, but their existence in the midst of such pollution, industry, and urban population is incredible.

The Bailly Homestead, dating from 1822, and the Chellberg Farm, built in the late 1880s, contain historical structures that the public can visit. There are hiking, bicycling, and horseback-riding trails to follow; in the winter they're used by cross-country skiers. At least 223 species of birds have been identified here, and many rare plants live among the dunes. Special programs and events are held all year long.

Although the national lakeshore actually lies in parts of three counties—Lake, Porter, and LaPorte—its visitor center is in Porter County, and this is where you should begin your visit. The center is located on Kemil Road, which runs south from US 12 about 3 miles east of the intersection of US 12 and State Road 49 near **Porter,** and is open daily year-round, 8:00 A.M. to 6:00 P.M. Memorial Day through Labor Day and 8:00 A.M. to 5:00 P.M. the rest of the year; closed major winter holidays. The park is open daily year-round; hours vary from area to area and are subject to change. A nominal parking fee is charged at West Beach from Memorial Day through Labor Day; everything else is free. For additional information write or call Indiana Dunes National Lakeshore, 1100 North Mineral Springs Road, Porter 46304; (219) 926–7561.

Completely surrounded by the national lakeshore are 2,182 acres that make up **Indiana Dunes State Park.** It offers a microcosm of the features found in its big brother and boasts the highest sand dune along the lakeshore—192-foot-tall Mt. Tom.

When conditions are just right, the drifting sand emits a low, humming sound, soothing to the ear and soul, that is akin to the sound produced by drawing a bow across the strings of a bass viola. The unique phenomenon is known locally as the music of the "singing sands."

Bird-watchers will find the park unique because both northeastern and southern bird species are found here. One, the Kirtland's warbler, is the rarest songbird in the nation and one of the rarest on earth; fewer than 2,000 exist worldwide.

The 1,500-acre **Dunes State Nature Preserve,** which lies within park boundaries, contains more species of trees than any other area of comparable size in the Midwest; from one spot alone you can identify thirty different varieties. In the summer the myriads of rare flowers and ferns found here create a near-tropical appearance. Recreational facilities include a modern campground, a nature center, a swimming beach, and trails for hiking, bicycling, and cross-country skiing. To reach the park, proceed north from Interstate 94 on State Road 49 for about 2 miles. The park is open year-round; a nominal vehicle

Diana of the Dunes

The story of Diana of the Dunes is one of the most enduring in Indiana lore. Born Alice Mable Gray, she was given the name by which she is remembered in legend when she rejected civilization in 1915 to move into an abandoned fisherman's shack nestled in the wilderness of Porter County's dune country.

Diana, a Phi Beta Kappa from Chicago, was believed to have been inspired by the poetry of Byron, who wrote in his poem "Solitude" that "In solitude . . . we are least alone." It is reported that, when weather permitted, she was often seen wandering over and among the dunes sans clothing.

Diana later married and shared her solitude with Paul Wilson, another lover of solitude who sought out Diana after reading about her unique lifestyle. The public, however, would not permit them their privacy, and when a man's charred body was found near their shack, many people believed the two were guilty of murder.

In 1925, Diana died and was buried in an unmarked grave in a nearby cemetery. Her grieving husband packed up and moved away. It is reported even today that her ghost can sometimes be seen at twilight flitting among the dunes she loved.

admission fee is charged from spring through fall. Write or call Indiana Dunes State Park, 1600 North 25 East, Chesterton 46304; (219) 926–1952.

When the Chicago World's Fair of 1933 closed, five homes from the *"Houses of the Future" exhibit* were placed on a barge and transported across Lake Michigan to the then-new community of *Beverly Shores.* Plans to make Beverly Shores the ultimate vacation resort were thwarted by the lingering effects of the Great Depression, but the houses are still there, lined up along Lake Front Drive and still of interest. Especially startling is the House of Tomorrow, a twelve-sided structure built like a wedding cake (the top two floors are each smaller in circumference than the floor below). You'll also see a reproduction of Boston's Old North Church; it, too, was carted over from the fair. For more information write or call the Porter County Convention and Visitors Bureau, 1420 Munson Road, Porter 46304; (219) 926–2255 or (800) 283–8687.

The magical kingdom of Oz is also a part of Dune Country. L. Frank Baum, author of the Oz books, used to summer here, and later his son established the International Wizard of Oz Club in this area. Today you can view a collection of Oz memorabilia in the *Wizard of Oz Fantasy Museum,* housed in the Yellow Brick Road shop in *Chesterton.* There's a nominal fee for the museum. The store is open 10:00 A.M. to 5:00 P.M. Monday through Saturday and 11:00 A.M. to 4:00 P.M. Sunday June through September; closed Monday October through May. It's easy to find: Just follow the yellow brick road (honestly!) to

109 East County Road 950 North, near that road's intersection with State Road 49; (219) 926–7048. Each September a **Wizard of Oz Festival,** complete with several real-life Munchkins from the movie's original cast, evokes memories of the Judy Garland screen classic. Contact the Yellow Brick Road or the Porter County Convention and Visitors Bureau (see previous entry).

The showpiece of **Valparaiso** in central Porter County is the striking **Chapel of the Resurrection** on the campus of Valparaiso University. This magnificent contemporary structure, which is the largest collegiate chapel in the nation, has received accolades from around the world. The entire building focuses on the chancel, whose limestone piers rise skyward for 98 feet and culminate in a roof shaped like a nine-point star. Try to visit here on a sunny day; from inside the chancel, the view of the awe-inspiring stained-glass windows will take your breath away. The largest Lutheran university in the country, Valparaiso counts the late Lowell Thomas among its alumni. Visitors are welcome at any time; the campus lies at the east end of Union Street. Call (219) 464–5093 or (888) 468–2576.

The **Hoosier Bat Company** produces more than 50,000 custom-made baseball bats each year for such teams as the Seattle Mariners, Chicago White Sox, Baltimore Orioles, Cleveland Indians, and Milwaukee Brewers. Sammy

Corn Off the Cob

The word *popcorn* and the name "Orville Redenbacher" have become virtually synonymous in the minds of snack lovers all over the world. An Indiana native and a graduate of Purdue University in West Lafayette, Orville began his rise to fame when he and a friend purchased a small agricultural company in Valparaiso. The unassuming entrepreneur dreamed of giving the world a fluffier, higher-quality popcorn, and the world is grateful for his efforts.

Originally marketed as Red Bow popcorn (a blending of Redenbacher and the name of his partner, Charles Bowman), it is now known as Orville Redenbacher's Gourmet Popping Corn. The two changed the name on the advice of a marketing firm, and sales soared. Perhaps in deference to his roots, one of Orville's trademarks was his red bow tie.

In later years, Orville's company was sold to Hunt-Wesson, Inc., and moved to California. However, until his death in 1995 at the age of eighty-eight, Orville never forgot his Indiana roots, returning to the state almost every year for the annual Valparaiso Popcorn Festival in September.

Today, Orville Redenbacher's Gourmet Popping Corn remains the top-selling microwave popcorn and is the only popcorn sold at Disney World in Florida and Disneyland in California.

Sosa of the Chicago Cubs used one to break his batting slump in 1998, then went on to become that year's National League Most Valuable Player and the first player in history to hit more than sixty home runs in consecutive seasons (1998 and 1999). The bat he used to hit his sixty-sixth home run in 1998 is now in the Baseball Hall of Fame. Owner Dave Cook says his company's ash bats are harder than typical bats. He also says that no cork is used in any of his bats. Visitors who tour the factory can see how the bats are made and, if they choose, buy a personalized bat. The tours are free, but an advance appointment is necessary. Hoosier Bat is located at 4511 East Evans Avenue in Valparaiso; call (219) 531–1006 or (800) 228–3787, or visit www.hoosierbat.com.

At the ***Strongbow Inn*** it's Thanksgiving all year long. You can have almost any part of the gobbler cooked nearly any way imaginable here. Turkey appears in salads, soups, sandwiches, crepes, pies, and pâtés, not to mention sliced up on a plate and accompanied by all the traditional fixings. Everything is made on the premises—breads, rolls, cranberry-orange relish, cakes, pies, and a delicious cup custard. If you're in the mood for something continental, try the veal Oscar, coquilles St. Jacques, or shrimp Pescatore. You'll find the inn at 2405 US 30 East, Valparaiso. Open 11:00 A.M. to 9:00 P.M. Monday through Thursday, 11:00 A.M. to 9:30 P.M. Friday and Saturday, and 10:30 A.M. to 8:00 P.M. Sunday; closed Christmas week. Reservations advised; (219) 462–5121 or (800) 462–5121. Stop at the Strongbow Bakery on the premises for some delectable take-home treats; (219) 464–8643.

St. Joseph County

If you ever wonder where all that spearmint in your Wrigley's chewing gum comes from, here's your chance to find out. Call the ***Martin Blad Mint Farm*** near ***South Bend*** and make an appointment to visit the place in July. That's when the bright yellow mint wagons haul a newly harvested crop into the mint-press building. You can watch as the oil is separated, picked up, guided through coils, and pumped into fifty-five-gallon containers. Then it's packed up and sent off to Wrigley's. The 2,500-acre farm is located at 58995 Mayflower Road (Highway 123), ½ mile north of its junction with State Road 23, just southwest of South Bend; (574) 234–7271.

From nearly every vantage point in South Bend, you can see the renowned golden dome that tops the administration building of the ***University of Notre Dame.*** A walking tour of the 1,250-acre campus will take you to such places as the Grotto of Our Lady of Lourdes, an exact reproduction of the original in France; the Sacred Heart Church, an awe-inspiring Gothic structure that contains one of North America's oldest carillons; the Snite Museum of Art, which houses rare religious artworks and masterpieces by such noted artists as Chagall, Picasso, and Rodin; and the Notre Dame Memorial Library, a huge, fourteen-story building noted for its rare-books room and the 132-foot-high granite mural that adorns its outer wall. To reach the university, go north from South Bend on U.S. Highway 31/33 to Angela Boulevard and turn east; call (574) 631–5000 for general information, (574) 631–5726 for tour information.

While on campus, be sure to visit the university's Main Building. Its restrooms were recognized in 2002 as the best in the country in an online pool that was conducted for nearly a year. Voters loved the imported tile floors, the solid oak doors on stalls, and the brass-accented faucets. Just as important, the restrooms are impeccably clean.

trivia

The original boundary line between Indiana and Michigan in St. Joseph County was established on June 30, 1805. When Indiana became a state in 1816, that line was moved 10 miles north. Hoosiers refused to agree to statehood that did not include waterfront property on Lake Michigan.

Of all the citizens of South Bend, past or present, Knute Rockne is perhaps the best known. The famous coach, who maintained that football was a game of brains rather than brawn, shaped the Fighting Irish into a legend. When he died in a plane crash in 1931, he was just forty-two years old. His funeral service, attended by an estimated 100,000 people and carried by radio across the nation and to Norway (the land of his birth), was one of the most emotional in American history. You can visit his grave in *Highland Cemetery* at 2557 Portage Avenue, not far from his beloved university.

The 1940 movie *Knute Rockne, All American* depicted a deathbed scene with Rockne and a dying George Gipp, one of Rockne's players who passed away in 1920. Gipp (portrayed by then-actor and later President Ronald Reagan) uttered the enduring words, "Tell them to win just one for the Gipper." Rockne later used those words to inspire his team, and the late President Reagan repeated them often during his political

trivia

In South Bend it is illegal for monkeys to smoke cigarettes.

career. Gipp's ghost is said to reside to this day in Notre Dame's Washington Hall.

Another name that's famous around South Bend is Studebaker. Clement Studebaker began his career as a wagon maker, supplying the Union Army during the Civil War and later the thousands who trekked west. As he progressed from wagons to carriages to automobiles, he kept a collection of company vehicles. They are housed today in the **Studebaker National Museum** at 201 South Chapin Street. Among the exhibits are a Conestoga wagon, the last Studebaker produced, the Studebaker carriage in which Abraham Lincoln rode to Ford's Theatre the night he was assassinated, a 1934 Bendix car, and a 1956 Packard Predictor Car of the Future. The museum is open from 10:00 A.M. to 5:00 P.M. Monday through Saturday and noon to 5:00 P.M. Sunday; closed for major holidays. Admission fee; call (574) 235–9714 or (888) 391–5600, or visit www.studebakermuseum.org.

trivia

Bendix Woods County Park in New Carlisle contains the world's largest living sign. Back in the 1920s, when the land was owned by the Studebaker Corporation, 8,200 pine trees were planted over an area 250 feet wide and a half mile long. The trees spell out "Studebaker," but the sign can only be read from the air.

By 1888 Studebaker had become a wealthy man, and he built himself a forty-room mansion worthy of his station, complete with twenty fireplaces and 24,000 square feet of space. Its massive stone walls, turrets, and irregular roofs gave it the appearance of a feudal castle. Today the historic mansion is called **Tippecanoe Place** and houses a fine gourmet restaurant that serves continental cuisine. Lunch is available from 11:30 A.M. to 2:00 P.M. Monday through Friday; dinner from 5:00 to 9:30 P.M. Monday through Friday, 4:30 to 10:00 P.M. Saturday, and 4:00 to 8:30 P.M. Sunday. A Sunday brunch is served buffet style from 10:00 A.M. to 2:00 P.M. Located at 620 West Washington Street; (574) 234–9077. Tours are available outside of dining hours. Reservations are strongly advised for both meals and tours.

The only artificial white-water course in North America and one of only three in the world is located in the heart of downtown South Bend. Called the **East Race Waterway,** it's a 2,000-foot-long channel that bypasses the South Bend Dam across the St. Joseph River. The elite of white-water paddlers from around the globe come here each summer to take part in national and international competitions. Because the flow of water can be controlled, the waterway can generate the churning rapids and 6-foot-tall waves needed for athletic events or can present a surface calm enough for whole families to paddle on. It's open to the public for

trivia

In 1863 one of the shortest business contracts ever written was signed by the Studebaker brothers for their wagon-making firm at South Bend. It contained two sentences: "I, Henry Studebaker, agree to sell all the wagons my brother Clem can make," and "I, Clem Studebaker, agree to make all the wagons my brother Henry can sell."

The Taking of Oliver

On the evening of December 24, 1889, friends and relatives gathered at the Matthew Larch farmstead near South Bend to celebrate the Christmas holiday. It was pitch black when eleven-year-old Oliver Larch was sent outside to fetch water from the well.

A few minutes later, Oliver's screams of pure terror reached the ears of those in the house. When they rushed outside to investigate, they clearly heard Oliver's voice from somewhere high above their heads proclaiming "Help! They've got me!" Horrified and helpless, people could only listen as Oliver's cries trailed off into the darkness.

The boy's footprints on the snow-covered ground simply ended. The oak bucket he had carried with him lay on the ground beside his trail. When questioned later by investigators, everyone present, including a local minister and a judge, told identical stories.

Oliver Larch was never seen again.

rafting, kayaking, and other water sports, under the watchful eyes of a well-trained rescue team, for approximately thirty hours per week throughout the summer; hours vary. The many adjacent walkways and bridges provide land-lubbers with a close-up view of waterway happenings. Located east of the St. Joseph River, along the west side of Niles Avenue, and between Jefferson Boulevard on the south and Madison Street on the north. For additional information about competitive events, hours open to the public, and watercraft rental, write to the East Race Waterway Corp., 126 North Niles Avenue, South Bend 46617; call (219) 233–6121 or contact the South Bend Parks Department, 321 East Walter Street, South Bend 46614; (574) 299–4765.

During March and August through November the East Race Waterway also functions as a fish ladder, one of four such ladders on the St. Joseph River. Steelhead trout and coho and Chinook salmon are able to detour around four dams and travel freely along the 63-mile stretch of river between Mishawaka and Lake Michigan. Some 600,000 of those fish are reared annually at the ***Richard Clay Bodine***

trivia

J. Paul Barnett of South Bend has a most unusual sideline—he plays the cannon. The original 1880 score of Tchaikovsky's *1812 Overture* calls for sixteen cannon blasts. When symphony orchestras across the country want to perform a historically accurate *1812*, they call Barnett. Barnett also owns South Bend Replicas, the company that makes the cannons he plays.

State Fish Hatchery in *Mishawaka.* Visitors can take a free, self-guided tour of the facilities daily between 8:00 A.M. and 3:30 P.M. Monday through Friday. Located at 13200 East Jefferson Boulevard; (574) 255–4199.

To sample one of Indiana's most delicious diversions, stop by the factory where the *South Bend Chocolate Company* makes its delectable treats (5,000 pounds daily and twice that around the holidays) and take a free twenty-minute tour. It's a good thing free samples are provided at the end of the tour, because you'll be salivating by then. A chocolate museum displays the world's largest collection of chocolate-related aritfacts, including a 1,300-year-old Mayan chocolate pot. Located at 3300 West Sample Street in South Bend; tours are offered hourly 9:00 A.M. to 4:00 P.M. Monday through Friday and 9:00 A.M. to 3:00 P.M. Saturday; large groups are asked to call ahead. Call (574) 233–2577 or (800) 301–4961, or visit www.sbchocolate.com for additional information and to make reservations.

Landscape architect Shoji Kanaoka went to Florida and designed the grounds at Epcot Center. He also came to Indiana and designed *Shiojiri Niwa,* a lovely 1.3-acre Japanese strolling garden located in the Merrifield Park Complex at 1000 East Mishawaka Avenue in Mishawaka. Among the garden's many pleasures are Oriental plantings, bridges, a tea garden, and dry waterfalls and streams. Visitors can sample its serenity at any hour of any day. Admission is free. Call the Mishawaka Parks and Recreation Department at (574) 258–1664.

On the campus of Bethel College in Mishawaka, you can visit the *Bowen Museum.* Dr. Otis Bowen, a physician from Bremen, Indiana, entered politics in 1952. After serving six years as Marshall County Coroner, he was elected to the Indiana House of Representatives, a post he held for fourteen years. Bowen was elected as Indiana's forty-second governor in 1972 and was reelected to a second term by a then-record high margin, the first Indiana governor to serve eight consecutive years. In 1985, at the request of the late President Ronald Reagan, Bowen became the first physician ever to fill the position of the U.S. Secretary of Health and Human Services. The museum honors the life of one of Indiana's most revered statesmen through displays of personal items, mementos, and official documents. Located in the Bowen Library at 1001 West McKinley Avenue on the campus of Bethel College; open from 2:00 to 4:00 P.M. on Wednesday and Saturday or by appointment. Admission is free, but donations are welcome. Call (574) 257–3347 for additional information.

Tippecanoe County

The tiny town of **Cairo** is home to the **Operation Skywatch Memorial,** a limestone statue honoring civilian volunteers in the Korean War. Because there was no national radar system during that conflict, the U.S. Air Force commissioned a nationwide system of observation towers that were manned around the clock by the Civilian Ground Observation Corps. Approximately ninety volunteers from the Cairo area worked in shifts, scanning the skies for enemy planes. The life-size figures of a man, woman, and child, faces turned upward, stand atop the base of the monument, which is inscribed with the words THEY ALSO SERVE WHO STAND AND WATCH. Located in Memorial Park at the junction of County Roads 850 North and 100 West; open during daylight hours.

On November 7, 1811, William Henry Harrison, then governor of the Indiana Territory, led his men in battle against the last all-Indian army to be assembled east of the Mississippi River. The Indians, representing a confederacy of tribes organized by Tecumseh and his brother, the Prophet, went down in defeat, ending any organized Indian resistance to the Europeans' settlement of the Northwest Territory. In later years Harrison's victory was a decisive factor in his successful bid for the presidency of the United States.

You can see an impressive 85-foot-tall monument and stroll the ninety-six-acre grounds where the battle was actually fought at the **Tippecanoe Battlefield State Memorial** near the town of **Battle Ground.** A scenic trail leads past several trees that stood during the battle; musket balls are still found in the older trees when they fall. The park is also a peaceful and lovely spot for a picnic—except on those summer weekends when two noisy annual events take place. Players of dulcimers, guitars, mandolins, and more hold all-day, all-night jam sessions during the **Indiana Fiddler's Gathering;** less lyrical sounds fill the air when various types of old machinery rev up their motors at the **Antique Farm Power Show.** The park is open daily, free of charge, year-round during daylight hours. A museum on the grounds presents the history of the battle from both sides' points of view. Open 10:00 A.M. to 5:00 P.M. daily, March through November; call for winter hours. There's a nominal admission fee. Located on Prophet's Rock Road just west of Battle Ground; follow signs; (765) 567–2147 or (800) 872–6569.

Nearby **Prophetstown State Park** can be viewed from the Tippecanoe Battlefield site. The 3,000-acre park is home to the **Woodland Native American Cultural Center,** the result of more than twenty Great Lakes tribes working together to create a world center for Native American education. Among the attractions are a re-created American Indian village, a living-history farm that features a replica of a 1918 Sears and Roebuck catalog house, and some 200 acres of prairie restoration containing plants native to Indiana. For additional information write or call Prophetstown State Park, 4112 East State Road 225, West Lafayette 47906; (765) 567–4919. Information is also available from the Museums at Prophetstown, Inc., 3534 Prophetstown Trail, Battle Ground 47920; (765) 567–4700.

trivia

In August 1859 the city of Lafayette became the site of the first official airmail flight by the United States Postal Service. Professor John Wise took off in his balloon, the *Jupiter,* with a mail pouch that included 123 letters and 23 circulars. Because of a capricious wind, he landed at the wrong destination, but the flight was officially recognized.

On certain nights, full moon or not, you can join a howling at Battle Ground's **Wolf Park.** The eerie but beautiful voices of the resident wolf pack drift through the air and send chills up and down your spine. If you like these misunderstood creatures, it is an experience you will never forget.

This unique wildlife park is a research facility, and you can visit during the day to watch scientists at work. Docents are on hand to tell you each wolf's name and rank order in the pack, and you can see the wolves interact with human beings whom they've come to accept as members of their "society." At 1:00 P.M. each Sunday from May through November, predators (wolves) and prey (bison) are placed together to demonstrate that a healthy animal has nothing to fear from wolves.

trivia

Movie director Sydney Pollack, born in Lafayette in 1934, won a Best Director Oscar for *Out of Africa.* Other movies he's directed include *Tootsie* and *The Way We Were.*

The park is operated by the non-profit North American Wildlife Park Foundation, which charges a nominal admission fee to the park to help offset expenses. Advance reservations are required for the wolf howls. The park is open 1:00 to 5:00 P.M. Tuesday through Sunday from the first weekend in May through November; howls are held at 7:30 P.M. on Saturday year-round and also at 7:30 P.M. on Friday from April through November (weather permitting). To reach the park, go north from Battle Ground on Harrison Road for about 1 mile; WOLF PARK signs point the way to the park at 4012 East 800 North. Write Wolf Park, c/o North American Wildlife Park Foundation, 4012 East 800 North, Battle Ground 47920; call (765) 567–2265; or visit www.wolfpark.org.

The Greatest Pacer of Them All

Long before Hoosier basketball fans fell in love with the Indiana Pacers, Hoosiers and the rest of the world fell in love with another pacer. To this day, Dan Patch remains a legend in harness racing.

Born near Oxford in Benton County on April 29, 1896, the mahogany-colored colt was at first a great disappointment to his owner. Dan's sire had been an outstanding pacer, and Dan's owner had hoped the son would inherit his father's greatness. When Dan was born bow-legged and awkward, that hope dimmed, but the ugly duckling grew into a swan.

Dan began racing in 1900 at age four and won every race he entered. By July 1902 there was no one left who wanted to match his horse against Dan, so Dan began racing only against the clock in exhibitions. At the 1906 Minnesota State Fair, Dan paced a mile in one minute, fifty-five seconds, a world record. Although unofficial, the record was generally accepted and remained unbroken for thirty-two years.

During his lifetime the charismatic Dan Patch became one of the most successfully merchandised sports figures in history. His name and likeness were used to endorse thirty products, including china, stopwatches, livestock feed, tobacco, washing machines, toys, and manure spreaders. There was a Dan Patch automobile that sold for $525. People danced the Dan Patch Two-Step to the song of the same name. Hollywood immortalized him in a 1949 movie called *The Great Dan Patch*. A Dan Patch thermometer, originally a promotional giveaway, was on sale at an Indiana antiques store in 1998 for $3,000.

Dan is still remembered in his hometown, too. Beginning in 1901, Oxford has honored its famous son with an annual event known as Dan Patch Days. The humble white barn near Oxford in which Dan Patch was born proudly bears the words "DAN PATCH 1:55" in large letters on a green-shingled roof.

Dan had more than one owner in his lifetime. His final owner, M. W. Savage of Minneapolis, cherished and provided well for his champion horse. Dan traveled around the country in a private railroad car adorned on each side with his portrait. The huge Minnesota barn in which Dan was stabled was so elaborate it was nicknamed the "Taj Mahal." It was in this barn that Dan died on July 7, 1916, at the age of twenty. His owner died thirty-two hours later.

On September 14, 1999, *USA Today* featured its choices for the eight great animal athletes of the century. Among them was Dan Patch, described by the newspaper as probably the greatest pacer of all time.

trivia

Amelia Earhart joined the staff at Purdue University in West Lafayette in 1935 as a visiting lecturer and counselor for women. In March 1937 she took off from the campus airport in a Lockheed Electra purchased for her by the university. She and her Electra were beginning the now famous around-the-world trip on which she vanished. To this day, her disappearance remains one of the world's great unsolved mysteries.

In *Lafayette* the twenty-acre *Clegg Botanical Gardens* perch on the high bank of Wildcat Creek. Wander along a mile of marked trails that lead past ancient white oaks, sugar maples, and dogwoods. Daffodils bloom in the spring; hybrid daylilies unfold their petals in June and July, followed by resurrection lilies in August and Japanese anemones in September. From Lookout Point you can see the Indiana countryside for miles around. Open 10:00 A.M. to sunset daily; free. Located at 1782 North County Road 400 East; call (765) 423–1325 or (800) 872–6648.

The *Red Crown Mini-Museum* in downtown Lafayette can be viewed only from the outside in. Housed in a restored 1928 Standard Oil gas station, one of only seven remaining Standard Oil Products buildings in the nation, the museum exhibits gas station memorabilia and antique cars. Admission is free. Located at 605 South Street, Lafayette; (765) 742–0280.

On a free tour of *Subaru of Indiana*, visitors walk along catwalks above the production lines and observe workers, robots, and some gigantic machines assemble complete automobiles. According to the company, this plant was designed with tours in mind. Tours are offered from 9:00 A.M. to 1:00 P.M. Monday through Friday; reservations must be made at least two weeks ahead by calling (765) 449–6262 or by completing a form online at www.subaru-sia.com. The plant is located at 5500 State Road 38 East in Lafayette; for additional information call (765) 449–1111.

White County

The small town of *Brookston* is home to the oldest and largest professional handmade-paper studio in the country that uses cotton and linen rag in its products. Located at 100 East Third Street (State Road 18), *Twinrocker Handmade Paper* produces a wide variety of quality papers that range from non-silver photography paper to archival paper to stationery and everything in between. Owners Kathryn and Howard Clark will design and produce any paper to any specifications a customer wants. Their clients include historical societies, museums, and libraries all over the country; among them are the Library of Congress, the Boston Museum, and the Lilly Library at Indiana University. Visitors can view the fascinating process on a thirty-minute tour offered at 1:30 P.M. on Tuesday and Thursday. No advance reservations are required. A nominal fee is charged, but after the tour, visitors can purchase paper products for a 25 percent discount. The mill is open from 8:00 A.M. to 5:00 P.M. Monday through Friday.

Twinrocker also sells papermaking supplies and offers workshops. For additional information write Twinrocker Handmade Paper, P.O. Box 413, Brookston 47923; call (765) 563–3119 or (800) 757–8946; or visit www.twin rocker.com.

Before leaving Brookston, stop in at the nearby **Klein Brot Haus,** a German bakery and cafe whose homemade breads are as unique as the papers made by its neighbor. A soup and bread bar includes five breads, five toppings for the breads (including homemade peanut butter), and two soups. Located at 106 East Third Street; (765) 563–3788.

One of the best small museums in the state is not far north of Brookston. Near the small town of **Monon,** you can see what may be the largest private collection of railroad artifacts and memorabilia on display in the country. The **Monon Connection Museum** is the outgrowth of a hobby that became a passion for owners Dale and Anne Ward. Over the years, their collection grew until it filled their house and six storage units to capacity, so they decided to build a museum and share it with the world.

Grateful railroad buffs will see such exhibits as elegant dining-car china and silverware, handheld lanterns from the Civil War, and some immaculately restored brass bells and whistles from steam locomotives. Although the museum is named after the Monon Railroad (also known as the Hoosier Line), other railroads are represented here, too. A completely furnished, full-size replica of an Illinois Central depot from the 1850s was transported here from Pennsylvania. Among the outside exhibits are a huge crane that formerly belonged to the Belt Railway of Chicago, a Wabash caboose, a Monon depot, an underground coal mine locomotive, and signs and signals galore. The **Whistle Stop Restaurant,** adjacent to the museum, offers a variety of sandwiches, dinner entrees, homemade pies, and ice cream in a railroad-themed dining room or on an outside patio.

The museum and restaurant are located at 10012 US 421 about 1 mile north of Monon. Museum hours are 11:00 A.M. to 7:00 P.M. Tuesday through Thursday, 11:00 A.M. to 8:00 P.M. Friday and Saturday, and noon to 6:00 P.M. Sunday; call (219) 253–4101. The restaurant is open from 7:00 a.m. to 8:00 P.M. Tuesday through Thursday, 7:00 A.M. to 9:00 P.M. Friday and Saturday, and 11:00 A.M. to 7:00 P.M. Sunday; call (219) 253–4100. If you eat at the restaurant, you'll receive a discount on your admission fee to the museum.

Now that the Wards have a museum, they can collect even more things. You can keep tabs on the renovation projects and other ongoing activities from afar by visiting the museum online at www.mononconnection.com.

Places to Stay in Northwest Indiana

ATTICA
Apple Inn B&B
604 South Brady Street
(765) 762–6574
Moderate

BEVERLY SHORES
Dunes Shore Inn
33 Lakeshore County Road
(219) 879–9029
Expensive

CHESTERTON
Gray Goose Inn
350 Indian Boundary Road
(219) 926–5781 or
(800) 521–5127
Moderate

LADOGA
Vintage Reflections
125 West Main Street
(765) 942–1002
Inexpensive

LAFAYETTE
Historic Loeb House Inn
708 Cincinnati Street
(765) 420–7737
Moderate

LAPORTE
Arbor Hill Inn
263 West Johnson Road
(219) 362–9200
Expensive

MICHIGAN CITY
Creekwood Inn
5727 County Road 600W
(219) 872–8357 or
(800) 400–1981
Expensive

Duneland Beach Inn
3311 Pottawattamie Trail
(219) 874–7729 or
(800) 423–7729
Expensive

Feallock Bed and Breakfast
402 East Eighth Street
(219) 878–9543
Moderate

The Hutchinson Mansion Inn
220 West Tenth Street
(219) 879–1700
Moderate

MONTICELLO
Black Dog Inn
2390 Untalulti Street
(574) 583–8297
Moderate

Quiet Water Bed and Breakfast
4794 East Harbor Court
(574) 583–6023
Moderate

The Victoria Bed and Breakfast
206 South Bluff Street
(574) 583–3440
Moderate

PORTER
Spring House Inn
303 North Mineral Springs Road
(219) 929–4600 or
(866) 386–3700
Moderate

SOUTH BEND
Cushing Manor Bed and Breakfast
508 West Washington Street
(574) 288–1990
Moderate

The Inn at Saint Mary's
53993 U.S. Highway 31/33 North
(574) 232–4000 or
(800) 947–8627
Moderate

The Oliver Inn Bed and Breakfast
630 West Washington Street
(574) 232–4545 or
(888) 697–4466
Moderate

Queen Anne Inn
420 West Washington Street
(574) 234–5959 or
(800) 582–2389
Moderate

VALPARAISO
Inn at Aberdeen
3158 South State Road 2
(219) 465–3753
Moderate

WEST LAFAYETTE

Commandant's Home B&B
3848 North River Road
(765) 463–5980 or
(877) 319–2783
Moderate

WINAMAC

Tortuga Inn
2142 North 125 East
(574) 946–6969
Inexpensive

Places to Eat in Northwest Indiana

BATTLE GROUND

TC's Restaurant
109 North Railroad Street
(765) 567–2838
Moderate
American

COVINGTON

Beef House
16501 North State Road 63
(765) 793–3947
Moderate
Steak/American

Maple Corner Restaurant
1126 Liberty Street
(765) 793–2224
Moderate
Home cooking

CROWN POINT

Bronko's
1244 North Main Street
(219) 662–0145
Inexpensive
American

Twelve Islands
114 South Main Street
Floor 2
(219) 663–5070
Inexpensive
Greek/American

CULVER

Cafe Max
113 South Main Street
(574) 842–2511
Inexpensive
American

Corndance Cafe
117 West Madison Street
(574) 842–3220
Inexpensive
Home cooking

HAMMOND

El Taco Real
935 Hoffman Street
(219) 932–8333
Inexpensive
Mexican

HEBRON

Marti's Place at Ramsey's Landing
17519 North 700 West
(219) 996–3363
Moderate
American

HOBART

Country Lounge
3700 Montgomery Street
(219) 942–6699
Moderate
American

KOUTS

Koffee Cup
105 South Main Street
(219) 766–2414
Inexpensive
American

LAFAYETTE

Arni's
2200 Elmwood Avenue
(765) 447–1108
Inexpensive
American

Bistro 501
501 Main Street
(765) 423–4501
Expensive
Provincial French

Pepe's
2625 Sagamore Parkway South
(765) 448–1888
Moderate
Mexican

Sarge Oak
515 South Street
(765) 742–5230 or
(800) 423–1137
Expensive
American

Sergeant Preston's of the North
6 North Second Street
(765) 742–7378
Moderate
American

LaPORTE

Christo's Family Dining
1462 West State Road 2
(219) 326–1644
Moderate
American

LOWELL

George's Family Restaurant
1910 East Commercial Avenue
(219) 696–0313
Inexpensive
American

SOURCES FOR ADDITIONAL INFORMATION ABOUT NORTHWEST INDIANA

**Greater Lafayette/West Lafayette
Convention and Visitors Bureau
(Tippecanoe County)**
301 Frontage Road at exit 172
Lafayette 47905
(765) 447–9999 or (800) 872–6648

**Greater Monticello/White County
Visitors Bureau**
116 North Main Street
P.O. Box 657
Monticello 47960
(574) 583–7220

**Lake County Convention and
Visitors Bureau**
7770 Corinne Drive
Hammond 46323
(219) 989–7979 or (800) ALL–LAKE
(255–5253)

**LaPorte County Convention
and Visitors Bureau**
1503 South Meer Road
Michigan City 46360
(219) 872–5055 or (800) 634–2650

Logansport/Cass County Tourism
300 East Broadway Street
Suite 103
Logansport 46947
(574) 753–6388

**Marshall County Convention
and Visitors Bureau**
220 North Center Street
P.O. Box 669
Plymouth 46563
(574) 936–1882 or (800) 626–5353

**Montgomery County
Visitors and Convention Bureau**
218 East Pike Street
Crawfordsville 47933
(765) 362–5200 or (800) 866–3973

**Newton County Chamber
of Commerce**
c/o Kentland Bank
111 North Fourth Street
P.O. Box 273
Kentland 47951
(219) 474–6665

**Porter County Convention and
Visitors Bureau**
1420 Munson Road
Porter 46304
(219) 926–2255 or (800) 283–8687

**South Bend/Mishawaka
Convention and Visitors Bureau
(St. Joseph County)**
401 East Colfax Avenue, Suite 310
South Bend 46634
(574) 234–0051 or (800) 519–0577

MICHIGAN CITY

Fortune House
312 West U.S. Highway 20
(219) 872–6664
Inexpensive
Chinese

Rodini's Restaurant
4125 South Franklin Street
(219) 879–7388
Expensive
American

Swingbelly's
100 West Washington Street
(219) 874–5718
Moderate
American

MILLER BEACH (GARY)

The Beach Cafe
903 North Shelby Street
(219) 938–9890
Moderate
American

Miller Bakery Cafe
555 Lake Street
(219) 938–2229
Moderate
International

MISHAWAKA

Doc Pierce's Restaurant
120 North Main Street
(574) 255–7737
Moderate
American

MONTICELLO

Oakdale Inn Restaurant
11899 West Oakdale Drive
(574) 965–9104
Moderate
American

MUNSTER

Giovanni's
603 Ridge Road
(U.S. Highway 6)
(219) 836–6220
Inexpensive
Italian

NEW CARLISLE

Miller's Home Cafe
110 East Michigan Street
(574) 654–3431
Moderate
Home cooking

PLYMOUTH

C&K Family Restaurant
12355 Michigan Road
(574) 936–7173
Inexpensive
American

PORTAGE

DaVinci's
6121 Melton Road
(U.S. Highway 20)
(219) 762–0509
Moderate
Italian

RENSSELAER

City Office and Pub
114 South Van
Rensselaer Street
(219) 866–9916
Inexpensive
American

Grandma's Home Cooking
9378 West State Road 114
(219) 866–4554
Inexpensive
Home cooking

ROLLING PRAIRIE

L&L Restaurant
5201 East U.S. Highway 20
(219) 778–4946
Inexpensive
American

SOUTH BEND

Chicago Steak House
222 South Michigan Street
(574) 234–5200
Moderate
Steak/seafood

East Bank Emporium Restaurant
121 South Niles Avenue
(574) 234–9000
Moderate
American

LaSalle Grill
115 West Colfax Avenue
(574) 288–1155
Expensive
American

VALPARAISO

Billy Jack's Cafe and Grill
2904 Calumet Avenue
(219) 477–3797
Moderate
American

China House
120 East Lincolnway
(219) 462–5788
Inexpensive
Chinese

Don Quijote
119 East Lincolnway
(219) 462–7976
Moderate
Spanish

Gaucho's Steakhouse
597 West U.S. Highway 30
(219) 759–1100
Expensive
Brazilian

WHITING

Purple Steer Restaurant
1402 Indianapolis Boulevard
(219) 659–3950
Moderate
American/Italian

Southeast Indiana

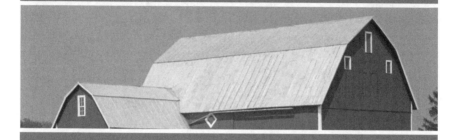

Beauty and history exist side by side in southeast Indiana. Although Interstate 70 on the north, Interstate 65 on the west, and Interstate 74 in between carve the landscape into two pie-shaped wedges, the land between those ribbons of highway is some of the loveliest the state has to offer. This is also the land where history began in Indiana, sweeping in on the waters of the beautiful Ohio River. The first settlers found woodlands so dense, it is said, that a squirrel could make its way across the state without ever once having to touch the ground.

Today a scenic highway winds along the banks of the Ohio, taking those who will spend the time on a voyage of discovery. Antiques lovers may think they've died and gone to heaven. History buffs will find museums galore, with unique treasures tucked away in their corners.

Bartholomew County

According to an article that appeared in the *New York Times Magazine* in recent years, "there is really no equivalent to **Columbus** anywhere." In its December 2005 issue, *Smithsonian Magazine* featured the city in an article that called Columbus the sixth most architecturally significant city in the country,

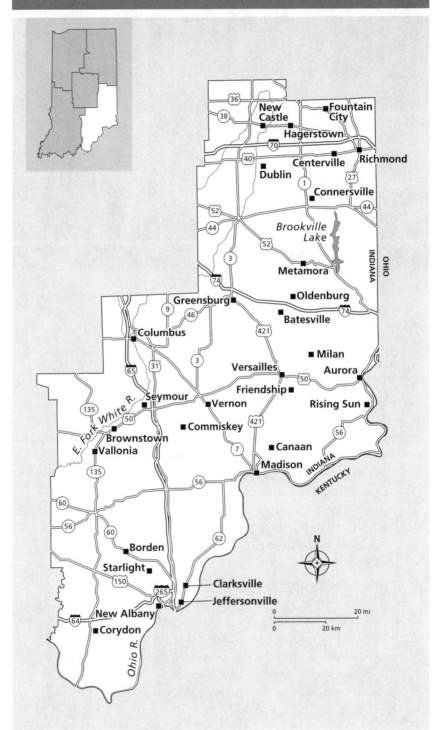

just behind Chicago, New York, San Francisco, Boston, and Washington, D.C. These are just two of the many tributes this town of 38,000 people has received from around the world in recognition of its architecture. More than sixty public and private buildings make up the most concentrated collection of contemporary architecture on Earth, and the names of the architects, artists, designers, and sculptors who created them are right from the pages of *Who's Who*. Where else, for instance, can you walk out of a church designed by Eliel Saarinen, cross the street, pass a Henry Moore sculpture, and enter a library designed by I. M. Pei?

One of the most visually striking buildings is the ***North Christian Church,*** designed by Eero Saarinen (Eliel's son). A low, hexagon-shaped building, it has a sloping roof centered by a 192-foot-tall needlelike spire that's topped by a gold-leaf cross. The multilevels of ***Smith Elementary School,*** created by John M. Johansen, are connected by several brightly colored, tube-shaped ramps—

AUTHOR'S FAVORITE ATTRACTIONS/EVENTS IN SOUTHEAST INDIANA

Canaan Fall Festival and Pony Express Mail Run
Canaan; September
(812) 839–4770

Celtic Celebration
Rising Sun; March
(812) 438–3532 or (888) 776–4786

Falls Fossil Festival
Clarksville; September
(812) 280–9970

Falls of the Ohio State Park
Clarksville
(812) 280–9970

Historic National Road Yard Sale
U.S. Highway 40 (RIchmond to Terre Haute); May/June
(765) 478–4809

Indiana Basketball Hall of Fame
New Castle
(765) 529–1891

National Muzzle Loading Rifle Association National Championship Shoot
Friendship; June and September
(812) 667–5131

Old-Fashioned Christmas Walk
Metamora; November/December weekends
(765) 647–2109

Scottish Festival
Columbus; September
(812) 378–2622 or (800) 468–6564

Squire Boone Caverns
Corydon
(812) 732–4381

Wayne County Historical Museum
Richmond
(765) 962–5756

Whitewater Canal State Historic Site
Metamora
(765) 647–6512

Wilbur Wright Birthplace Festival
Millville; June
(765) 332–2495

Zimmerman Art Glass Factory
Corydon
(812) 738–2206

pure delight for the children who use them. *Clifty Creek Elementary School* was designed by Richard Meier, the architect who also designed the spectacular J. Paul Getty Fine Arts Center that sprawls atop a Brentwood, California, hilltop. The sanctuary of *St. Peter's Lutheran Church,* topped by a 186-foot-tall, copper-clad steeple, rises in Byzantine-like splendor above its surroundings— beautiful at any time, but especially so when touched by the sun. Just east of town, the sprawling *Otter Creek Clubhouse,* designed by Harry Weese, lies adjacent to one of the finest public golf courses in the country; the late Robert Trent Jones, who laid out the course, once said its thirteenth hole is the single best hole he'd ever designed.

trivia

The only car to ever complete the Indianapolis 500 without a single stop was a diesel-powered car entered in the 1931 race by Cummins Engine Company of Columbus.

The beauty of the downtown area is enhanced by a sprawling white structure that serves as the world headquarters of *Cummins Engine Company,* Columbus's oldest and leading firm. Outside, graceful fountains feed shallow ponds and fingers of vines meander up the walls. Inside, within the glassed-in lobby, a diesel engine—the product that first brought fame to the company—is displayed as an abstract sculpture. Since 1957, as part of its commitment to a quality environment for all town residents, the Cummins Foundation has paid the fees of all leading architects chosen by the town leaders, contributing to the overall design of the city itself.

Not all of these buildings will knock your socks off at first sight. To fully appreciate them, you should learn something about the innovative functions and attention to details that lie behind the facades. The *First Christian Church,* built in 1942, could just as easily have been built yesterday.

trivia

Flambeau Products Corporation in Columbus supplies the world with Duncan yo-yos. In 1998 yo-yo sales were estimated at fifty million, breaking the company's previous record of forty-two million sold in 1962.

Columbus also has its share of renovated and historical buildings, but it is the modern architecture that has brought this small town fame as the "Athens of the Prairie." In 2001 six of the city's buildings were designated National Historic Landmarks, a rare honor because five of the six did not meet the usual criterion of being more than fifty years old.

Begin your tour at the *Columbus Area Visitors Center,* housed in a nineteenth-century home at 506 Fifth Street; (812) 378–2622 or (800) 468–6564.

You'll find interactive exhibits that call up images of the area's best-known architecture, including a special child-oriented section, a fifteen-minute video presentation about the city's architectural heritage, and an eye-catching yellow neon chandelier that highlights a two-story bay window.

Measuring 9 feet high by 6 feet across and weighing 1,200 pounds, the chandelier is the creation of world-renowned glass artist Dale Chihuly. The unique work of art contains 900 pieces of handblown glass in four shades of yellow and 50 feet of neon tubing. Chihuly, who studied glassblow-

North Christian Church

ing in Italy, is the first American glassblower ever permitted to work on the island of Murano, a carefully guarded and isolated Italian glassmaking center that dates from the thirteenth century. Former President Bill Clinton has given smaller Chihuly pieces as gifts to world leaders when he travels abroad.

You can also pick up brochures, maps, and descriptive cassette tapes for self-guided tours of the city or make advance reservations for a minibus guided tour, available daily April through October. The center is open 9:00 A.M. to 5:00 P.M. Monday through Saturday and 10:00 A.M. to 2:00 P.M. Sunday, April through October; hours vary the rest of the year.

There's nothing contemporary about **Zaharako's Confectionery** in downtown Columbus—it's pure nostalgia. Located at the same address since October 1900, the store is now a Columbus institution. Its fixtures carry you back to the beginning of the twentieth century—Mexican onyx soda fountains purchased from the St. Louis World Exposition in 1905, a full-concert mechanical pipe organ brought here from Germany in 1908 that rings out with tunes of the Gay Nineties, an exquisite Tiffany lamp, and accessories of carved mahogany. Amid these ornate surroundings you can enjoy homemade ice cream, fountain treats, and an assortment of candies and sandwiches. You'll find the store at 329 Washington Street; (812) 379–9329. Open 10:00 A.M. to 3:00 P.M. Monday through Thursday and 10:00 A.M. to 5:00 P.M. Friday and Saturday.

Across the street from Zaharako's is Columbus's ultramodern, award-winning shopping mall and special-events center, **The Commons,** designed by Cesar

Effective Living

One of the most successful self-help books in recent years is *The 7 Habits of Highly Effective People*. It has sold some fifteen million copies worldwide and has been translated into thirty-four languages. Stephen Covey, its author, is a former business professor at Brigham Young University in Provo, Utah.

A few years back, Covey signed up six "experimental" communities to be the beneficiaries of *7 Habits* training. One of those communities was Columbus (population 38,000). Covey's goal is to train every citizen in the 7 Habits, thereby improving (theoretically) the performance of every organization and the quality of life for every citizen.

One Columbus Chamber of Commerce executive expressed the purpose of the city's participation: "What we want is to have productive, happy people. . . . I think this can be life-changing."

Only time will tell, of course, but Columbus would seem an ideal choice for such an experiment. It is a community that personifies civic pride.

Pelli. Completely enclosed, The Commons houses *Chaos I,* a seven-ton, 30-foot-tall, in-motion sculpture crafted out of scrap metal by Swiss artist Jean Tinguely; the piece becomes more intriguing the longer you look at it.

In 1895 the Romanesque Revival building at the corner of Fifth and Franklin Streets was the brand-new Columbus City Hall. Today it is an elegant bed-and-breakfast inn that ranks as one of the Midwest's finest. Meticulously renovated, the **Columbus Inn** combines the best of past and present. Each of the thirty rooms and five suites contains American Empire–style cherry furnishings—including beds that were custom-made in France—and some beautiful antiques. The efficiency kitchens in the suites boast microwave ovens, linen napkins, and French crystal. For breakfast, guests are served such fare as an egg casserole (a unique dish that has contributed greatly to the inn's growing fame), fruit salad, homemade bread, and imported tea. Rates for two, which include a buffet breakfast, range from about $120 to $299 per night. For reservations write the inn at 445 Fifth Street, Columbus 47201, or call (812) 378–4289.

On the north side of Columbus is the city's municipal airport, originally built during World War II as the Atterbury Air Base. The **Atterbury-Bakalar Air Museum** at the airport pays tribute to military aviators who served their country from 1942 to 1970. Among the memorabilia are uniforms, flight jackets, and scale models of vintage aircraft. Homage is also paid to one of the least-known units of World War II—the pilots who flew the 6,000 gliders known as the "Silent

Wings." Towed aloft by C-47s, the engineless planes were cut loose to silently infiltrate enemy territory and deliver their cargoes of infantrymen and munitions. The U.S. Army trained the pilots to fight on the ground as well, but each flight was obviously a one-way mission, and casualties were high.

The museum also honors the famous Tuskegee Airmen, a special unit of black Americans that was composed of graduates of the Tuskegee Institute in Alabama. During World War II, some of those men trained at Atterbury Air Base in B-25 bombers. Their combat record was unblemished—no bomber flown by a Tuskegee Airman was ever lost to the enemy. In addition to an indoor exhibit, the airmen are memorialized in an outdoor monument that stands on Bakalar Green just south of the airport terminal. The museum is located at 4742 Ray Boll Boulevard; admission is free. Open 10:00 A.M. to 2:00 P.M. Tuesday through Friday and 10:00 A.M. to 4:00 P.M. Saturday; hours for the museum, which is currently staffed by volunteers, may be expanded in the near future. For up-to-date information call (812) 372–4356 or visit www.atterburybakalarairmuseum.org.

Clark County

Along the banks of the Ohio River in **Clarksville** lies a 400-million-year-old fossil bed that is one of the world's greatest natural wonders. Its rare and unusual formations date back to the Devonian age and have for decades attracted sightseers and scientists from around the world. Once the reef was covered by the Falls of the Ohio, a raging, 2-mile stretch of water below Louisville in which the Ohio River dropped 22 feet over limestone ledges. Now the Ohio has been reduced to a series of pools by a string of dams, and the controlled water levels have left the reef high and dry. Its fossil corals archaeological sites are among the best in the country, and the variety of its migratory bird life is unparalleled at any other inland location.

For years efforts have been under way to preserve this area. The first step in realizing that dream occurred in October 1984, when the U.S. Senate approved funding for the creation of the **Falls of the Ohio National Wildlife Conservation Area.** In 1990 sixty-eight acres of land were dedicated as an Indiana state park. Although relatively small itself, the **Falls of the Ohio State Park** lies within the 1,404 acres of the federally protected conservation area, providing lots of wide-open space to explore.

A 16,000-square-foot interpretive center, perched atop a bluff overlooking the fossil beds, opened to the public in January 1994. The building's exterior features horizontal bands of Indiana limestone alternating with bands of earth-toned bricks, creating a layered look reminiscent of the geological treasure that sprawls below it.

Indiana Fried Chicken?

Few people know that Col. Harland Sanders was born in the tiny southern Indiana town of Henryville. As a matter of fact, few people who live in Henryville knew it until recently. Young Harland loved to cook even as a boy, a skill that served him and his family well. Harland was just five years old when his father died in 1895, and his mother had to go to work to support her family. It fell to Harland to take care of many of the household chores, including much of the cooking. One of his specialties was fried chicken.

When he was barely into his teens, the young man went to work as a farmhand and then as a streetcar conductor in New Albany before enlisting in the army as an underage recruit (easy to do in those days). He later sold insurance in Jeffersonville; started a ferry company that ran boats across the Ohio River between Jeffersonville and Louisville, Kentucky; and worked as a secretary for the Columbus, Indiana, Chamber of Commerce. There he also launched a manufacturing company that went belly-up when his firm's product became obsolete. Off Harland went to Kentucky, where he progressed from tire salesman to gas station manager to restaurant owner. Finally, it seemed, Harland had found his niche. Kentucky Fried Chicken became one of the most successful food franchises in history.

Harland also knew talent when he saw it. During a visit to a Fort Wayne franchise, he was impressed with the work ethic of a young man who worked there and predicted that the industrious employee would someday amount to something. Indeed, the young man did. Dave Thomas moved on to found Wendy's.

Inside, exhibits lead visitors back through the millennia to a time when ancient Indiana lay about twenty degrees south of the equator beneath the warm waters of a tropical sea. An orientation video employs the latest laser technology to portray the history of the falls. The use of underwater oceanic photography to re-create a 400-million-year-old tropical sea is a first in the film industry. In a wildlife observation room, visitors can view some of the area's 265 species of avian visitors in a small garden area. Elsewhere, the center offers panoramic views of the Ohio River, a historic railroad bridge, the McAlpine Dam and Locks, and the fossil bed itself (best seen from August through October, when the river is at its lowest level).

Low-water periods also provide the best opportunity to explore the fossil bed. More than 600 fossil species have been identified, and two-thirds of those were discovered here for the first time anywhere in the world. Visitors may walk among the eroded rock slabs and search for fossils freed from the bedrock by the powerful waters of the river. Handling of the fossils is encouraged, but they must be returned to their original locations. Collecting is strictly forbidden.

Other activities include fishing, picnicking, and hiking along park trails. A log cabin in the park is a historically accurate reconstruction of the nineteenth-century home of Gen. George Rogers Clark, the Revolutionary War hero who founded Clarksville. Built on the site of Clark's original home, the cabin sits atop a hill overlooking the foot of the Falls of the Ohio.

The park is located on the south side of Riverside Drive, about a mile west of U.S. Highway 31. Visitors to the park alone pay a nominal parking fee; a nominal admission fee for the interpretive center includes free parking. The center is open 9:00 A.M. to 5:00 P.M. Monday through Saturday and 1:00 to 5:00 P.M. Sunday. For additional information write or call Falls of the Ohio State Park, 201 West Riverside Drive, Clarksville; (812) 280–9970.

The Falls of the Ohio area played a major role in the national celebration of the bicentennial of the Meriwether Lewis and William Clark expedition of 1803. It was here that the two explorers and their Corps of Discovery assembled at the home of Gen. George Rogers Clark, William's older brother, before departing on their epic journey. The explorers traveled westward to the Pacific Ocean, mapping the area included in the Louisiana Purchase of earlier that year that doubled the size of the country at that time. As part of the remembrance, Clarksville dedicated its **Lewis and Clark Park** on November 5, 2006, 300 years after the expedition's return to this spot. The new park, which is part of a planned Lewis and Clark Plaza, extends westward from the George Rogers Clark homesite. For up-to-date information call the Indiana Lewis and Clark Commission at (317) 232–4020 or visit www.lewisandclark.in.gov.

Presiding over Clarksville is the town's own version of London's Big Ben. The main building of the **Colgate-Palmolive plant** at State and Woerner Streets is topped by the second-largest clock in the world, which is a monstrous 40 feet in diameter and has a 16-foot-long hour hand that weighs 500 pounds. (The largest clock in the world, 50 feet in diameter, sits on the former site of a Colgate plant in Jersey City, New Jersey.) No one in Clarksville gets away with saying he doesn't know the time—the electric-powered clock is said to be accurate to within fifteen seconds a month, the clock's face can be read from a distance of 2½ miles, and the clock is illuminated at night by neon tubes.

You can take a free tour of Colgate's facilities at 9:00 A.M. each Tuesday if you make an advance appointment; call Employee Relations at (812) 283–6611. The plant, which produces an array of household and personal care products, is housed in a building at the corner of State and Woerner Streets that once served as Indiana's first state prison. You'll have to hurry, though—the plant is scheduled to close in January 2008. The clock, however, will remain.

Jeffersonville, which adjoins Clarksville to the east, is home to the biggest inland boatbuilding company in North America. You can see workers along the

ANNUAL EVENTS IN SOUTHEAST INDIANA

Madison Regatta
Madison; July
(812) 265–2956 or (800) 559–2956

Swiss Wine Festival
Vevay; August
(800) 435–5688

Labor Day Antiques and Vintage Collectibles Market
Town of Vernon; Labor Day weekend
(812) 346–4865 or (800) 928–3667

Lanesville Heritage Festival Weekend
Lanesville; September
(812) 952–2600

Madison Chautauqua
Madison; September
(812) 265–2956 or (800) 559–2956

Tree City Fall Festival
Greensburg; September
(812) 663–2832

Canal Days
Metamora; October
(765) 647–2109

Ethnic Expo
Columbus; October
(812) 378–2622 or (800) 468–6564

Lewis and Clark River Festival
Clarksville; October
(812) 280–5566 or (800) 552–3842

Stumlers Applefest
Starlight; October
(812) 923–3832

waterfront building cruise ships, ferries, towboats, barges, and—with the recent arrival of riverboat gambling in Indiana—gaming boats. The company, known as *Jeffboat, Inc.,* has its offices at 1030 East Market Street; call (812) 288–0200.

Until 1931 the Howard Shipyards were in Jeffersonville. During their 107 years in business, the yards produced some 3,000 steamboats, reported to be the finest ever to ply the waters of North and Central America. The *J. M. White,* the most luxurious steamboat in history, was built here, as were the *Glendy Burke,* which inspired the Stephen Foster song of the same name; the *City of Louisville,* the fastest steamboat ever built; and the *Cape Girardeau,* captured on film for all time in *Gone with the Wind.*

The steamboat era was flourishing in the 1890s when construction began on the elaborate twenty-two-room Howard mansion at 1101 East Market Street that today houses the *Howard Steamboat Museum.* A striking late-Victorian structure, the house features stained- and leaded-glass windows, a Moorish-style music room that contains its original Louis XV furniture, and intricate embellishments that were hand-carved from fifteen types of wood.

You can see all this today, plus a priceless collection of relics that played a role in the golden era of steamboating, miniature models of Howard-built steamboats, and rooms furnished like staterooms on the finest turn-of-the-twentieth-century boats. Open 10:00 A.M. to 4:00 P.M. Tuesday through Saturday and 1:00 to 4:00 P.M. Sunday; closed Monday and major holidays. There's a nominal admission fee. For further details write the Clark County Historical Society at P.O. Box 606, Jeffersonville 47131; call (812) 283–3728 or (888) 472–0606.

An old-fashioned candy store complete with soda fountain and tin ceiling, **Schimpff's Confectionery,** 347 Spring Street in Jeffersonville, open since 1891, is one of the oldest continuously operated family-owned candy businesses in the country. Its cinnamon red-hot squares are a particular favorite, ordered through the mail by people from around the world. The folks in Bakersfield, California, for example, order sixty to eighty pounds of red hots annually. All candies are handmade, just as they were a century ago. They're all scrumptious, and the ice cream's good, too! There's even a candy museum to explore. Open 10:00 A.M. to 5:00 P.M. Monday through Friday and 10:00 A.M. to 3:00 P.M. Saturday; (812) 283–8367.

trivia

Southern Indiana is the only place in the world where Deam's foxglove, a vascular plant, occurs naturally.

Something's always going on at the 550-acre Huber Farm near **Borden.** Officially billed as the **Huber Orchard, Winery, and U-Pick Farm,** it's open to the public year-round. Strawberries are ripe for the picking from mid-May through mid-June. Twelve varieties of apples are in season from late summer through December. You can select your own pumpkin right from the patch in the fall and cut your own Christmas tree in December. Cider made on the farm each fall is available for purchase at any time.

Brothers Gerald and Carl Huber, along with their families, also produce commercial wines, and thus far they've garnered more than one hundred awards for their efforts, including "Best of Show" at several Indiana State Fairs and a silver medal at the prestigious Eastern International Wine Competition in 1991. Visitors can sample their many varieties and tour the winery. The

trivia

The chief engineer on the Hoover Dam project on the Colorado River at the Arizona-Nevada state line was Dr. Elwood Mead of Patriot. Upon completion of the project in 1936, the huge reservoir created by the dam was named Lake Mead in honor of the Hoosier native.

Hubers also make cheese on their farm, and visitors can watch this process as well. You can buy the makings of a picnic lunch, as well as ready-made sandwiches and cheese trays, right on the farm. Additions to the farm include a bakery, a petting zoo, and a cafe. Open 10:00 A.M. to 6:00 P.M. daily May

OTHER ATTRACTIONS WORTH SEEING IN SOUTHEAST INDIANA

CAMBRIDGE CITY

Huddleston Farmhouse Inn Museum
838 National Road
(765) 478–3172

CHARLESTOWN

Charlestown State Park
12500 State Road 62 East
(812) 256–5600

COLUMBUS

Irwin Home and Sunken Gardens
608 Fifth Street
(812) 378–2622 or (800) 468–6564

CORYDON

Corydon Capitol State Historic Site
200 South Capitol Avenue
(812) 738–4890

KNIGHTSTOWN

Carthage, Knightstown & Shirley
Railroad Round-Trip Excursion
CKS Depot, 112 West Carey Street
(765) 345–5561

Trump's Texaco Museum
39 North Washington Street
(765) 345–7135

MADISON

Madison Railroad Station and
Jefferson County Historical
Society Museum
615 West First Street
(812) 265–2335

NEW ALBANY

Culbertson Mansion State
Historic Site
914 East Main Street
(812) 944–9600

RICHMOND

Gaar Mansion and Farm Museum
2593 Pleasant View Road
(765) 966–7184 or (800) 828–8414

RISING SUN

Ohio County Historical Museum
212 South Walnut Street
(812) 438–4915 or (888) 776–4786

SALEM

John Jay Center and Stevens
Memorial Museum
307 East Market Street
(812) 883–6495

VEVAY

Switzerland County Historical
Society Museum
210 West Market Street
(812) 427–3560

through December; 10:00 A.M. to 6:00 P.M. Tuesday through Saturday and noon to 6:00 P.M. Sunday January through April. Call (812) 923–WINE or (800) 345–WINE for hours and directions, or write the Hubers at 19816 Huber Road, Starlight 47106. You can also visit the Hubers online at www.huberwinery.com.

Just down the road, on a 360-acre farm, cousin Joe runs the ***Joe Huber Family Farm and Restaurant.*** The down-home country cooking features fried chicken, fried biscuits, and fresh fruit and vegetables; all menu items are prepared from scratch. Open 11:00 A.M. to 8:00 P.M. Monday through Thursday, 11:00 A.M. to 9:00 P.M. Friday and Saturday, and 11:00 A.M. to 7:00 P.M. Sunday, May through October; 11:00 A.M. to 8:00 P.M. Monday through Saturday, and 11:00 A.M. to 6:00 P.M. Sunday, January through April and November through December 23; closed December 24 through January 1. Located at 2421 Scottsville Road; call (812) 923–5255 or (877) 563–4823, or visit www.joehubers.com.

After visiting the ***Forest Discovery Center*** in ***Starlight,*** you may never look at a tree in the same way again. Step into the massive building and enter an indoor forest, complete with trees, a stream, the natural music of the woodlands (recorded), and re-creations of the creatures that live there. A television set embedded in a tree trunk plays a video describing the many uses of a tree. Elsewhere you'll find a giant, walk-through oak tree, a 1,000-square-foot mural created from small pieces of wood, a children's play area with interactive games, and a gift shop. Artisans and craftspeople display their creations and discuss woodworking techniques.

The center was built by the Koetter family, who owns and operates ***Koetter Woodworking,*** a state-of-the-art lumber mill that's adjacent to the center. Visitors can access the plant via a glass-enclosed sidewalk and watch the manufacturing process from a series of elevated catwalks. You'll see logs enter one end of the building and exit the other as a finished product. Along the way, the logs are sawed, planed, dried, ripped for width, and chopped for length—all done by high-tech computerized equipment. What's more, not one bit of a log goes to waste. The sawdust generated along the way is burned to provide the electricity that powers the plant, and the steam created by the burning provides the heat used in the kilns to dry the lumber.

The center is open 9:00 A.M. to 5:00 P.M. Tuesday through Saturday. The mill can be toured during the same hours but can be seen in operation only on weekdays. Both are included for a nominal admission fee. For additional information write or call the Forest Discovery Center, 533 Louis Smith Road, Starlight 47106; (812) 923–1590.

Dearborn County

Atop a wooded hillside overlooking the village of ***Aurora*** stands a splendid yellow frame house filled with the memories of a bygone era. It was built in the 1850s by Thomas Gaff, a wealthy industrialist and shipping magnate whose steamboats regularly plied the waters of the Ohio River far below.

Gaff's love for the river ran deep, and that love is reflected in his home, **Hillforest Mansion,** whose architectural style is often referred to as "steamboat Gothic." And indeed it does resemble a steamboat in part, with its rounded front porticoes and cupola, coupled columns, and suspended interior staircase—all features that were typical of the "floating palaces" that graced the nation's rivers in the heyday of river transportation.

trivia

The ministry of Henry Ward Beecher, a noted nineteenth-century clergyman, began in 1837 at a Presbyterian church in Lawrenceburg. He spoke eloquently against slavery, a cause that was further espoused by his sister, Harriet Beecher Stowe, in her novel *Uncle Tom's Cabin.*

Now restored and filled with antique furniture, the entire mansion can be toured, from its wine cellar up to the observatory at the top of the house. The view of the Ohio River is just as beautiful as it was when Thomas Gaff himself stood here. Around the one-of-a-kind home are ten acres of grounds laid out in the grand manner of an Italian villa. Open 1:00 to 5:00 P.M. Tuesday through Sunday, April through December 23 and December 26 through December 30; admission fee. Located at 213 Fifth Street; (812) 926–0087.

Decatur County

It's easy to tell the visitors from the hometown folks in **Greensburg**—the visitors are all looking up. Up, that is, at a tree that's growing where we've all been led to believe trees can't grow—on a roof. Eye-catching, to be sure.

The tree adorns the tower that tops the **Decatur County Courthouse.** When the first tree appeared here in 1870, local authorities, who knew a tree's proper place, grubbed it out. Five years later a second tree appeared. The amazed citizenry, admiring its tenacity, merely stood by and watched this time. That tree thrived until 1929, when it failed to leaf and was removed to the local **Decatur County Museum** for preservation.

At the time of its removal another tree had already started growing on the opposite side of the tower. Other trees appeared through the years, growing without any apparent nourishment (although local comedians conjecture that they are fed by the springs in the tower's clock). The current tree is the eleventh offspring of the original. The townsfolk have long since made their peace with this peculiar situation, and they even celebrate each September with a **Tree City Fall Festival.**

What type of tree had implanted itself on the courthouse roof? For years no one could agree on the answer, and finally scientists at the Smithsonian Institution in Washington, D.C., were consulted. They declared the trees to be large-toothed aspens. For additional information contact the Greensburg/Decatur County Visitor Center, 232 North Franklin Street, P.O. Box 345, Greensburg 47240; (812) 222–8733 or (877) 883–5447.

While in Greensburg, you may want to try body-flying. The nation's fourth vertical wind tunnel and free-fall simulator can be found at the Greensburg/Decatur airport. Located at *Skydive Greensburg,* a Midwest center for skydiving, the simulator allows you to experience the thrill of free falling without jumping out of an airplane. Folks who have tried it describe feeling akin to a Ping-Pong ball caught in an updraft. Actually, they're floating atop a column of air created by a huge propeller that can create winds up to 135 miles per hour. Body position determines how high a person rises inside the 17-foot-tall Plexiglas cylinder; and a screen over the top keeps anyone from flying out. The primary purpose of the wind tunnel is to help skydiving students prepare for free-falling from a plane, but it's not necessary to be a skydiver to enjoy the wind tunnel. It's open to anyone in reasonably good physical shape who is at least six years old, with parental consent required for those under eighteen.

trivia

Carl Fisher, born poor and half-blind in Greensburg in 1874, had to quit school and go to work at age twelve. Nevertheless, he founded the town of Speedway, helped create the Indianapolis Motor Speedway (home of the Indianapolis 500), was instrumental in marking the route for the first transcontinental road for automobiles, and created the resort town of Miami Beach, Florida, from a mangrove swamp.

The wind tunnel is open on weekends and by appointment on weekdays during warm weather months. For rates and additional information, write Skydive Greensburg, P.O. Box 276, Greensburg 47240; call (800) SKY–DIVE or (812) 663–DIVE; or visit www.skydivegreensburg.com.

If you'd like to experience the real thing, Skydive Greensburg offers some of the best skydiving facilities, equipment, and instructors in the country. Former Green Beret Jay Stokes came here in 2006 to challenge the world record of 534 parachute jumps in twenty-four hours. He succeeded, achieving a new record of 640. It will replace the old one—also set by Jay Stokes—in the next edition of the *Guinness Book of World Records.*

Fayette County

The *Whitewater Valley Railroad,* the longest steam railroad in Indiana, travels 32 scenic miles between *Connersville* and Metamora each Saturday, Sun-

Whitewater Valley Railroad

day, and holiday from May through November. All the sights and sounds of old-time steam travel have been re-created to transport you back in time, and places of interest, including some of the original locks of the old Whitewater Canal, are pointed out along the way. Two rare Baldwin locomotives, vintage 1907 and 1919, pull New York Central and Erie Stillwell passenger cars over tracks laid along the canal's towpath. At Metamora (see Franklin County) there's time to disembark and explore a restored canal town.

Both round-trips and one-way trips, as well as caboose rides and special Christmas runs, are available. Round-trips, which are approximately five hours long, originate at the Connersville station, located 1 mile south of town on Highway 121. For a schedule and additional information, write the Whitewater Valley Railroad, Inc., 455 Market Street, P.O. Box 406, Connersville 47331; call (765) 825–2054.

Seven miles southwest of Connersville on County Road 350 South is the **Mary Gray Bird Sanctuary,** a 684-acre wildlife preserve owned and operated by the Indiana Audubon Society. These peaceful surroundings are crisscrossed by several miles of hiking trails, and a full-time naturalist is on hand to answer your questions. A small museum depicts local flora and fauna. The preserve is open daily, free of charge, from dawn to dusk. Write the sanctuary at 3497 South Bird Sanctuary Road, Connersville 47337; call (765) 827–0908.

Floyd County

In the mood for something exotic to eat in a setting that's unique? Then head for the **Creekside Outpost Cafe** in **New Albany** and indulge in one of the more than three dozen types of game served there. How about some ground

A Labor of Love

If you happen to travel through northeastern Floyd County during the Easter or Christmas holidays, you may see one of southern Indiana's most cherished landmarks.

Atop a rise that overlooks the tiny town of St. Joseph, a 50-foot-tall lighted cross dominates the landscape. It was erected in the early 1950s by the Clark County REMC (Rural Electric Management Company) and became an instant holiday tradition. Equipped with three 350-watt lamps and 105 100-watt lamps, it could be seen by pilots from more than 100 miles away.

The cross was a fixture on the holiday scene until the mid-1960s, when repeated damage by some incorrigible vandals forced REMC to discontinue the tradition. In 1972, however, the congregations of three local churches asked REMC to resume operation of the cross, and the company responded by repairing it. The cross has illuminated the skies ever since, a lovely and enduring symbol of the holidays.

camel? Or an elk steak? Maybe a bison burger or some buffalo jerky? Then, of course, there's always ground beaver.

Owners Phil and Donna "Ladyhawk" Young once operated a more conventional restaurant in New Albany. That was before Ladyhawk came down with a mysterious illness that even the famed Mayo Clinic could not treat. In desperation, they turned to an alternative treatment that involved a special macrobiotic diet. Ladyhawk recovered and, to supply the special foods that she needed, the Youngs opened up a health food store in a converted stable behind their home. Before long, they were back in the restaurant mode and serving meals, too.

In addition to their exotic meats, the Youngs serve a wide range of vegetarian foods and, each week, a different macrobiotic special. Some of the fare can be a bit pricey (it isn't cheap to import camel to southern Indiana), but that doesn't seem to deter the clientele. Thus far, the Youngs have expanded three times.

The Creekside Outpost Cafe is located at 614 Hausfeldt Lane in New Albany. Call (812) 948–9118 for hours.

Franklin County

Not too long ago, **Metamora** was a dying town, its days numbered by the end of the canal era. That was before the state of Indiana decided to restore a 14-mile section of the old **Whitewater Canal,** originally a 76-mile waterway constructed in the mid-1800s. Now the small village hums with activity.

An 80-foot-long covered wooden aqueduct in Metamora was built in 1848 to carry the canal 16 feet above Duck Creek. Believed to be the only such structure in existence, it was once featured on *Ripley's Believe It or Not.*

A horse-drawn canal boat takes visitors for a leisurely thirty-minute cruise through the aqueduct and a restored lock. Occasionally the Whitewater Valley Railroad's steam train chugs by, carrying passengers between its Connersville station (see Fayette County) and Metamora.

Many of the town's fine arts, crafts, and specialty shops are housed in pre–Civil War buildings that cling to the banks of the canal; others occupy reconstructed and reproduced buildings elsewhere in a section known as Old Metamora. An aged brick gristmill still grinds and sells flour, cornmeal, and grits. The total effect is that of a country village suspended in the 1830s.

Of the many special events scheduled throughout the year, the loveliest is the Christmas Walk that's held evenings on the first three Fridays and Saturdays after Thanksgiving. Some 3,000 lights line the banks of the canal, roads, and walkways. Carolers stroll through the streets; horses clippity-clop along, pulling carriages behind them. The aroma of hot spiced cider perfumes the air. Quite a show for a town that has a population of about sixty permanent residents!

If while in Metamora you experience a bit of déjà vu, it may be because you've seen the movie *Rain Man.* Dustin Hoffman and Tom Cruise came here to shoot part of the film.

Most shops are open 10:00 A.M. to 4:00 P.M. Tuesday through Friday and 10:00 A.M. to 5:00 P.M. Saturday, Sunday, and holidays, from mid-April to late December, while some are open only on weekends. Head for the shops flying bright yellow flags; that's Metamoraese for "Come on in! We're open!" For additional information write or call the Metamora Visitor Center, P.O. Box 117, Metamora 47030; (765) 647–2109.

The canal boat operates on the hour from noon to 4:00 P.M. Wednesday through Sunday, May through October (by reservation only on May weekdays); a nominal fee is charged. Write or call the Whitewater Canal State Memorial, 19083 North Clayborn Street, P.O. Box 88, Metamora 47030; (765) 647–6512.

Oldenburg is another architectural and historical gem that has dwelt in the past since it was founded in 1837. Known as the ***"Village of Spires"*** because of its many soaring steeples, Oldenburg is the home of the **convent and academy of the Sisters of St. Francis,** an order that originally came here from Austria. The peaceful grounds, which invite leisurely strolls, include a cemetery reserved for the sisters. In warm-weather months the cemetery is a stunning mosaic in green and white—paths edged by low-cut green hedges, emerald lawns shaded by the sprawling branches of ancient shade trees, and row on row of small, white, identical stone crosses. The convent itself, renowned for its ceiling frescoes, basilica-like chapel, iron stairways, and solid oak woodwork, can be toured by appointment. Call (812) 934–5675.

Elsewhere in the picturesque community are houses and storefronts adorned with the ornate tinwork of master craftsman Gasper Gaupel. The lovely tree-lined streets bear German names, ranging from the mundane Haupstrasse (Main Street) to the lyrical Schweineschwantz Gasse (Pigtail Alley). Every so often the aroma of brats and sauerkraut escapes from a local eatery. If you'd like to sample some German cuisine, just follow your nose.

Harrison County

A few miles south of **Corydon** is a peaceful valley laced with subterranean caverns and edged by forested hills. Squire Boone first saw this area in the late 1700s while hunting with his older brother, Daniel, and eventually returned here to settle down, building a home for his family and a gristmill that provided their means of support. When he died in 1815 he was buried at his own request in the cave that today bears his name, and the walnut coffin that contains his remains can be seen on a guided tour.

Squire Boone Caverns offer a wondrous mix of colorful stalactites and stalagmites, underground streams, waterfalls, twisted helictites, massive pillars of stone, and the world's largest travertine dam formation. Cave crickets, blind crayfish, isopods, amphipods, and a few bats live in the cave's deepest recesses. The tour guides are extremely well informed about this cave and about caves in general. At one point along the way, in the belly of the cave, all lights are turned out—an eerie experience that gives new meaning to the word *black*. This is not the largest cave around, but it is certainly one of the most dazzling. Visitors should be aware that the subterranean temperature is a constant fifty-four degrees, and there is a steep spiral staircase to climb at the end of the fifty-five-minute, ⅓-mile tour.

Topside, you can visit an operating gristmill rebuilt on the original foundation used by Squire Boone, watch the miller at work, and buy his products. A cluster of log cabins near the cave's entrance houses various crafts shops, an art gallery, a homemade-candy store, and a bakery; the craftspeople who work here are as authentic as the log cabins that shelter them. Children can get acquainted with farm animals at a petting zoo, uncover fossils at the Fossil Dig, pan for gold and gems, and learn something about earth science at the Rock Shop.

To reach Squire Boone Caverns and Village, go south from Corydon on State Road 135 for about 10 miles, then turn east on Squire Boone Caverns Road for another 3 miles; look for signs. Guided one-hour-long cave tours start every thirty minutes from 9:00 A.M. to 5:00 P.M. daily from Memorial Day

Gone Too Soon

Lova Cline, born in 1902, was the only child of George and Mary Cline of Arlington, Indiana. Unfortunately, Lova suffered from a serious illness and had to spend much of her short life in bed. Her father, hoping to bring some joy to his daughter's life, built her a dollhouse. He and Lova's mother filled it with toys, dolls, and love.

When Lova died at the age of six, her parents placed her beloved dollhouse above her grave. That dollhouse still marks the spot in the Rush County cemetery where little Lova lies.

Lova's parents have long since joined her in death, but they bequeathed the upkeep of the dollhouse to Lova Wooten, the daughter of some friends of the Clines who was named after the first Lova. The second Lova, who faithfully tended the unusual monument until her own death, filled it with handmade items of sentimental value.

Now fitted with aluminum siding and anchored by a cement foundation, the dollhouse draws visitors from across the state and beyond. Visitors may see it in the East Hill cemetery along U.S. Highway 52, just east of Arlington—a poignant monument to a little girl who died much too soon.

weekend through Labor Day; 10:00 A.M. to 4:00 P.M. every two hours daily after Labor Day through December 31, and from March 1 through the day before Memorial Day weekend; 10:00 A.M. to 4:00 P.M. every two hours Saturday and Sunday the rest of the year; closed major winter holidays. Village hours are 10:00 A.M. to 5:00 P.M. Memorial Day weekend through mid-August and 10:00 A.M. to 6:00 P.M. mid-August through Labor Day. The gristmill, which lies just outside the cave-village complex, is open, free of charge, when the village is open. Write Squire Boone Caverns, 100 Squire Boone Caverns Road Southwest, Mauckport 47142, or call (812) 732–4381.

trivia

The Edwardsville Railroad Tunnel near Corydon is Indiana's longest tunnel. Completed in 1881, the 4,311-foot-long passageway cost nearly $1 million to build.

Back in Corydon at the *Zimmerman Art Glass Factory* you can observe a process that is now nearly extinct. Brothers Bart and Kerry Zimmerman handblow every piece of glassware they make, and no two pieces are identical. The Zimmermans specialize in paperweights—clear crystal balls, large and small, that enclose unfolding blossoms—but will try just about anything that tickles their fancy. Their glass menagerie includes trays of glass fruits, sugar bowls and creamers, and an assortment of baskets, lamps, vases, and perfume decanters—some clear, some in exquisite color.

Many customers order items made to their specifications. An example is the lady from Australia who dropped by to describe the lamp she wanted and asked the partners to send it to her home—the shipping charges cost more than the lamp.

Although small, the company is nationally known, and its artistic

wares are displayed in many museums, including the Smithsonian Institution. You're welcome to drop in and watch these skilled craftspeople breathe life into molten glass; free glass-sculpting demonstrations are given from 9:00 A.M. to 3:00 P.M. Tuesday through Friday. The factory, open from 8:00 A.M. to 4:00 P.M. Tuesday through Saturday except major holidays, is housed in a green, corrugated-metal shed at 395 Valley Road on the south edge of Corydon; (812) 738–2206.

Henry County

In Indiana it's known as "Hoosier Hysteria"; to the rest of the world it's known as basketball. Almost anyone, after spending about five minutes in Indiana, can tell you that basketball holds a special place in the hearts of Hoosiers. It is not unheard of, for instance, for whole towns—gas stations, restaurants, and shops included—to shut down totally so that everyone can go to the local high school basketball game. After a short visit to the state, former CBS news anchor Dan Rather was heard to remark that "a ball and a net would make a perfect state flag" for Indiana. The world's record attendance for an indoor basketball game occurred in 1984, when 67,596 persons attended an exhibition game between the National Basketball Association All-Stars and the U.S. Olympic team in Indianapolis. In 1990 two Indiana teams playing for the state championship set a national record for attendance at a high school basketball game—41,046 persons showed up to cheer on their favorites. Eighteen of the twenty largest high school gyms in the country are in Indiana.

It should therefore surprise no one that there is an ***Indiana Basketball Hall of Fame;*** the citizenry would have it no other way. Previously located in Indianapolis, the Hall of Fame moved to newer and roomier quarters in ***New Castle*** in 1990. Within its walls visitors can see multimedia presentations, use computers to research the basketball history of state schools, play a trivia game, try to outwit a mechanical guard, attempt to make the winning shot as a clock counts down the last five seconds of a game, and learn basketball lore in abundance. The museum stands, appropriately, next door to the New Castle High School gym—the largest high school gym in the world. It's located at 1 Hall of Fame Court; there's a nominal admission fee. Open 10:00 A.M. to 5:00 P.M. Tuesday through Saturday and 1:00 to 5:00 P.M. Sunday; closed major winter holidays and Easter. Call (765) 529–1891.

Few people realize that the older half of the famous Wright Brothers was born in Indiana. Wilbur Wright's extraordinary life began in the town of Millville, a small town near New Castle, on April 16, 1867. Although the Wright family lived here for only six months, the town pays homage to Wilbur's memory with the *Wilbur Wright Birthplace and Museum.*

Most people would agree that few events in the twentieth century surpass in importance that defining moment when Wilbur and Orville first flew their airplane above the sand dunes of Kitty Hawk, North Carolina, in 1903. The Wright Flyer housed in the museum building is an exact replica of that plane and is believed to be the only one other than the original that is flightworthy. Parked outside the museum building, in stark contrast to the Flyer inside, is an F–84 jet fighter.

The museum also includes a simulator plane in which youngsters can test their flying skills and a wind tunnel like the one in which the Wright Brothers tested some of their ideas. Wright Village is an indoor street scene from the late 1800s; among the business facades is the Wright Brothers Bicycle Shop.

The house in which the future inventor was born burned down some time ago, but the small, two-story white frame dwelling has been reconstructed on

The Legend of the Raintree

It is a legend carved from dreams, a tale of a mystical tree that poets have sung about in every language in every land. Ross Lockbridge, Jr., wrote about it in his classic Civil War novel, *Raintree County:* "Luck, happiness, the realization of dreams, the secret of life itself—all belong to he who finds the raintree. Stand beneath its rain of golden blossoms and discover love."

The beautiful and exotic raintree about which he wrote, it is said, grows somewhere in Indiana's Henry County, but its exact location remains a mystery. Its seed may have been brought here by Johnny Appleseed, who wandered the Midwest in the first half of the nineteenth century planting apple orchards in what was then wilderness. With him, he carried one special seed—the seed of the golden raintree—searching for the one place where the seed might take root and flourish. Somewhere in Henry County, as legend has it, he found that place, and somewhere in Henry County, it endures to this day.

the home's original foundation, and the smokehouse behind it is the original structure used by the Wright family.

Tour guides humanize the brothers with fascinating true stories about their personal lives. Among them are anecdotes about their numerous failed business ventures, Orville's proclivity for practical jokes, and Wilbur's attempts at cooking.

To reach the birth site, go east from New Castle on State Road 38 to Wilbur Wright Road, turn north, and follow the signs. It's open from 10:00 A.M. to 5:00 P.M. Tuesday through Saturday and 1:00 to 5:00 P.M. Sunday, mid-March to mid-November,

trivia

The first train robbery in the United States was committed by the Reno brothers near Seymour in October 1866.

and by appointment the rest of the year. A small admission fee is charged. For additional information write or call the Wilbur Wright Birthplace and Museum, 1525 North County Road 750 East, Hagerstown 47346; (765) 332–2495.

Jackson County

The heavenly aroma that sometimes tantalizes the nostrils in **Brownstown** is a vanilla bean on its way to becoming vanilla extract. This metamorphosis takes place each working day at the **Marion-Kay Spice Company** plant, which turns out an array of spices, herbs, extracts, and seasonings. You can learn about the whole process, as well as the history of spices, on a free tour. The Marion-Kay plant and outlet store are located at 1351 West U.S. Highway 50 on the western edge of town. Open 8:00 A.M. to 4:30 P.M. Monday through Friday; call (812) 358–3000 for tour hours or visit the company's Web site, www.marionkay.com.

Indiana's **Skyline Drive** meanders across a series of knobs for some 6 miles through the **Jackson-Washington State Forest** and offers spectacular hilltop vistas. The poorly surfaced road is narrow, hilly, and treacherous, so plan on taking your time. A clearing at its peak 929-foot elevation offers picnic facilities and a panoramic view that extends into four counties. If you climb the fire tower that you'll see along the way, you'll see seven counties. To reach the drive, head south from Brownstown on South Poplar Street and follow the signs. Write the Jackson-Washington State Forest, 1278 East Highway 250, Brownstown 47220, or call (812) 358–2160, for information about the drive and the many recreational opportunities elsewhere in the forest.

Vallonia was established circa 1811, making it Jackson County's oldest community. Its longevity may be attributed in part to the fact that it has its own guardian angel.

Made of French marble and soaring to a height of more than 15 feet, the **Angel on Angel Hill** has stood atop a pedestal in a small family cemetery just south of town since 1887. The daughter of a prominent local businessman, who wanted to memorialize her father with a very special monument, had the sweet-faced angel shipped from Paris to New York. There she was placed aboard a train to Seymour and then carted on a log wagon to her permanent home in Vallonia, where she has been a curiosity ever since for both tourists and locals.

The cemetery over which she stands guard, wings unfurled and right arm extended, is atop a small rise in the midst of a soybean field along State Road 135 South. A narrow path leads through the field to the graveyard and its angel.

Two notable **covered bridges** can be seen in Jackson County. Both of them span the East Fork of White River. To view what's billed as one of the longest covered bridges in the world, head east from Medora for 1 mile on State Road 235. The 434-foot-long span, built in 1875, is certainly the longest in Indiana. It carried traffic across the river until 1974, when it was bypassed by a new bridge. Sadly, the old **Medora Bridge** is slowly falling into decay—the cost to preserve it has thus far been out of reach.

The **Shieldstown Covered Bridge,** constructed in 1876, is 231 feet long. To visit it, go southwest from Seymour on US 50 for about 6½ miles, then turn northwest onto a country road leading to Crane Hill and proceed about 1 mile; look for signs along the way.

A third bridge, the 325-foot-long **Bell's Ford Bridge,** recently collapsed into the White River, a gradual process that culminateed in 2006. It was the only triple-burr-arch covered bridge in Indiana and the only known Post truss bridge in existence anywhere. Erected in 1869, the Post truss represented a period when bridges were evolving from all-wood into all-metal or concrete structures. Its sides and floor featured iron rods and straps covered with wood. Funds are being raised to restore it. The bridge was located on State Road 258, 3 miles west of Seymour.

For additional information about the county's bridges, write or call the Jackson County Visitor and Convention Bureau, Tanger Outlet Center, 357 Tanger Boulevard, Suite 231, Seymour 47274; (812) 524–1914 or (888) 524–1914. You might want to also ask for information about the county's three round barns.

When rock star John Mellencamp penned his popular song "Small Town," he was describing his hometown of **Seymour.** Tourism officials in this still-small community say that not a day goes by that they don't receive inquiries about John, so they've created a brochure titled **John Mellencamp's Seymour and Jackson County,** which includes fourteen stops on a self-guided tour of landmarks associated with the town's most famous native son. The brochures are available at various businesses around town and at the Jackson County Visitor and Convention Bureau (see previous paragraph for contact information).

One of the stops is the ***Southern Indiana Center for the Arts (SICA),*** home to the only permanent exhibit of John's oil paintings. John comes by his artistic ability naturally. He was exposed to art throughout his life because his mother, Marilyn, is a painter; her paintings are also displayed at the center. A garden on the grounds is dedicated to the memory of John's grandmother, Laura. There's also a crafts barn with a resident potter who helps visitors take a turn on the pottery wheel.

SICA's newest attraction is the ***Conner Museum of Antique Printing.*** A working print shop that employs period presses from the 1800s, the museum offers a hands-on history lesson on printing. Visitors can feel different types of papers and take home examples of type. Special tours can be arranged. Admission is free. SICA is located at 2001 North Ewing Street; (812) 522–2278. Open noon to 5:00 P.M. Tuesday through Saturday or by appointment; closed major winter holidays.

Wildlife lovers will want to stop at ***Muscatatuck National Wildlife Refuge,*** located 3 miles east of Seymour on the south side of US 50. Covering more than 7,700 acres, it was established primarily as a sanctuary for wood ducks. Each spring and fall thousands of migrating waterfowl pause to rest on the open water and are occasionally joined by flocks of sandhill cranes. White-tailed deer and wild turkeys make their homes here all year long. Once extinct in Indiana, the bald eagle has begun returning to the Hoosier state; this majestic bird can occasionally be seen nesting here. Rare whooping cranes pass over and sometimes pause for a bit during fall and spring migrations between Wisconsin and Florida. The refuge is open daily year-round, from dawn to dusk; there's a nominal admission fee. Write or call the Muscatatuck National Wildlife Refuge, 12985 East US 50, Seymour 47274; (812) 522–4352.

Jefferson County

The late Charles Kuralt once called ***Madison*** the most beautiful river town in America. The curator of a Michigan museum, when he first saw Madison, said, "Put a fence around the entire town and don't let anyone touch anything in it!" During World War II the Office of War Information selected Madison as the "typical American town" and made movies of it in thirty-two languages to distribute around the world to remind our troops what they were fighting for. *Life* magazine chose Madison as the most pleasant small town in the country in which to live. Its nineteenth-century architecture, a mix of several styles, has been praised as the most beautiful in the Midwest, and its setting on the banks of the Ohio River, against a backdrop of wooded hills and limestone bluffs, is equally lovely. In 2006, the entire town was designated a National Historic Landmark. Obviously, if you're going to tour Indiana, Madison is one place you shouldn't miss.

Once Madison was a thriving river port and the largest town in the state. When railroads arrived on the scene, the river traffic departed, and Madison, in keeping with the times, built its own railroad. What no one foresaw was that nearly everyone would get on the train and leave town. For many years no one came to replace the populace that had moved on, and 133 blocks of buildings thus survived an era when it was fashionable to tear down anything old and replace it with something new in the name of progress. It is this legacy of architectural splendor that can be seen today.

The most notable building is the *Lanier Mansion* at 511 West First Street, a palatial home built in the 1840s for about $50,000—quite a chunk of money in those days. Its owner, James Lanier, was an astute banker whose loans to the state government during the Civil War helped Indiana avert bankruptcy. Facing a broad lawn that rambles down to the Ohio River, the Lanier Mansion is an outstanding example of the Greek Revival style. Its two-story portico is supported by tall Corinthian columns and hemmed in by wrought-iron grillwork. Inside, a spiral staircase climbs three stories, unsupported except by its own thrust, and each of the rooms is decorated with period furniture and accessories. Now a state historic site, the five-acre estate is open free of charge year-round. Hours are 10:00 A.M. to 5:00 P.M. Tuesday through Saturday and on Monday holidays, and 1:00 to 5:00 P.M. on Sunday mid-April to mid-November; 10:00 A.M. to 5:00 P.M. Saturday, 1:00 to 5:00 P.M. Sunday, and by appointment the rest of the year. Closed Easter, Thanksgiving, December 24 and 25, and January 1; (812) 265–3526.

Among the other attractions in Madison's historic district are the *office and private hospital of Dr. William Hutchings,* with all the original medications and possessions of the late-nineteenth-century doctor still intact; a restored *pioneer garden* with vintage roses and other period plantings; and the *Francis Costigan House,* home of the architect who designed Lanier Mansion. The restored *Schroeder Saddletree Factory* at 106 Milton Street, a living museum of industry complete with operable antique machinery, is the only museum in the country that explores the saddletree maker's craft. Everywhere in Madison you'll see elaborate ornamental ironwork reminiscent of New Orleans but forged locally (as was much of New Orleans's ironwork). *"Little Jimmy,"* a locally famous weathervane, sits atop the firehouse bell tower.

Maps and guides for walking tours are available from the Madison Area Convention and Visitors Bureau at 601 West First Street; (812) 265–2956 or (800) 559–2956.

At the **Gatehouse Museum** on the grounds of Madison State Hospital, you can see artifacts and exhibits that trace changes in the treatment of mental illness. The hospital, which opened in 1910 as a treatment center for mental patients, is located at 711 Green Road. The museum is open 10:00 A.M. to 4:00 P.M. Thursday through Saturday from late April through mid-November; there's a nominal admission fee. For more information contact the Jefferson County Historical Society, 615 West First Street, Madison; (812) 265–2335.

Railroad buffs will want to take a look at one of the world's steepest noncog train tracks. Cut through limestone bluffs in 1835, the track rises 413 feet in elevation in little more than a mile. Eight-horse teams drew the first trains up the incline but were eventually replaced by a wood-burning steam engine. The tracks can be viewed from State Road 56 at the west edge of town.

Not far west of Madison via State Road 56 you can stay at the **Clifty Inn** at Clifty Falls State Park. It features guest rooms for $74 to $167 per night for two; some rooms have private balconies that overlook the Ohio River valley. The dining room serves three meals a day for reasonable rates. Write Clifty Inn, P.O. Box 387, Madison 47250; call (812) 265–4135 or (877) 925–4389.

Noted for its natural beauty, **Clifty Falls State Park** sprawls over 1,360 hilly acres. The prettiest area, **Clifty Canyon State Nature Preserve,** is accessible only on foot. The great boulder-strewn canyon is so deep that sunlight can penetrate it only at high noon. Mosses, lichens, and ferns cling to the precipitous cliffs along Clifty Creek. In the spring, when the water is running fast, there are spectacular waterfalls; Big Clifty Falls, the granddaddy of them all, drops 60 feet. The park also offers an Olympic-size swimming pool, a modern campground, a nature center, an exercise trail, and breathtaking views from atop a 400-foot bluff. Nominal admission fee. Write or call Clifty Falls State Park, 1501 Green Road, Madison 47250; (812) 273–8885.

Canaan's annual Fall Festival, held the second weekend in September, features a potpourri of such events as a frog-jumping contest, a bucksaw woodcutting contest, a greased-pole climbing contest, and the Chief White Eye painting contest. It is the unique **Pony Express Run,** however, that has made the festival famous far and wide. Mail is specially stamped at Canaan, packed in authentic pony express mailbags on loan from the Smithsonian Institution in Washington, D.C., and delivered to the Madison post office by a rider on horseback. For further information write or call the Jefferson County Convention and Visitors Bureau, 601 West First Street, Madison 47250; (812) 265–2956 or (800) 559–2956.

For years few people knew the story behind the three-story stone structure that sits atop a hill in rural Jefferson County. When the building was first erected by abolitionists in 1848, it was known as **Eleutherian College,** and what went on there was illegal.

The educational institution was quietly set up in the rural community of Lancaster to offer college-level courses to all, regardless of race or gender. As such, it was the first school in Indiana to offer a higher education to African Americans. The name it was given attested to its purpose. *Eleutherian* is a Greek word meaning "freedom and equality."

After falling into a period of decay, Historic Eleutherian College, Inc., was formed as a nonprofit organization to purchase and restore the structure and to research its history. Remnants of cupboards and benches remained, along with a couple of long-abandoned pianos, but a cast-iron bell in the belfry rang as true as the first day it was placed there. One bit of lore claims that two of the children born to Thomas Jefferson and Sally Hemmings attended school here. An important first step in the preservation effort was to have the college designated a National Historic Landmark, an honor that was bestowed upon it at a dedication ceremony in October 1997. A visitor center features exhibits depicting the history of the area's ties to the Underground Railroad.

Eleutherian is located at 6927 West State Road 250, about 10 miles northwest of Madison. Call (812) 273–9434 for hours or to make an appointment for a guided tour. A donation is required for admission.

Jennings County

Each weekend from mid-April to mid-December, visitors trek to tiny **Commiskey** to enjoy the pleasures of **Stream Cliff,** Indiana's oldest herb farm. They come to wander through the flower gardens or to enjoy the salads, sandwiches, and teas served at the Twigs & Sprigs Tearoom. They browse through the three arts-and-crafts shops to the accompaniment of dulcimer music. They sit beneath a shaded arbor or watch the goldfish glide by in the farm's two ponds. If they're so inclined and register in advance, they can take one of the many classes offered here. Various experts demonstrate such things as the uses of different herbs and how to create craft items. Whatever you choose to do, you will find a quiet and serene retreat in which to do it. Open 10:00 A.M. to 4:00 P.M. Wednesday through Saturday and noon to 4:00 P.M. Sunday in warm weather months. Located at 8225 South County Road 90 West; (812) 346–5859.

Every Labor Day weekend for more than forty years, the population of **Vernon** swells from 300 to 30,300. That's when the Jennings County Historical Society holds its annual **Antiques, Collectibles, Crafts, and Farmers' Mar-**

ket. Actually, it's one huge yard sale, and word has gotten around. Dealers and shoppers alike come from more than 1,000 miles away to sell or shop from sunrise to sunset. If time permits, visitors can explore the town of Vernon itself. It is rich in history and has preserved that history well. For additional information call the Jennings County Visitors Center at (812) 346–4865 or (800) 928–3667.

trivia

The late President Richard Milhous Nixon had deep roots in Jennings County. His mother, Hannah Milhous Nixon, and his cousin, noted novelist Jessamyn West, were both born near Butlerville.

Ohio County

In the small Ohio River community of **Rising Sun,** you can visit **Harps on Main** and watch as William Rees and his sons Bryant and Garen design and construct fine hardwood harps. Mr. Rees, a nationally known harp builder who makes harps used by Grammy-winning harpists, also is the inventor of the Harpsicle, a smaller, more affordable, lighter-weight harp that sounds full-sized. He, his wife, Pamela, and his sons moved to Rising Sun from California a few years back, lured by the town's charm and its growing reputation as an arts center. You can also purchase Celtic music, jewelry, and other gift items here. Harps on Main is located at 222 Main Street. Open 10:00 A.M. to 5:00 P.M. Monday through Saturday and sometimes from 11:00 A.M. to 2:00 P.M. on Sunday; call (812) 438–3032 or visit www.tradionalharps.com.

Harps on Main is also a concert venue. Concerts featuring a variety of music are held in a 250-seat theater at 7:00 P.M. and 8:15 P.M. on the first Saturday of every month, except January; a nominal admission fee is charged.

Ripley County

Many a visitor, while traveling through the small town of **Versailles,** has stopped to stare in wonderment at the unusual looking church on the corner of Tyson and Adams Streets. Known officially as the **Tyson United Methodist Church** and unofficially as the Tyson Temple, it is a continuous flow of rounded corners, arches, columns, windows, and roof lines. Its striking spire is a rounded, inverted cone of openwork aluminum. Inside, the altar is framed by columns that duplicate those in the Taj Mahal. The rounded ceiling above the pews is painted with the stars and constellations that appear over Indiana in October. To enhance the effect of a nighttime sky, the ceiling is illuminated by light reflected from wall fixtures. The dome over the choir loft is covered with gold leaf from Germany. Pulpit furnishings come from Italy, and the windows are from Belgium. The grand but small Tyson Church (it seats only 200 people) draws visitors from across the country. Free tours are offered by appointment; call (812) 689–6976.

The tiny town of **Milan** (population 1,861) is arguably the sports mecca of Indiana. In 1954 its high school basketball team, playing in what was then a single-class state championship tournament, defeated a mighty Muncie Central team 32-30 when Bobby Plump sank a last-minute jump shot. Milan walked away with the championship and walked into sports history. In 1999 that team, whose story inspired the movie *Hoosiers,* was named the twelfth greatest team of the last century by *Sports Illustrated.* In 2004 *USA Today* referred to the game as "the most legendary upset in American high school sports history." Also in 2004, *Hoosiers* was voted the top sports movie of the last twenty-five years for the first time by the viewers of ESPN, cable television's sports channel, and it remains at the top of that list today. Perhaps the greatest award bestowed upon the movie, however, was its listing by the Library of Congress as an American icon, an honor bestowed upon only a few movies.

The David-over-Goliath victory is still referred to as the Milan Miracle by basketball fans everywhere, and the town is honoring its heroes by establishing the **Milan '54 Museum.** Visitors will see such memorabilia as photos of the players (then and now), most of their black-and-gold letter jackets, and an autographed hunk of the old maple gym floor on which the championship game was played. A blackboard with a diagram of Bobby Plump's final shot stands in a corner. Other exhibits include twelve lockers decorated with items from each player, Bobby Plump's satin warm-ups, Coach Marvin Wood's good-luck ties, an Indiana All-Star jersey, and hundreds of other items, such as posters, newspaper stories, and pictures.

Artifacts are still being collected, and an empty building has been purchased for the museum. In the meantime the exhibits can be seen at the **Milan Station Antique Shop** at 113 West Carr Street. The shop is open 10:00 A.M. to 4:00 P.M. Thursday through Saturday and noon to 4:00 P.M. Sunday year-round; closed major holidays. Call (812) 654–2772.

Shop owner Roselyn McKittrick says that Milan has thousands of visitors each year, all lured by the feel-good story of the scrappy little team that pulled off the biggest upset in Indiana basketball history. They visit both her shop and Milan High School, where a display case holds the 1954 game ball and the championship trophy.

In **Batesville** you can enter the old-world atmosphere of the **Sherman House** and enjoy some of the tastiest food in southern Indiana. Diners can select one of twenty moderately priced entrees or the specialty of the day, but fresh Maine lobster from the restaurant's tank, chateaubriand, veal cordon bleu, New York sirloin steaks, and Hoosier-fried chicken are among the longtime favorites. The Sherman House also offers overnight accommodations at a rate of $65 to $85 for two. Although the inn has undergone several renovations since opening in 1852, the 30-inch-square, 90-foot-long yellow poplar timbers used in the original structure are still in place and in perfect condition. Restaurant open 6:30 A.M. to 8:45 P.M. Monday through Thursday, 6:30 A.M. to 9:45 P.M. Friday and Saturday, and 6:30 A.M. to 7:55 P.M. Sunday; closed Christmas and New Year's; reservations recommended. Located at 35 South Main Street (State Road 229); (812) 934–2407 or (800) 445–4939.

trivia

Batesville is the Casket Capital of the World. The origins of the Batesville Casket Company date back to the nineteenth century, when the area was forested with an abundance of oak, cherry, and walnut trees.

When the late Carl Dyer moved to **Friendship** in 1982, he thought he was retiring from a long career of moccasin making, but relentless customers who demanded his products drew him back into the business. He also discovered that he loved his craft too much to give it up.

Dyer never advertised his mostly mail-order business—he didn't have to. Even people from abroad somehow obtained his phone number and called to place their orders.

The son of an accomplished bootmaker (his father crafted the aviation boots that Charles Lindbergh wore on his historic flight across the Atlantic), Dyer learned his trade early. Today, although Dyer himself is gone, the business, known as **Carl Dyer's Original Moccasins,** continues to produce several thousand pairs of handmade moccasins in eight different styles each year. The double-soled, heavy leather, waterproof moccasins range in price from approximately $165 to $396.

Customers include celebrities and *Fortune* 500 company executives, all of whom rave about the molded-to-your-feet comfort. Interestingly, one order was from Charles Lindbergh's grandson, who was unaware that he was ordering his moccasins from the same family that had made his grandfather's boots.

The shop is located at 5961 East State Road 62. Because hours vary, call before visiting; (812) 667–5442. You can also visit online at www.carldyers.com.

Wayne County

Every state has one, and in Indiana it's in Wayne County. The distinguished (at least to Hoosiers) spot sits in the middle of a bean field and is marked by a pile of rocks with a stick in it. Officially known as *Hoosier Hill,* it soars to 1,257 feet above sea level and is the highest point in Indiana.

It's a lonely site. In a good year, it lures about 200 visitors from around the country. Many are members of the National Highpointers Club, a group dedicated to visiting the highest point in each of the United States.

The current high point has not always been the highest point in Indiana. Originally that honor belonged to a spot approximately 200 yards to the southwest. But when that spot was resurveyed by satellite a decade or so ago, it was discovered that the original high point had shrunk. The popular belief is that it was done in by the repeated attacks of a manure spreader. That fate will not soon befall the current high point. It was purchased in 1982 by Kim Goble, a resident of nearby Richmond, so that its unique status could be preserved. For additional information write or call Ms. Goble at 3501 National Road West, Richmond 47374; (765) 966–5674.

Getting to Hoosier Hill is an adventure in itself. The noted landmark is located in the northeastern corner of Wayne County, not far from the small town of Bethel. From Bethel, go north on State Road 227 for about 1¼ miles to Randolph County Line Road (also known as Bethel Road) and turn west. Go west 1 mile and turn south onto Elliot Road. Proceed about 1¼ mile to an access road on the west. Park on the access road, climb over the adjacent fence on a stile provided by some Highpointers Club members, and walk about 100 feet along a rock-lined path to the top of the hill. There you'll find a picnic table and a sign that identifies this as Indiana's Highpoint. For additional information write or call the Richmond/Wayne County Convention and Tourism Bureau, 5701 National Road East, Richmond; (765) 935–8687 or (800) 828–8414.

trivia

The first newspaper in Rushville, the *Dog-Fennel Gazette,* was reportedly printed on one side of a single sheet of paper. When subscribers finished reading it, they returned the paper to the Gazette's office so that the next issue could be printed on the blank side.

Although it may seem an unlikely location for such an enterprise, *Richmond* boasts one of the largest rose-growing industries in the world. *Hill Floral Products, Inc.,* pioneers in greenhouse rose growing since 1881, annually ships more than thirty million cut roses to midwestern and southern states. The famed American Beauty Rose was developed here, and new hybrids continue to be produced each year. Free tours are conducted during the annual Richmond Area Rose Festival each June; free tours for groups of ten or more are available year-round by appointment. Located at 2117 Peacock Road; call (765) 962–2920.

The luxurious *Hill Memorial Rose Garden* in Glen Miller Park, which displays more than 1,600 rose-bushes, was established in tribute to the local flower industry. Located at 2500 National Road East, the park is also the site of the All-America Rose Garden, the German Friendship Garden, and a small zoo. Peak blooming periods are June and September. Admission is free; the park is open 6:00 A.M. to 11:00 P.M. daily. Call (765) 962–1511, (765) 935–8687, or (800) 828–8414.

At the *Hayes Regional Arboretum,* a 355-acre botanical preserve, you can view regional plant species—all labeled—on a 3½-mile auto tour. Also on the grounds are Indiana's first solar-heated greenhouse, a fern garden, a wild bird sanctuary, 10 miles of hiking trails (one of which passes an Indian mound), and a nature center housed in a barn close to two centuries old, where a telephone line permits you to eavesdrop on a colony of bees busily at work making honey. The arboretum is open 9:00 A.M. to 5:00 P.M. Tuesday through Saturday, March through October; open only for special events November through February. The nature center is open 9:00 A.M. to 5:00 P.M. Tuesday through Saturday and 1:00 to 5:00 P.M. Sunday, April through November. The arboretum is closed major winter holidays. Admission is free. Write or call Hayes Regional Arboretum, 801 Elks Road, Richmond 47374; (765) 962–3745.

Following a disastrous gas explosion and fire in 1968 that destroyed much of the downtown business district, Richmond covered its physical scars by building an unusual *Downtown Promenade.* The 5 blocks of flowing fountains, soft music, and unique specialty stores have been nationally acclaimed for their beauty. You'll find the promenade on Main Street between Fifth and Tenth Streets; (765) 962–8151.

The *Wayne County Historical Museum,* not far from the promenade area, is generally recognized as one of the best county museums in the state. Its diverse collection ranges from vintage cars made in Richmond to a Japanese samurai warrior's uniform, from a nineteenth-century general store to a 3,000-year-old Egyptian mummy (X-rays of the mummy taken by two local physicians can be seen by visitors). Open 10:00 A.M. to 4:00 P.M. Tuesday through Friday and 1:00 to 4:00 P.M. Saturday and Sunday, April through October; 10:00 A.M. to 4:00 P.M. Tuesday through Friday and 1:00 to 4:00 P.M. Saturday the rest of the year; closed major holidays. There's a nominal admission fee. Write or call the Wayne County Historical Museum, 1150 North A Street, Richmond 47374; (765) 962–5756.

All That Jazz

The sounds emanating from the small town of Richmond in the 1920s were some of the sweetest on earth. Musicians from all over the country came here during that decade to a tiny recording studio perched on the banks of the Whitewater River.

Our country was in the throes of the Jazz Age then, and many now-legendary jazz artists signed their first recording contracts at Gennett Studios. Among them were Fred "Jelly Roll" Morton, Bix Beiderbecke (his Rhythm Jugglers featured Tommy Dorsey on the trombone), King Oliver, Duke Ellington, and the incomparable Louis Armstrong.

Hoagy Carmichael made the first recording of *Stardust* here, but it was nearly lost to posterity when a Gennett employee almost threw it in the trash. Thankfully, the error was caught in time. Although that original version was recorded in an upbeat dance tempo, *Stardust* has evolved into a more mellow rendition that the world now regards as one of the most beautiful love songs ever written.

Blues musicians also recorded at Gennett, and the recordings of a young Gene Autry introduced old-time country music to the world. Billy Sunday, a popular preacher of the day, and poet James Whitcomb Riley, a native Hoosier, added the spoken word to Gennett's repertoire. The company also produced copies of William Jennings Bryan's famous 1896 "Cross of Gold" speech; they were taken to Tennessee and sold outside the courthouse where Bryan was participating in the 1925 Scopes "monkey" trial.

From 1916 to 1934 the studio produced thousands of recordings, featuring any recorded sound that had or could have a market. All this was accomplished despite the fact that the studio had no electricity until 1926 and had to halt recording every time a train came by on the adjacent railroad track.

Unfortunately, like many other businesses of the day, the Gennett label was done in by the Great Depression, but Richmond has not forgotten its rich heritage as the "cradle of recorded jazz." Visitors can currently learn more about the Gennett studio at the Wayne County Historical Museum, and plans are under way for a new museum devoted solely to the history of the "label of legends."

Although every other sport takes a backseat to basketball in Indiana, the state has also produced some football heroes. They're all honored in the *Indiana Football Hall of Fame,* located at 815 North A Street. Among the inductees are O. J. Simpson, Bart Starr, and Jim Thorpe, all of whom once played football in the Hoosier State; Knute Rockne, the legendary coach of Notre Dame; Tom Harmon (the father of actor Mark Harmon), who is the only Indiana native to ever have won the Heisman Trophy; and Weeb Ewbank, a local great who coached the Baltimore Colts and New York Jets. Tony Hulman, whose name is synonymous with the Indianapolis 500, is remembered here as an All-American end on the undefeated Yale University team of 1923. Open 10:00 A.M. to 4:00 P.M. Monday through Friday and weekends by appointment, May through September, and from 10:00 A.M. to 2:00 P.M. the rest of the year; closed holidays. There's a nominal admission fee; (765) 966–2235.

Earlham College, located on the south side of U.S. Highway 40 just west of downtown Richmond, is the home of the *Joseph Moore Museum of Natural History.* Such

trivia

The Ohio County Courthouse in Rising Sun, built in 1845, is the oldest Indiana courthouse in continuous use.

wonders as a prehistoric mastodon, an extinct giant beaver, and authentic *Allosaurus* skeletons are displayed, along with Ordovician fossils, arthropods, live snakes, Indiana birds of prey, and a mummy. The free museum is open from 1:00 to 5:00 P.M. Monday, Wednesday, and Friday, mid-September through mid-December and mid-January through April; also open 1:00 to 5:00 P.M. Sunday year-round and other times by appointment. Admission is free, but donations are appreciated. Write or call Earlham College, 801 West National Road (US 40), Richmond 47374; (765) 983–1303 or (765) 983–1200.

Whitewater Gorge Park, which borders the Whitewater River in the heart of Richmond, is one of only two known places in the United States where a unique type of limestone is exposed to the surface. Geologists, paleontologists, and amateur collectors have been coming to this site for more than a century to examine the abundance of fossils in the gorge's 425-million-year-old rock formations. The park also contains an Audubon bird sanctuary, Thistlethwaite Falls, Middlefork Reservoir, and some scenic fossil collection sites. A 3½-mile-long footpath leads through the gorge, but it's necessary to hike the entire length of it. Trail maps and additional information can be obtained by contacting the Richmond Parks and Recreation Department, Administration Office, 50 North Fifth Street, Richmond 47374; (765) 983–7275; or the Richmond/Wayne County Convention and Tourism Bureau, 5701 National Road East, Richmond 47374; (765) 935–8687 or (800) 828–8414.

Centerville, about 5 miles west of Richmond on US 40, claims to have the greatest concentration of antiques shops in the United States. *Webb's Antique Mall* alone covers approximately two acres and boasts nearly 500 dealers. The mall is open 8:00 A.M. to 6:00 P.M. daily March through November and 9:00 A.M. to 4:00 P.M. daily December through February. Contact the mall's office at 200 West Union Street in Centerville; (765) 855–5551.

Fountain City is the home of the *Levi Coffin House,* known as "the Grand Central Station of the Underground Railroad." Levi and Catharine Coffin, Quakers

trivia

Indiana was the first state in the country to commercially produce wine. The industry began in Vevay in 1802.

who were opposed to slavery, opened their 1839 Federal-style home to approximately 2,000 fugitive black slaves during the Civil War era. You may know the Coffins better as Simeon and Rachel Halliday, characters in *Uncle Tom's Cabin*. Eliza Harris, the heroine of the same book, was a refugee who stayed with the Coffins for several days. The house, located at 113 U.S. Highway 27 North, is open to the public from 1:00 to 4:00 P.M. Tuesday through Saturday, June through August and 1:00 to 4:00 P.M. Saturday only, September through October; closed July 4; there's a nominal admission fee. For more information write the Levi Coffin House State Historic Site, P.O. Box 77, Fountain City 47341; call (765) 847–2432 or (765) 847–2076; or visit www .waynenet.org/nonprofit/coffin.htm.

Since Guy Welliver bought his **Hagerstown** restaurant in the 1940s, he has increased its seating capacity from about fifty to 500—and still customers stand in line. They do so patiently, secure in the knowledge that what awaits them at **Welliver's Smorgasbord** is well worth it. Regular patrons include the 2,000 or so lucky people who live in Hagerstown and don't have far to go, as well as diners from all over central Indiana and neighboring Ohio. What lures them is the specialty of the house—an elaborate but moderately priced buffet that features steamed shrimp in all-you-can-eat quantities. The homemade bread and salad bar are also highly recommended. Welliver's Smorgasbord, located at 40 East Main Street, is open 5:00 to 8:00 P.M. Thursday, 5:00 to 8:30 P.M. Friday, 4:00 to 9:00 P.M. Saturday, and noon to 7:00 P.M. Sunday (shrimp only after 4:00 P.M. on Sunday); (765) 489–4131; www.wellivers.com.

Abbott's Candy Shop, the oldest continuously operating business in Hagerstown (circa 1890), uses old family recipes to turn out a cornucopia of confections that are sold at its store at 48 East Walnut Street and by mail throughout the country. Its specialty and most popular sweet is the caramel, but many other varieties await visitors, too. Open 9:00 A.M. to 5:00 P.M. Monday through Friday; also open 9:00 A.M. to 5:00 P.M. Saturday from Thanksgiving to Christmas Eve. Call (765) 489–4442 to arrange a free tour (yes, free samples *are* included).

The redbrick storefront in **Dublin** gives little hint of the treasure trove inside. Owner Patricia McDaniel is an antiques dealer extraordinaire. She is also one of Hollywood's aces-in-the-hole.

It all began in 1987, when movie director John Sayles needed some props for *Eight Men Out,* a baseball movie that was filmed partly in Indiana. McDaniel was able to supply them; the word spread, and Hollywood has beat a path to her door ever since. Her period props, many of them hard to find elsewhere, have appeared in about sixty major movies, including *Legends of the Fall, Avalon, This Boy's Life, A League of Their Own, Munich, The Good Shepherd,* and *Charlotte's Web.*

McDaniel's store is amazing to behold. Something appears to occupy every centimeter of shelf space and very nearly all of the floor space. Yet McDaniel knows her stock. She always knows *where* something is, even if she's not sure *what* it is. A case in point is an item called Stop and Go. She originally thought it was a laxative but later learned it was a vitamin.

McDaniel's shop, called ***Old Storefront Antiques,*** is located at 2191 East Cumberland Street. Store hours are by chance or appointment; for additional information call (765) 825–6295 or (765) 478–4809, or visit www.oldstore frontantiques.com.

McDaniel also conceived the idea of a ***Historic National Road Yard Sale.*** The first sale in 2003 included a portion of the National Road (also known as US 40) in Indiana. By 2006, it was such a success that the sale passed through six states (Maryland, West Virginia, Pennsylvania, Ohio, Indiana, and Illinois) and stretched more than 800 miles in length. The 2007 event will be held from May 30 through June 3 during daylight hours. McDaniel will be happy to provide details; her phone number and Web site appear in the previous paragraph. You can also obtain up-to-date information from the Historic National Road Association, P.O. Box 284, Cambridge City 47327; (765) 478–3172; www.indiananationalroad.org.

Places to Stay in Southeast Indiana

BETHLEHEM

Storyteller's Riverhouse Bed and Breakfast
101 Bell Street
(812) 293–3845
Moderate

BROOKVILLE

Four Governors Inn
1049 Main Street
(765) 647–6731
Moderate

The Hermitage Bed and Breakfast
650 East Eighth Street
(765) 647–5182 or
(877) 407–9198
Moderate

CENTERVILLE

Historic Lantz House Inn
214 West Main Street
(765) 855–2936 or
(800) 495–2689
Moderate

COLUMBUS

Country Chalet
624 North Hickory
Hills Drive
(812) 342–7806
Very expensive

Ruddick-Nugent House
1210 Sixteenth Street
(812) 379–1354 or
(800) 814–7478
Moderate

CONNERSVILLE

The Over House Bed and Breakfast
1826 Indiana Avenue
(765) 825–2371
Moderate

CORYDON

Kintner House Inn
101 South Capitol Avenue
(812) 738–2020
Inexpensive

GREENSBURG

Nana's House Bed and Breakfast
3126 East Base Road
(812) 663–6607 or
(877) 669–3870
Moderate

JEFFERSONVILLE

1877 House Country Inn
2408 Utica-Sellersburg Road
(812) 285–1877 or
(888) 284–1877
Moderate

Market Street Inn B&B
330 West Market Street
(812) 285–1877 or
(888) 284–1877
Moderate

The Old Bridge Inn Bed & Breakfast
131 West Chestnut Street
(812) 284–3580 or
(866) 284–3580
Moderate

KNIGHTSTOWN

Old Hoosier House
7601 South Greensboro Pike
(765) 345–2969
Moderate

LIBERTY

Liberty Motel
303 North Main Street
(785) 458–6894
Inexpensive

MADISON

Carriage House Bed and Breakfast
308 West Second Street
(812) 265–6892
Expensive

Schussler House Bed and Breakfast
514 Jefferson Street
(812) 273–2068 or
(800) 392–1931
Moderate

Vintage Views Inn
411 West First Street
(812) 265–6856 or
(888) 833–7378
Moderate

MAUCKPORT

High Ridge Log Cabin Rentals
9100 Cabin Lane Southwest
(812) 732–8802
Moderate

METAMORA

The Grapevine Inn
10083 Bridge Street
(765) 647–3738
Moderate

Thorpe House Country Inn
19049 Clayborne Street
P.O. Box 36
(765) 647–5425
Moderate

MILAN

Huntington at Hillbrook Farm
918 North County Road 450 East
(812) 654–2143 or
(888) 298–8855
Moderate

Milan Railroad Inn
Main and Carr Streets
(812) 654–2800 or
(800) 448–7405
Moderate

NEW ALBANY

Honeymoon Mansion B&B
1014 East Main Street
(812) 945–0312 or
(800) 759–7270
Moderate

NEW CASTLE

Mulberry Lane Inn
5256 North County Road 75 West
(765) 836–4500
Moderate

OSGOOD

Victorian Garden B&B
243 North Walnut Street
(812) 689–4469
Moderate

RICHMOND

Hilltop Hide-A-Way Log House
1088 Boston Township Line Road
(765) 935–5752
Moderate

Philip W. Smith Bed and Breakfast
2039 East Main Street
(765) 966–8972 or
(800) 966–8972
Moderate

RISING SUN

Mulberry Inn and Gardens
118 South Mulberry Street
(812) 438–2206 or
(800) 235–3097
Moderate

VEVAY

Rosemont Inn
806 West Market Street
(812) 427–3050
Moderate

Places to Eat in Southeast Indiana

AURORA

Applewood by the River
215 Judiciary Street
(812) 926–1166
Moderate
American

BROOKVILLE

Dairy Cottage Restaurant
1116 Main Street
(765) 647–5451
Inexpensive
Home cooking

Ye Olde Shack
Third and Main Streets
(765) 647–5571
Moderate
American

CENTERVILLE

Jag's Cafe
129 East Main Street
(765) 855–2282
Inexpensive
American

CLARKSVILLE

Mark's Feed Store
513 East State Road 131
(812) 285–1998
Inexpensive
Barbecue

Texas Roadhouse
201 East Lewis and
Clark Parkway
(812) 280–1103
Moderate
American

COLUMBUS

Grindstone Charley's
2607 Central Avenue
(812) 372–2532
Moderate
American

New Japan
3820 Twenty-fifth Street
(812) 372–1128
Moderate
Traditional Japanese

Smith's Row Restaurant
418 Fourth Street
(812) 373–9382
Expensive
American

FLOYDS KNOBS

RockWall
3426 Paoli Pike
(812) 948–1705
Moderate
Bistro/American

GREENSBURG

**Heritage Acres
Call-Ahead Restaurant**
(Reservations required)
5084 West State Road 46
(812) 663–1088 or
(888) 663–1088
Moderate
Home cooking

Storie's Restaurant
109 East Main Street
(812) 663–9948
Inexpensive
American

Trackside Cafe
533 West Main Street
(812) 663–9903
Inexpensive
American

GUILFORD

Chateau Pomije
25043 Jacobs Road
(812) 623–8004 or
(800) 791–9463
Moderate
French

JEFFERSONVILLE

Frank's Steak House
520 West Seventh Street
(812) 283–3383
Moderate
American

Mai's Thai Restaurant
1411 East Tenth Street
(812) 282–0198
Inexpensive
Thai

Rocky's Italian Grill
715 West Riverside Drive
(812) 282–3844
Moderate
Italian

LAWRENCEBURG

Whisky's
334 Front Street
(812) 537–4239
Moderate
American

MADISON

**Nex-Dor Restaurant
and Lounge**
Best Western Inn
700 Clifty Drive
(812) 273–5151
Moderate
American

Ovo Cafe
209 West Main Street
(812) 273–8808
Moderate
Italian

SOURCES FOR ADDITIONAL INFORMATION ABOUT SOUTHEAST INDIANA

Brookville/Franklin County Convention, Recreation, and Visitors Commission
813 Main Street
P.O. Box 97
Brookville 47012
(765) 647–6522 or (866) 647–6555

Clark/Floyd Counties Convention and Tourism Bureau
Southern Indiana Visitor Center
315 Southern Indiana Avenue
Jeffersonville 47130–3218
(812) 282–6654 or (800) 552–3842

Columbus/Bartholomew County Visitors Center
506 Fifth Street
P.O. Box 1589
Columbus 47202
(812) 378–2622 or (800) 468–6564

Connersville/Fayette County Tourism Bureau
115 East Sixth Street
Connersville 47331
(765) 825–2561

Dearborn County Convention, Visitor, and Tourism Bureau
320 Walnut Street
Lawrenceburg 47025
(812) 537–0814 or (800) 322–8198

Greensburg/Decatur County Visitor Center
232 North Franklin Street
P.O. Box 345
Greensburg 47240
(812) 222–8733 or (877) 883–5447

Harrison County Convention and Visitors Bureau
310 North Elm Street
Corydon 47112
(812) 738–2138 or (888) 738–2137

Henry County Convention and Visitors Bureau
2020 South Memorial Drive
Suite I
New Castle 47362
(765) 593–0764 or (800) 676–4302

Jackson County Visitor Center
357 Tanger Boulevard
Suite 231
(Tanger Outlet Center)
Seymour 47274
(812) 524–1914 or (888) 524–1914

Jennings County Visitors Center
325 North State Road 7 and State Road 3
P.O. Box 415
North Vernon 47282-0415
(812) 346–4865 or (800) 928–3667

Madison/Jefferson County Convention and Visitors Bureau
601 West First Street
Madison 47250
(812) 265–2956 or (800) 559–2956

Richmond/Wayne County Convention and Tourism Bureau
5701 National Road East
Richmond 47374
(765) 935–8687 or (800) 828–8414

Ripley County Tourism Bureau
102 North Main Street
P.O. Box 21
Versailles 47042
(812) 689–7431 or (888) RIPLEY4

Pine's
2700 Michigan Road
(812) 273–4645
Moderate
Home cooking

METAMORA

Hearthstone Restaurant
18149 U.S. Highway 52
(765) 647–5204
Inexpensive
Home cooking

Rileybrook Hall
16049 Duck Creek Road
(765) 647–3316 or
(800) 406–5169
Inexpensive
American

MILAN

Milan Railroad Inn
Main and Carr Streets
(812) 654–2800 or
(800) 448–7405
Moderate
American

The Reservation
1001 North Warpath Drive
(812) 654–2224
Inexpensive
American

Villa Milan Vineyard
7287 East County Road
50 North
(812) 654–3419
Inexpensive
Italian

NEW ALBANY

Ranch House
2612 Charlestown Road, #B
(812) 944–9199
Inexpensive
American

NORMAN

Hitching Post
5401 North O'Neal Street
(812) 995–8425
Inexpensive
American

NORTH VERNON

Joe's Pizza & Pickin' Parlor
41 North Madison Avenue
(812) 346–2238
Moderate
Pizza/sandwiches

OLDENBURG

Brau Haus
22170 Wasserstrasse
(Water Street)
(812) 934–4840
Inexpensive
German

Wagner's Village Inn
22171 Main Street
(812) 934–3854
Inexpensive
American

RICHMOND

**Country Rib Eye
Steakhouse**
725 Progress Drive
(765) 966–4902
Moderate
American

Jade House
4710 National Road East
(765) 935–4575
Inexpensive
Chinese

Olde Richmond Inn
138 South Fifth Street
(765) 962–2247
Moderate
American

SCOTTSBURG

Jeeves and Company
64 South Main Street
(812) 752–6559
Moderate
American

SEYMOUR

Larrison's Diner
200 South Chestnut Street
(812) 522–5523
Inexpensive
American

The Pines
4289 North U.S. Highway 31
(812) 522–4955
Moderate
Buffet/American

STARLIGHT

Stumler Restaurant
10924 Saint John's Road
(812) 923–3832
Inexpensive
Home cooking

VERNON

Log Cabin Inn
59 East State Road 3 and 7
(812) 346–7272
Inexpensive
American

VEVAY

The Ogle Haus
1013 West Main Street
(812) 427–2020
Expensive
German/American

Southwest Indiana

Generally described as the most beautiful part of the Hoosier State, southwest Indiana is filled with uninterrupted stretches of dense forests, jutting cliffs, and clear streams. Scenic highways wind through hills lush with greenery in the spring and summer and blazing with color in the fall. Where the Wabash River, which forms much of the state's western border, meets the Ohio River, which bounds the state on the south, there are misty bayous and cypress swamps reminiscent of the Deep South.

The banks of the Ohio River are dotted with small towns in which historic sites and nineteenth-century architecture have been carefully preserved. Beneath the earth's surface lies Indiana's world-famous limestone belt, laid down by an ancient sea 300 million years ago.

This is the land that shaped a young Abraham Lincoln. It is the place the founders of New Harmony viewed as Utopia. In the 1920s and 1930s, movie stars and gangsters came here to relax and rejuvenate themselves in the waters of the region's abundant mineral springs. It is still a place where life plays out in its own sweet time, a place that invites the visitor to explore and discover.

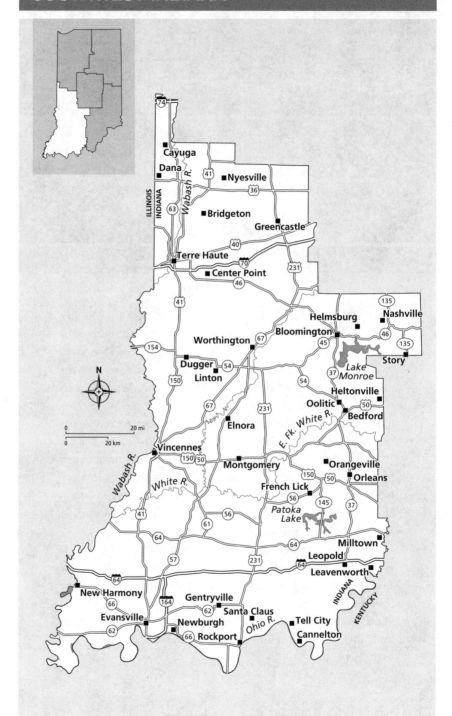

Brown County

Things don't change much in Brown County. The population today is nearly the same as it was in 1880. Each morning the mists rise from hills still draped with forests. Log cabins, hemmed in by split-rail fences, nestle in isolated hollows. Like as not there's a woodpile in the yard, and on cool days fingers of wood smoke spiral up from stone chimneys. Narrow, twisting country roads lead to picturesque places with picturesque names—Gnaw Bone, Bean Blossom, Scarce O'Fat Ridge, Bear Wallow Hill, Milk-Sick Bottoms, Slippery Elm Chute Road, and Booger Holler. No billboards mar your view along the way—

AUTHOR'S FAVORITE ATTRACTIONS/EVENTS IN SOUTHWEST INDIANA

Antique Auto Hill Climb
Newport; October
(765) 492–4220

Bluegrass Hall of Fame and Uncle Pen Day Festival
Bean Blossom; September
(812) 988–6422 or (800) 414–4677

Brown County State Park
Nashville
(812) 988–6406

Gasthof Amish Village
Montgomery
(812) 486–3977 or (800) 225–8655
www.gasthofamishvillage.com

Lilly Library of Rare Books and Manuscripts
Indiana University, Bloomington
(812) 855–2452;
www.indiana.edu/~liblilly

Limestone Heritage Festival
Bedford; June and July
(812) 849–1090 or (800) 798–0769

Little Italy Festival
Clinton; September
(765) 832–7254

New Harmony (entire town)
(812) 682–4488 or (800) 231–2168

Parke County Covered Bridge Festival
Rockville; October
(765) 569–5226

Red Skelton Festival
Vincennes; June
(812) 886–0400 or (800) 886–6443

Spirit of Vincennes Rendezvous
Vincennes; May
(812) 886–0400 or (800) 886–6443

Tulip Trestle
near Solsberry
(812) 384–8995

Turkey Trot Festival
Montgomery; September
(812) 486–3649

West Baden Springs National Historic Landmark
West Baden
(812) 936–4034 or (800) 450–4534

Wyandotte Cave
Leavenworth
(812) 738–2782 or (888) 702–2837

they're not allowed in Brown County. No air pollution muddies the landscape and offends your nostrils—Brown County has no industry. And if you're in a hurry, you're out of luck—Brown County doesn't cater to people in a hurry.

trivia

Freshwater jellyfish are known to exist at twenty-five sites in Indiana. About the size of a nickel or dime, they are clear or translucent white and consist of more than 90 percent water. One of their known habitats is Yellowwood Lake, which lies within Yellowwood State Forest in Brown County.

Nashville, the county seat and largest town in the county, normally has a population of about 700 people, but on October weekends that figure swells to more than 100,000. Brown County is best known for its dazzling fall color. Most folks head for **Brown County State Park,** some 15,000 acres of natural beauty near Nashville. It regularly ranks as one of the top ten most visited parks in the nation—and the other nine are all *national* parks! **Yellowwood State Forest** in western Brown County and a portion of the southern part of the county offer equally spectacular and less-crowded panoramas.

In spring Brown County is glorious when its redbud and dogwood trees and myriad wildflowers are abloom. In summer the woods offer a cool green retreat, and for wintertime visitors there are cross-country ski trails.

Brown County first gained fame as a mecca for artists and craftspeople, who have been inspired by the peace and beauty of these hills since the 1870s. Today many open their studios to the public. The **Brown County Craft Gallery,** the **Brown County Art Barn,** and the **Brown County Art Gallery,** all in Nashville, are among the galleries that exhibit some of their works.

Nashville is the hub of activity in Brown County—a potpourri of some 300 shops, museums, and restaurants. Craftspeople make and sell quilts, pottery, wood carvings, metal sculptures, hand-carved candles, leather goods, silver and gold jewelry made to order, stained-glass wares, dollhouses, teddy bears, handblown art glass, dulcimers, and much more. At many shops you can watch the artisans at work. Each Saturday and Sunday in June, July, and September, the beautifully handcrafted **Melchior Marionettes** delight onlookers at an outdoor theater on South Van Buren Street; call (800) 849–4853 for schedule and ticket information.

With no chair more than ten rows from the stage, the **Brown County Playhouse** in the heart of Nashville doesn't have a bad seat in the house. This is Indiana's oldest professional stock theater; performers are from the Theatre and Drama Department at Indiana University in nearby Bloomington (see Monroe County). Actors Kevin Kline, Patricia Kalember, and Jonathan Banks, as well as the late Howard Ashman, the Academy Award–winning lyricist of the Disney films *Aladdin, Beauty and the Beast,* and *The Little Mermaid,* are just a few of the people who have honed their skills on this stage before going on to bigger things. Showtime is at 8:00 P.M., with nights of performance varying from Wednesday through Sunday during summer and fall months. For an exact schedule and other information, call the Indiana University Auditorium at (812) 855–1103. In season you can also write the Brown County Playhouse, P.O. Box 1187, Nashville 47448, or call (812) 988–2123 from 10:00 A.M. to 5:00 P.M. daily and from 10:00 A.M. to 8:30 P.M. on performance days.

A complex of authentic nineteenth-century buildings just northeast of the courthouse in Nashville is known collectively as the ***Brown County Historical Museum.*** Carding, spinning, and weaving are demonstrated in an old log barn. You'll also see a country doctor's office, a blacksmith's shop, and a log

ANNUAL EVENTS IN SOUTHWEST INDIANA

Chocolate Fest
Bloomington; February
(812) 332–9615

French Lick Springs Jazz Festival
French Lick; March
(800) 457–4042

Lotus Dickey Hometown Reunion
Paoli; June
(812) 723–4318 or (877) 422–9925

Shoals Catfish Festival
Shoals; July
(812) 247–2828

Jasper Strassenfest
Jasper; July/August
(812) 482–6866

Knox County Watermelon Festival
Vincennes; August
(812) 886–0400 or (800) 886–6443

Schweizer Fest
Tell City; August
(812) 547–7933 or (888) 343–6262

Amish Quilt Show and Auction
Cannelburg; Saturday on Labor Day weekend
(812) 486–3491 or (800) 449–5262

Herbstfest
Huntingburg; September
(812) 683–5699

Native American Days
Evansville; September
(812) 853–3956

Persimmon Festival
Mitchell; September
(812) 849–1090 or (800) 798–0769

Lotus World Music and Arts Festival
Bloomington; September/October
(812) 336–6599

cabin home, all complete with furnishings, and an unusual log jail that claims the distinction of being the only one in the state that ever permitted a prisoner to be his own keeper. While serving a sentence for bootlegging, the prisoner went wherever he wanted to during the day, locked himself up at night, acted as a guide for tourists, and once aided the sheriff in making an arrest. For a nominal admission fee, the buildings can be toured from 1:00 to 5:00 P.M. Saturday, Sunday, and holidays, May through October. They can be viewed free of charge at all times, however, from the outside.

One of the newest experiences in Brown County is a tour of a sock factory. Visitors to *For Bare Feet* will see the entire process of how socks are made, from cones of yarn to the finished product. Owner Sharon Rivenbark started the factory to provide a job for her son Tim, who had a rare brain disease that forced him to drop out of college. Tim has since passed away, but the business that was founded for and with him in 1984 has flourished beyond anyone's expectations. What started as a small business has become a national success. Customers of For Bare Feet include national parks, resorts, sporting goods chains, department stores, college bookstores, and theme parks; special orders have even come from the White House and from NASA. The company is also a league-licensed producer of socks, headbands, and wristbands for the National Basketball Association, National Football League, National Hockey League, and Major League Baseball. Socks can be personalized or purchased ready-made in literally thousands of unique designs at one of two For Bare Feet shops in the town of Nashville; you'll find For Bare Feet Originals at 75 South Jefferson Street and For Bare Feet Too at 40 West Main Street. The factory is located in Helmsburg, which lies a few miles north of Nashville on State Road 45. Tour schedules vary according to the season, but they generally begin at 1:00 P.M. and last about one hour. The nominal admission fee includes a pair of socks. For additional information call (812) 988–2067 or visit www.forbarefeet.com.

To bluegrass music fans, the late Bill Monroe is the father of bluegrass and Bean Blossom is a bluegrass mecca. Monroe held annual festivals on his sprawling Bean Blossom property starting in the mid-1960s, making this the locale of the longest-running bluegrass festival in the country. The thousands of devotees who still come here from all over the country and beyond say the bluegrass festivals at the *Bill Monroe Memorial Music Park* have an ambience unlike any other in the world. When professional musicians aren't playing on stage, amateur musicians in the audience are playing in their own impromptu groups. It's a rare moment when there's no music to be heard anywhere. If you love the sound of bluegrass, there is no better place to be.

Most people stay on the festival grounds for the three or four days a festival is held. A campground on the property offers both modern and primitive campsites. Several rustic log cabins may be rented by advance reservation. In 1992 Monroe brought his extensive collection of bluegrass and country music memorabilia to Bean Blossom and opened the ***Bluegrass Hall of Fame and Museum.*** Monroe accumulated his collection throughout more than sixty years of entertaining.

One of the fourteen rooms in the 5,000-square-foot museum is filled with Bill Monroe's personal mementos, including items once owned by Johnny Cash, Dolly Parton, and Dottie West. On the grounds near the museum is a cabin that was moved here log by log from Nashville, Tennessee. Known as Uncle Pen's Cabin, it belonged to a relative who took young Bill Monroe into his home when Monroe's parents died. Fans will recognize the name from a song Monroe wrote about his uncle. (It was recorded by Ricky Skaggs and Porter Wagoner.)

Originally home to two annual bluegrass festivals, the park has expanded its offerings to include additional music festivals, a flea market (open weekends, holidays, and special events April through October), and a gift shop.

The park is located at 5163 State Road 135 North in Bean Blossom, about 5 miles north of Nashville. Open daily spring through fall; hours may vary. For additional information call (812) 988–6422 or (800) 414–4677, or visit www .beanblossom.com.

East of Nashville on State Road 46 is the northern entrance to Brown County State Park, accessible via Indiana's only divided, two-lane covered bridge (circa 1838). Enjoy 27 miles of scenic roads, approximately 6 miles of mountain-bike trails, hiking and bridle trails, a nature center, campgrounds (including one for horseback riders), an archery range, an Olympic-size swimming pool, a lodge with a restaurant, and rustic rental cabins. You can also climb the fire tower atop Weed Top Hill, the state's second highest point, for a panoramic view. A nature trail leads through ***Ogle Hollow State Nature Preserve,*** noteworthy for its rare yellowwood trees. Open year-round during daylight hours; there's a vehicle entrance fee April through October. Write or call Brown County State Park, P.O. Box 608, Nashville 47448; (812) 988–6406. For lodge and cabin reservations, write or call Abe Martin Lodge, P.O. Box 547, Nashville 47448; (812) 988–4418 or (877) 265–6343. You can also make reservations online at www.indianainns.com.

Continuing east from the park on State Road 46, you'll come to State Road 135, which leads south into a secluded and untrammeled part of Brown County. Follow State Road 135 to an area referred to locally as ***Stone Head,*** so called because of the unique monument by the side of the highway that serves as a road sign—a white stone head atop a stone pillar. Every once in a while a prankster makes off with the carving, but the persistent community has always managed to recover the monument.

OTHER ATTRACTIONS WORTH SEEING IN SOUTHWEST INDIANA

BLOOMINGTON

Indiana University Art Museum
Fine Arts Plaza
900 East Seventh Street
(812) 855-5445

EVANSVILLE

**Evansville Museum of
Arts and Science**
411 Southeast Riverside Drive
(812) 425-2406

FERDINAND

Monastery Immaculate Conception
802 East Tenth Street
(812) 367-1411

JASPER

Indiana Baseball Hall of Fame
Vincennes University
State Road 162 and College Avenue
(812) 482-2262 or (800) 968-4578

Saint Joseph Church
Thirteenth and Newton Streets
(812) 482-1805 or (800) 968-4578

NASHVILLE

Forth Dimension Hologram Museum
90 West Washington Street
(812) 988-8212

The Joybell Theatre
79 North Van Buren Street
(812) 988-2166 or (800) 462-1241

T. C. Steele State Historic Site
4220 T. C. Steele Road
(812) 988-2785

TERRE HAUTE

**Children's Science and
Technology Museum**
523 Wabash Avenue
(812) 235-5548

Clabber Girl Museum
900 Wabash Avenue
(812) 232-9446

Native American Museum
5170 East Poplar Drive
(812) 877-6007

Sheldon Swope Art Museum
25 South Seventh Street
(812) 238-1676

VINCENNES

Indiana Military Museum
2074 North Old Bruceville Road
(812) 882-8668

**Lincoln Memorial Bridge and
USS *Vincennes* Monument**
West Vigo Street at the Wabash River
(812) 886-0400 or (800) 886-6443

Proceed on State Road 135 to the tiny community of **Story.** Virtually unchanged since its founding in the 1850s, the peaceful hamlet exudes the charm of a long-ago Brown County whose rural serenity and beauty first lured artists and craftspeople to these forested hills. Here, amid a cluster of tumble-down buildings that bear mute testimony to old dreams, the **Story Inn** offers food and shelter so pleasing that the Indiana Division of Tourism bestowed its Best Bed-and-Breakfast in the State award on it. On the outside, the tin-faced, tin-roofed building resembles the general store it once was. On the inside, antiques and knickknacks line the walls of the dining room, and a potbellied stove stands ready to serve on cold winter days. The food, however, is pure gourmet. Such offerings as rabbit New Orleans, chicken Provençal, and Greek spinach pie appear on a menu that changes weekly but always features fresh fish and a pasta dish. No matter what entree you decide on, save room for dessert—the turtle cheesecake, with its chocolate graham cracker crust and thick caramel topping, is to die for. Guests can stay in one of the inn's upstairs bed-rooms or in one of the renovated village cottages nearby; a full country break-fast is included in the rates. All rooms have private baths and air-conditioning but no television or telephone. If you stay in the Garden Room and you're lucky (or unlucky, depending on your point of view), you may see the "Blue Lady," the Story Inn's resident ghost. The inn's gourmet restaurant serves three meals a day; breakfast and lunch are served from 8:00 A.M. to 2:00 P.M., and dinner is served from 5:00 to 9:00 P.M. Tuesday through Sunday; hours may vary from November through March. Prices are moderate to expensive. Advance reserva-tions are recommended for meals and are required for overnight accommoda-tions. The inn also sponsors many special events and concerts throughout the year. One of the more unusual events is the annual Celebrity Duct Tape Con-test; some of the celebrities who have been recognizably sculpted from the sil-ver tape are Lucille Ball and native Hoosiers John Mellencamp and David Letterman. For additional information contact the Story Inn at 6404 South State Road 135, Nashville; (812) 988–2273 or (800) 881–1183; www.storyinn.com.

To experience a bit of splendid solitude and delve into a mystery that has defied explanation for decades, continue southwest from Story on Elkinsville Road to **Browning Mountain.** The journey is an adventure in itself. The paved road soon gives way to a gravel one. Hills and ridges rise above you, and Salt Creek meanders across the valley floor. The road becomes rougher, the bridges narrower. Eventually, you'll drive through rather than over dry creek beds. Then, approximately 4 miles after leaving Story, at the juncture of Elkinsville and Combs Roads, the mountain appears before you.

The mountain, of course, is actually a hill, but once you have ascended the steep path that leads to its summit you'll understand why it has come to be popularly known as a mountain. Atop the hill is the mystery you are seeking—Indiana's own version of Stonehenge (the world-famous site near Salisbury, England, where huge stone blocks arranged in an orderly fashion have stood for nearly 1,000 years). No one is sure how the enormous slabs at Stonehenge could have been transported there so long ago, just as no one is sure how the scattering of giant hunks of limestone atop Browning Mountain made their way there. One theory is that a bed of limestone was laid down long ago when Brown County was covered by an ancient sea, then broken up and tossed about by natural forces when the sea waters receded. Another theory is that the stones once marked a place sacred to Native Americans. It is true, however, that these huge rocks must weigh many tons each, and some look as though they might have been cut to size and placed in some sort of significant arrangement.

Over the years, attempts were made to quarry the stones, but so many accidents occurred that all further attempts were abandoned. This gave rise to the legend of an Indian spirit watcher who makes sure no one disturbs the stones and to tales of the ghosts of men who died when they disturbed this spot and were condemned to roam the area forever.

If you still can't solve the mystery, you're in good company. A few years ago, a group of scientists journeyed here from South America to examine these stones, but they couldn't come up with a plausible explanation either. Even if you come away from Browning Mountain with more questions than answers, the journey that takes you there, through one of the most beautiful and unspoiled areas of Indiana, will likely be so rewarding you won't mind at all.

Another mystery has recently come to light in Brown County. It was discovered by a hunter who was tracking a wild turkey in Yellowwood State Forest on a cold February morning in 1998. He found his turkey in a most unlikely spot—perched atop a huge, refrigerator-size rock that was cradled in the limbs of a chestnut oak tree about 80 feet above the ground.

Any explanation as to how the rock got there or how long it's been there is purely speculative. No heavy equipment could have placed it there. The area is so remote and so densely forested that any activity involving heavy equipment would be easily spotted. Another theory is that the rock might have been flung there by blasting in a nearby area, but there has been no nearby blasting. Perhaps the most logical suggestion thus far is that a tornado deposited the rock in the branches, but there's no sign of any tornado damage anywhere else in the vicinity. And of course there are a few people who hint at UFO involvement. Whatever the explanation, ***Gobbler's Rock,*** as it has been officially named, was firmly entrenched in its treetop perch until the tree was uprooted in 2006. The rock now lies on the ground, entangled in the oak's branches, but you can still visit the site and ponder the mystery.

Since the discovery of Gobbler's Rock, the mystery has deepened. Hikers sighted two more giant sandstone boulders sitting in the top limbs of two sycamores growing about 100 yards apart in a remote area of the 23,000-acre forest. In intervening years, four more treetop rocks have shown up. Locals have dubbed the rocks URBs (Unexplained Resting Boulders). Word of the strange phenomena has spread, and the forest office has been getting inquiries about their exact locations. If you would like to view the rocks yourself and are willing to walk a bit to see them, stop by the forest office and ask for directions. You'll likely need a GPS to locate them. The office is located at 772 Yellowwood Lake Road; take State Road 46 west from Nashville for about 6 miles and turn north at the YELLOWWOOD STATE FOREST sign; call (812) 988–7945 for office hours.

Tourists, as well as armies, travel on their stomachs. The most popular of the many fine eateries in Nashville is **The Nashville House,** located on the corner of Main and Van Buren Streets in the center of town. Its charming, rustic atmosphere is enhanced by antique furniture, checkered tablecloths, and a huge stone fireplace. The menu lists such Hoosier favorites as fried ham steak, baked ham, barbecued ribs, roast turkey, country-fried chicken, and hot or iced sassafras tea, but the highlight of any meal has to be the fried biscuits. These delicious deep-fried dough balls, served with baked apple butter, could make an addict of anyone. Owner Andy Rogers says they were invented by his father, Jack Rogers, around 1947. The Nashville House is no place for dieters—not only is everything sinfully fattening, but unless you're a lumberjack, you might be hard put to eat everything that's placed in front of you. Although the menu is limited, the food is country cooking at its finest. Prices range from moderate to expensive, and there's a children's menu. Open 11:30 A.M. to 7:00 P.M. Sunday, Monday, Wednesday, and Thursday and 11:30 A.M. to 8:00 P.M. Friday and Saturday; also open 11:30 A.M. to 8:00 P.M. daily in October; closed for two weeks during the Christmas season. Reservations are accepted except during October; (812) 988–4554.

The entrance to the Nashville House is through the **Old Country Store,** a pleasant place to browse if you have to wait for seating in the restaurant. It's just what the name implies—a delightful clutter of goods that includes many hard-to-find items from yesteryear.

Overnight facilities in and near Nashville range from resort inns to motels, from bed-and-breakfast rooms in private homes to furnished log cabins with equipped kitchens. Many are booked up as far as two years in advance, especially on weekends from spring through fall and the week before Christmas, so plan ahead.

For more information about Brown County and its attractions, contact the Brown County Convention and Visitors Bureau, 10 North Van Buren Street,

P.O. Box 840, Nashville 47448; (812) 988–7303 or (800) 753–3255; www.brown county.com.

While in Nashville, buy a copy of the **Brown County Democrat,** which has been honored as Indiana's finest weekly newspaper more times than anyone can remember. The "Sheriff's Log" therein is a Brown County classic. You'll find such entries as:

> *Man called and said he just put on a pot of coffee if any officers are in the area and want coffee.*
>
> *Girl at restaurant requests a conservation officer. An owl is sitting on the pizza oven.*
>
> *Trouble reported at the city dump. Someone abandoned a person there.*
>
> *A coon is asleep on the shelf [of a local shop] with a teddy bear.*
>
> *Man wants deputy [any deputy] to meet him so that he can borrow $5 or $10.*
>
> *Man requests Nashville town marshal go to restaurant and check the stove to see if he left a pot of beans on.*
>
> *Caller says someone has been cow tipping. His cows were asleep in the field and someone tipped them over.*
>
> *Woman reports that a white space ship with an El Camino on the back of it has been going into her neighbor's house. The man driving the space ship has been dead for several years.*
>
> *Man wants to know if the sheriff would like to come watch his snakes eat.*
>
> *Cancel burglar alarm. A grouse flew through a window, setting off the alarm, but the house cat ate the grouse.*
>
> *Wild cow reported in Fruitdale.*
>
> *Three UFOs hovering over house near Bean Blossom. Keep changing colors and shapes.*
>
> *Woman wants to know what she has to do to get arrested so she can spend Thanksgiving weekend in jail with her sister.*
>
> *Man says a naked woman walked into his house.*

Like the mythical sheriff's office in Mayberry, North Carolina, made famous by a television series, this one's run with a lot of heart.

A tiny town in a rural county in Indiana may seem an unlikely venue for an upscale coffeehouse and art gallery, but that's where you'll find the ***Figtree***

Gallery and Coffee Shop. A few years back, owners Glenn and Thomi Elmore traveled to Africa and fell in love with the beauty and culture of Kenya. Then they came to Brown County and fell in love with ***Helmsburg.*** The Figtree evolved from that love and, with its blend of premier coffee and original African art, has become a popular gathering place for tourists and locals alike. Coffees from the Americas, Africa, and Indonesia are available by the cup or in bulk; Dancing Goat, a house blend, is favored by many. Other offerings include specialty cold drinks (the Gorilla Freeze is recommended) and pastry items. The artwork is a mix of paintings, carvings, and colorful fabrics. Generally open 9:00 A.M. to 4:00 P.M. Wednesday and Saturday and 9:00 A.M. to 9:00 P.M. Thursday and Friday, April through mid-December; varying hours the rest of the year. It's best to call before going; (812) 988–1375. Check out their Web site at www.figtreegallery.com. Located at 4865 Helmsburg Road about 5 miles northwest of Nashville.

Clay County

Folks from Wisconsin have munched on cheese curds for years, but they're a relatively new treat for most Hoosier palates. At the ***Swiss Connection,*** not only can you purchase these delectable treats; you can also watch them evolve from start to finish on a free tour. Among the things you'll learn is that a 1,500-pound batch of milk yields 160 to 180 pounds of cheese. You can also purchase the curds and more conventional types of cheese at an on-site store. Owners Alan and Mary Yegerlehner are not content to rest on their cheese curd laurels, however. They also make and sell butter, grass-fed meat products, and two dozen flavors of ice cream. The Swiss Connection and the farm on which it's located are at 1087 East County Road 550 South, not far north of Clay City. Open 9:00 A.M. to 5:00 P.M. Monday through Friday and 9:00 A.M. to 4:00 P.M. Saturday. Tours must be scheduled in advance; call (812) 939–2813.

At the ***Exotic Feline Rescue Center*** in ***Center Point,*** visitors can see more big cats than they would at most zoos. At this writing the center is the "forever home" to approximately 180 lions, tigers (including a rare white tiger), bobcats, mountain lions, leopards, ocelots, servals, one lynx, and one caracal. An overnight adult-only guest facility overlooks two large tiger enclosures; the cost includes two all-day passes and special after-hours tours. Founder Joe Taft, who

trivia

Indiana was the first state to begin reforesting strip mines. The system was initiated in fall 1920, when thousands of trees were planted by coal companies operating in Clay County.

operates the center, takes in animals that have been abused or whose owners can no longer care for them. Currently, the center brings in about two cats per month. The center is located at 2221 East Ashboro Road; a nominal admission fee includes a guided tour. To schedule a tour or make an overnight reservation, call the center at (812) 835-1130 or visit www.exoticfelinerescuecenter.org.

A book entitled *Saving the Big Cats*, published in 2006, tells the story of the center; a portion of the funds from each sale will be donated to the center. Written by Stephen D. McCloud, it's available from Indiana University Press; order it directly from the center, online at www.iupress.indiana.edu, or by calling (800) 849-6796.

Crawford County

Most spelunkers are aware of the subterranean wonders that exist in the Hoosier State, but few other people know that there are numerous caves in southern Indiana. Several are in Crawford County and open to the public.

Thanks to mentions in both *Ripley's Believe It or Not* and the *Guinness Book of World Records*, **Wyandotte Cave** has become world famous for its Monument Mountain—the highest underground mountain in any known cave on earth. It stands 135 feet tall, the focal point of an awe-inspiring room known as Rothrock's Cathedral, which is approximately 185 feet high, 360 feet long, and 140 feet wide. Your tour guide may introduce you to the ghost of Chief Wyandotte, an apparition defined by a weird and entertaining play of shadows at the top of the cathedral. Superlatives apply elsewhere in the cave, too: an area ½ mile in circumference and 200 feet high is the largest subterranean room known anywhere in the world, and a resplendent stalagmite 35 feet high and 75 feet around is believed to be the world's largest formation of its kind. With some 25 miles of known passages explored, the cave itself is believed to be among the Earth's largest. You'll also see delicate and exquisite formations called helictites that are extremely rare. A two-hour walk covers miles; if you're the rugged type, opt for a five- or eight-hour tour during which you'll not only walk but also crawl, climb, descend a pole once used by Indians, and, in places, travel by lantern light.

Just south of Wyandotte Cave is **Little Wyandotte Cave,** which can be toured in about thirty minutes. This cave is much more ordinary but is enjoyable for those who've never been in a cavern.

To reach the caves, travel west from Corydon on State Road 62 for about 12 miles and turn north on a blacktop road; signs point the way. There are admission fees; reservations are necessary for the five- and eight-hour tours. Although available all year, tours are conducted more frequently in the sum-

mer. Nature provides a constant temperature of fifty-two degrees all year long in
both caves. The caves and visitor center
are open daily 9:00 A.M. to 6:00 P.M. Memorial Day through Labor Day; open 9:00
A..M. to 5:00 P.M. Tuesday through Sunday

the rest of the year. Contact Wyandotte Caves, RR 1, Box 85, Leavenworth
47137; (812) 738–2782.

The state-owned caves are part of a larger recreation area known as the
Harrison-Crawford Wyandotte Complex. Besides the caves it includes
O'Bannon Woods State Park and the **Harrison-Crawford State Forest,**
both of which straddle the Harrison-Crawford county line. Wyandotte Woods
offers developed campsites, hiking and bridle trails, a nature center, a restored
1850 hay press, and views of the Ohio River. For those who enjoy roughing it,
Harrison-Crawford State Forest has primitive campsites and overnight back-
packing trails. To reach both, travel west from Corydon on State Road 62 for
about 8 miles to State Road 462 and turn south; State Road 462 runs through
the forest and ends in Wyandotte Woods. The forest and state park offices are
located at 7240 Old Forest Road Southwest, Corydon 47112; call the forest
office at (812) 738–7694 and the park office at (812) 738–8232.

Not far north of Wyandotte Caves is **Marengo Cave,** a national natural
landmark that was discovered in 1883 by a young brother and sister exploring a
sinkhole. The cave, a comfortable fifty-four degrees at all times, has been open
to the public ever since, and its beauty has been acclaimed throughout the world.
Concerts were once held in a subterranean room noted for its acoustics, and an
early-day evangelist preached his fiery message from Pulpit Rock. Underground
weddings and dances were regular occurrences throughout the years, and a
square dance is still held in the Music Hall Chamber each July.

A ⅓-mile cave tour is highlighted by a visit to Crystal Palace, acknowledged by speleologists as one of the ten most beautiful cavern rooms anywhere. A 1-mile tour through a different part of the cave features totem pole
stalagmites and a cavern that looks big enough to build a highway through.
Physically fit visitors may opt to explore two different undeveloped sections of
the cave. Above the cavern is a 122-acre park, complete with camping cabins,
campsites, and trail rides atop horses from the park's stables and such special
activities as rock climbing, gemstone mining, and a simulated cave maze crawl.
There's a separate fee for each tour, as well as special combination rates. The
cave is open daily year-round, except Thanksgiving and Christmas: 9:00 A.M. to
6:00 P.M. weekdays and 9:00 A.M. to 6:30 P.M. weekends Memorial Day through
Labor Day, and 9:00 A.M. to 5:00 P.M. the rest of the year. Marengo Cave is just

northeast of the town of Marengo; go east from Marengo on State Road 64/66 and follow the signs. Write or call Marengo Cave Park, Marengo Cave Road, 400 East State Road 64, P.O. Box 217, Marengo 47140; (812) 365–2705 or (888) 70–CAVES.

Twisting its way southward through Crawford County is the lovely, spring-fed **Blue River,** Indiana's first officially designated natural and scenic river and an ideal canoe stream. Several outfitters offer trips, ranging from 7 to 58 miles; on longer trips you spend the night on the river. Depending on the trip you take, you'll float quiet waters and shoot rapids; pass caves, springs, limestone bluffs, and walls of trees; or make your way around rock gardens and through narrow gorges. The fishing is some of the best in the Midwest, producing catches of bass, crappie, bluegill, and catfish, and the serenity can be well-nigh incredible. In its lower stretches, just before it joins the Ohio River, the Blue River turns sluggish—perfect for tubing. Rates for canoeing include paddle, life jacket, and shuttle service; there are special rates for children. The season is usually April through October, but water levels are best for canoeing before mid-July. For names of outfitters in the area, write or call the Crawford County Tourism Center, P.O. Box 227, Leavenworth 47137; (812) 739–2246 or (888) 846–5397.

About 5 miles south of **Milltown** is one of Indiana's most curious landmarks—a white oak known locally as the **Shoe Tree,** where hundreds of pairs of shoes of all shapes, sizes, and colors can be seen dangling from its branches. No one seems to know exactly when the custom started, but it's generally believed to date back to the early 1960s. Local folks speculate that someone thought of his shoes as longtime friends that had served him faithfully and well and deserved a better fate than to be unceremoniously dumped in the garbage, so he decided to display them in a permanent place of honor.

Although old shoes hang from many places these days, the folks in Milltown, who refer to this tree as the town's "branch office," will tell you that their Shoe Tree is the original. In fact, they claim, they've even copyrighted it. To reach the fabled tree, head south from Milltown on County Road 23 to its intersection with County Road 30, a distance of about 5 miles. The shoe-laden oak tree dominates the landscape at the junction of these two roads.

Just west of Milltown, on the north side of State Road 64, is an **old limestone quarry** with an intriguing maze of tunnels dug into the side of a hill. Inside the cavernous excavations, eerie echoes bombard your ears—the flutter of birds' wings, dripping water, your own footsteps. Ceilings at least 20 feet high, supported by great stone buttresses, and the silent halls they enclose create the impression that you are entering some ancient catacombs or perhaps a cathedral, now hushed and still, whose days of glory have been lost in the mists of time. Explore at your own risk.

The little town of **Leavenworth** on the Ohio River likens its history to that of Noah and the ark—the oldest establishments in town date back to just after the flood. The granddaddy of all floods on the Ohio occurred in 1937, and most of the riverside town of Leavenworth was washed away to points south. Undaunted, residents moved up to a blufftop and started over. Lack of money, like politics, can make for strange bedfellows, so a small cafe and a grocery store shared the second floor of a chicken hatchery. From those humble beginnings has evolved a family restaurant called **The Overlook,** which now occupies the entire building. Through the years the restaurant has specialized in good home cooking and reasonable prices, and people go out of their way to stop here. Even if the food weren't so good, it would be worth stopping at The Overlook just for the view—a sweeping panorama of forested hills and the broad Ohio River as it arches around a horseshoe bend. The Overlook, located at 1153 West State Road 62 in Leavenworth, is open 8:00 A.M. to 9:00 P.M. daily year-round, except Christmas Eve and Christmas, for breakfast, lunch, and dinner. Prices are inexpensive to moderate. Write The Overlook, P.O. Box 9, Leavenworth 47137; call (812) 739–4264; or visit www.theoverlook.com.

trivia

Forty-two species of orchids are native to Indiana. Hawaii is home to only three native species.

Also on State Road 62, not far east of The Overlook, is a shopping experience not to be missed. You can find most anything imaginable at **Stephenson's General Store and Old Rivertown Museum,** where items of every ilk have been accumulating since the store opened in 1915. There are craft items, antiques, groceries, furniture, and hardware items—in no discernible order. Some mole traps, rusty though they may be, do not detract from the exquisite beauty of the pottery shelved near them. Cookie mixes are on a shelf below sleigh bells, and slabs of bologna are found behind a display of ball gloves. The museum mentioned in the store's name, a bit worse for years of wear, is housed in the basement; among the exhibits is a rare wicker casket. Wander the aisles and browse a bit, and you'll find that, as much as anything, Stephenson's contains memories. Open 10:30 A.M. to 5:30 P.M. Monday through Saturday year-round; also 1:00 to 5:00 P.M. Sunday, April through December. For additional information call Stephenson's at (812) 739–4242.

Daviess County

Along about 1972 the local folks decided they needed a unique attraction to put Daviess County on the map, and their idea brought them fame that exceeded their wildest expectations. They combined Indiana's best-known event, the Indianapolis 500, with Daviess County's best-known product—turkeys—and gave birth to the ***Turkey Trot Festival.***

Come September, turkeydom's finest make their way to Ruritan Park in ***Montgomery*** for four days of the most laughable racing imaginable. Because there are about forty turkeys to every human being in Daviess County (with a noticeable but temporary change in the ratio just after the Thanksgiving and Christmas holidays), there can be a lot of birds to face off. This requires many preliminary heats, and only the cream of the crop survive the grueling schedule to race in the final championship run.

On the last, fateful day, anxious jockeys lead their tethered birds to the starting line, eager to put weeks of training to the test. Some raw talent is always on hand, too, since many owners believe that training a bird with a brain the size of a thumbnail is a waste of time. Onlookers cheer their personal favorites—such racing greats as Dirty Bird, White Lightning, and Turkey Lurkey.

On signal, the turkeys head down a 213-foot-long straightaway track toward a finish line that, for a top turkey trotter, is approximately twenty seconds away. Alas, prima donnas are inevitable. Some refuse to start at all. The more befuddled go sideways or backward. Still others tire along the way and pause to peck at whatever turkeys like to peck at. Some even take to the air, disdainfully rising above it all. Eventually, however, one galloping gobbler manages to cross the finish line and is declared the grand champion.

Another big event is the best-dressed turkey contest, which inspires elaborate costumes. One winner devastated the judges when she modeled her stunning powder-blue bikini, then further charmed them by coyly batting her false eyelashes.

And if you think they don't take all this seriously in Daviess County, consider the fact that these are the only turkey races in the world sanctioned by the National Turkey Federation. The races have received national attention from the day of their inception, and stories about them have been translated into a half dozen languages and printed all around the globe. Spectators come from all over.

Although the turkeys are obviously the main attraction, the festival also features mud volleyball, a demolition derby, tractor pulls, and entertainment by top country music stars. For additional information write or call the Daviess County Visitors Bureau, 1 Train Depot Street, P.O. Box 430, Washington 47501; (812) 254–5262 or (800) 449–5262.

Montgomery is located in the heart of southern Indiana's Amish country, a fact that until a few yeas ago was little known beyond the borders of Daviess County and its immediate neighbors. To celebrate this heritage, the sixty-five-acre ***Gasthof Amish Village*** has been constructed on the Henry Wittmer farm near Montgomery. Visitors will find **Der Deutsche Gasthof,** a restaurant that features authentic Amish cooking; a gift shop that sells items handmade by Amish craftspeople; an outdoor flea market (Tuesday, Wednesday, and Saturday, May through October); an inn; a petting zoo; and shops that house various Amish businesses. Located just north of Montgomery on County Road 650E, the village is open 11:00 A.M. to 8:00 P.M. Monday through Thursday, 11:00 A.M. to 9:00 P.M. Friday 7:00 A.M. to 9:00 P.M. Saturday, and 11:00 A.M. to 3:00 P.M. Sunday, May through October; 11:00 A.M. to 8:00 P.M. Monday through Thursday, 11:00 A.M. to 9:00 P.M. Friday and Saturday, and 11:00 A.M. to 3:00 P.M. Sunday the rest of the year. Hours may vary; call (812) 486–3977 or (800) 225–8655, or visit www.gasthofamishvillage.com.

Guided tours of the surrounding area are available for groups of fifteen or more; visitors are taken to Amish communities and to such Amish businesses as a quilt shop, a buggy factory, a candy factory, and a country store. Tours, which include a meal at the village's restaurant, are offered at 9:00 A.M. and 1:00 P.M. Monday through Saturday year-round; reservations must be made at least ten days in advance. For tour reservations and information about the village, write or call the Gasthof Amish Village, P.O. Box 60, Montgomery 47558; (812) 486–2600.

The **Graham Farms Cheese Company** at **Elnora** has been producing cheese for Hoosiers since 1928. Visitors are invited to stop by this family-owned business and watch the entire process. The free tours, which are available Monday through Friday, are accompanied by free samples. All finished products, including unique Indiana University, Purdue University, and State of Indiana cheeses, can be purchased on the premises. Open 8:00 A.M. to 6:00 P.M. Monday through Saturday and noon to 5:00 P.M. Sunday. Located on State Road 57 North; call (812) 692–5237 or (800) 472–9178, or visit www.grahamcheese.org.

Greene County

No matter what you've read or been told, there is no way to fully prepare you for your first glimpse of the **Tulip Trestle** (sometimes called the Greene Country viaduct). One minute you're driving along an isolated rural road that winds through wooded hills and hollows; the next minute you're suddenly confronted with an open valley and the massive railroad trestle that spans it—one of the most spectacular sights in the state.

Completed in 1906 as part of the Illinois Central Railroad line, the trestle is 180 feet high and 2,295 feet long—the second longest in the world. (To see the longest, you'll have to travel to Cantal, France.) Park beneath the massive steel girders that support it, and climb a well-worn path up the hill at the north end for a sweeping view.

The trestle is located just south of a road that links Solsberry and the hamlet of Tulip. Head west from Solsberry on the country road that parallels the railroad tracks. After driving about 5 miles, you'll come to County Road 480E, which turns off to the south and leads beneath the trestle.

It's best to stop at the general store in Solsberry and ask for exact directions. Roads are not well marked hereabouts, and besides, it's great fun to listen to the yarns being spun by any occupants of the store's "liar's bench." Maybe they'll tell you the one about the man wearing gum rubber boots who fell off the trestle while it was being constructed and bounced for three days. He finally had to be shot to keep him from starving to death. For additional information write or call the Bloomfield Chamber of Commerce, 6 East Main Street, P.O. Box 144, Bloomfield 47424; (812) 384–8995.

In the vast, dense forest that covered most of Indiana during the last century, there grew a **huge sycamore** that was the largest tree in the eastern half of the United States. Naturalists and historians advised everyone to go to **Worthington** and see this wonderful tree, which stood 150 feet high, spread its branches to a length of 100 feet, and measured more than 42 feet in circumference at 5 feet above the ground.

In 1920 a storm toppled it, and the town of Worthington decided to preserve one of its limbs in a place of honor. That limb, more than 23 feet in circumference and larger than the trunks of most trees in Indiana today, can be seen in Worthington's City Park at the north end of town. You can't miss it—it's the only tree in the park with a roof over its head.

The town of **Linton** was the birthplace of the late bandleader and show business personality Phil Harris, who never forgot his Indiana roots. Older folks will remember him for his bits on Jack Benny's radio and television shows. Younger folks will remember him as the resonant baritone voice heard in various Disney movies (Little John in *Robin Hood*, Baloo the Bear in *The Jungle Book*, and Thomas O'Malley in *The Aristocats*). For many years, Harris and his late wife, movie actress and singer Alice Faye, returned to Linton for the annual Phil Harris Festival. Ms. Faye reportedly loved this small town, and she and Harris donated their collection of numerous show business memorabilia to his boyhood home. A virtual history of show business, the **Harris-Faye collection** includes photographs, awards, scrapbooks, letters, and trophies. Also seen here are souvenirs from well-known personalities in the fields of entertainment, sports, and government. The collection is housed in the basement of the Regions Bank, at 89 West Vincennes Street. Because it's staffed entirely by volunteers, the collection is not open on a regular basis, but it can be seen by appointment when the bank is open. Contact the curator, Regina Kramer, by writing Route 1, P.O. Box 918, Lone Tree Road, Linton 47441; call (812) 847–4635. Admission is free.

Knox County

Vincennes, Indiana's oldest city, has a colorful history, and the town abounds with monuments to its past. George Rogers Clark came here during the American Revolution to battle the British, and his deeds are memorialized in the twenty-four-acre ***George Rogers Clark National Historical Park,*** located at 401 South Second Street (open 9:00 A.M. to 5:00 P.M. daily, except major winter holidays). Within a magnificent round stone structure are seven murals depicting Clark's military campaigns. Living-history programs, featured on some summer weekends, re-create camp life with military drills and firearm demonstrations. There's a nominal admission fee for the memorial building, but the visitor center is free; (812) 882–1776, ext. 110.

At the ***Vincennes State Historic Sites,*** at the corner of First and Harrison Streets on the western edge of the ***Vincennes University*** campus, is a two-story white frame building that served as the ***Indiana Territory Capitol*** from about 1805 to 1813. Nearby is the **Western Sun *Print Shop*** where the territory's first newspaper was published on July 4, 1804; the wooden printing press seen by today's visitors is the same type as the original. Legend has it that Abe Lincoln, a faithful reader of the *Sun,* came here as a young man to study a printing press in operation and actually helped print the Saturday, March 6, 1830, edition of the paper on the day of his visit. Donations are requested. Open 9:00 A.M. to 5:00 P.M. Tuesday through Saturday and 1:00 to 5:00 P.M. Sunday, April through November. For information write or call Vincennes State Historic Sites, 1 West Harrison Street, P.O. Box 81, Vincennes 47591; (812) 882–7422.

Grouseland, an early-nineteenth-century Georgian mansion, was the home of William Henry Harrison when he served as the first governor of the

Grouseland

Indiana Territory. (He later became the ninth president of the United States and was the grandfather of the twenty-third.) As part of his official duties, he once invited Indian Chief Tecumseh to his home to discuss their differences. Tecumseh refused to come inside, saying he preferred to sit on the Earth, his mother, and so the two men held council in a walnut grove on the front lawn. Located at 3 West Scott Street; (812) 882–2096. Open 9:00 A.M. to 5:00 P.M. Monday through Saturday, 11:00 A.M. to 5:00 P.M. Sunday, March through December, except Thanksgiving and Christmas; 11:00 A.M. to 4:00 P.M. daily January and February, except New Year's Day. There's a nominal admission fee.

trivia

Indiana is on top of several earthquake faults. The largest concentration, known as the Wabash Valley fault system, lies in the southwestern part of the state. Most earthquakes centered in Indiana are relatively minor events, but recently discovered evidence indicates that a quake of magnitude 7.5 occurred near Vincennes about 5,000 years ago.

The boundaries of the Indiana Territory first encompassed the present-day states of Indiana, Illinois, Michigan, and Wisconsin and part of Minnesota, and later the lands included in the 1803 Louisiana Purchase. So tiny Vincennes, with Harrison at its helm, was for a while the seat of government for most of the United States territory from the Alleghenies to the Rockies.

Harrison also served as one of the first trustees of Vincennes University. Founded in 1801, it is the oldest university west of the Alleghenies.

St. Francis Xavier Cathedral, dating back to 1702, is the oldest Catholic church in Indiana. The present redbrick building is actually the fourth church to stand on this site; its first two predecessors were built of logs, while the third, also a brick structure, was built in 1826 and rebuilt later the same year after a storm nearly destroyed it. Rich, dark cedars shelter the serene grounds of the *Old French Cemetery* adjacent to the cathedral, where priests, parishioners, natives, soldiers, and African slaves lie buried, many in unmarked graves. The first interment was in 1741, the last in 1846. The cathedral is located at 205 Church Street; open 7:00 A.M. to 4:00 P.M. daily. Call (812) 882–5638.

Behind the cathedral, housed in a modern redbrick building, is *Brute Library,* the oldest library in Indiana, containing more than 11,000 rare books and documents. Bishop Simon Brute (1779–1839), the first Bishop of Vincennes, assembled the collection in France and brought it with him to the wilderness that was the Indiana Territory. He was called by President John Quincy Adams "the most learned man of his day in America."

A papal bull of Pope John XXII, dated 1319 and written on heavy parchment, is the oldest manuscript in the library. The oldest book, dated 1476,

The Marrying Man

Until his demise on June 10, 1997, at the age of eighty-eight, Glynn "Scotty" Wolfe was acknowledged to be the world's most married man. Reportedly, until the day he died, he was still chasing women at the nursing home in which he was living—even though he was by then confined to a wheelchair.

Wolfe, who lived in California at the time of his death, was a native of Knox County. Between 1927 and 1996, he married twenty-nine times. His longest marriage lasted six years, his shortest just nineteen days. The flamboyant Wolfe claimed that he left one of his wives because she ate sunflower seeds in bed and walked out on another because she used his toothbrush.

According to the man himself, his colorful life included stints as a Baptist minister, a pilot in Britain's Royal Air Force, a sailor on the USS *Arizona* (before it was bombed and sunk at Pearl Harbor), and a bodyguard for Al Capone.

Wolfe is survived by his several children (believed but not confirmed to be nineteen in number) and his twenty-ninth wife—Linda Essex-Wolfe of Anderson, Indiana, who at the time of their marriage had been married twenty-three times and was the world's most married woman.

glows with the lustrous colors of hand illumination, and the parchment still bears the holes made by the pins that held the pages in place while the illuminating was done. Another interesting volume contains the Lord's Prayer in 250 different languages. In addition, there are old maps, letters, and a certified copy of a license issued on March 6, 1833, to Abraham Lincoln and William Berry, permitting them to operate a tavern in New Salem, Illinois. There's a nominal admission fee. The library is open 1:00 to 4:00 P.M. daily, Memorial Day through Labor Day; (812) 882–5638.

Built about 1806, the ***Brouillet French House*** at 509 North First Street is one of the few remaining upright log-and-mud houses in North America. Inside are the original fireplace and warming oven, along with authentic period furnishings. An Indian museum is located behind the house, which is open 8:00 A.M. to 4:00 P.M. Monday through Friday; admission is free. Call (812) 882–7422.

A remnant of prehistory, the 40-foot-high ***Son of Tabac Mound*** is a natural formation dating to 600–1000 B.C. and is known to be an Indian burial site. The grounds are open daily, dawn to dusk; admission is free. The mound is located on the south side of Wabash Avenue about ½ mile east of Thirteenth Street; look for signs. Several other mounds lie to the east and south of Vincennes. Call (812) 882–7422.

The late **Red Skelton,** the beloved comedian, was born in Vincennes at 111 West Lyndale Avenue. A sign in front of the house commemorates the occasion.

When Red was just ten he joined the Hagenbeck-Wallace Circus (which wintered in Peru, Indiana) as a clown. That was the beginning of his illustrious career, which included the starring role in some thirty movies, hosting his own television show for twenty years, and performing for eight U.S. presidents.

In February 2006, the 63,000-square-foot **Red Skelton Performing Arts Theater** opened on the campus of Vincennes University just across the street from Red's birthplace. His widow, Lothian, said Red, who died in 1997, would have been thrilled because it was a lifelong dream of his to have a theater of his own.

Construction has also started on a Red Skelton museum next to the theater. It will house a collection of the comedian's memorabilia, donated by Red's widow, that's valued at three million dollars. The tentative opening date is fall 2007. A **Red Skelton Festival,** which debuted in June 2006, will become an annual event.

For additional information write or call the Vincennes/Knox County Convention and Visitors Bureau, 102 North Third Street, Vincennes 47591; (812) 886–0400 or (800) 886–6443.

Lawrence County

For more than one hundred years, many of the great public edifices in this country and elsewhere have been constructed with Indiana limestone. Architects favor it because it lends itself easily to carving and the most delicate tracery when first quarried, then becomes hard and durable when exposed to atmospheric agents. Just a few of the structures that are built at least partly of oolitic limestone (so called because of its granular composition, which suggests a mass of fish eggs) from the Bedford area are the Empire State Building and Rockefeller Center in New York City; Washington National Cathedral (eighty-three years in the making, it was completed on September 29, 1990, when a crane placed a 1,000-pound chunk of intricately carved Indiana limestone atop one of the church's towers); the Pentagon; the Lincoln and Jefferson Memorials; Chicago's Merchandise Mart; and the University of Moscow.

The **limestone quarries** are quite impressive to see—great gaping cavities in the earth from which are extracted immense blocks of stone that average 4 feet in thickness, 10 feet in width, and from 50 to 100 feet in length. Before being removed from the quarry floor, they're broken into small blocks for easy transportation to a processing mill. To view the quarries, go north from

Bedford on Highway 37 through Oolitic; the quarries are about ½ mile north of Oolitic.

When you pass through **Oolitic,** stop and meet one of the town's residents—the limestone **statue of Joe Palooka,** which stands in front of the town hall on Main Street. A famous comic strip character from the not-too-distant past, Joe was at the peak of his popularity in the 1940s. A paragon of good, Joe was an earthbound Superman of sorts who championed democracy and decency and was an inspiration to the youth of his day. He was also a boxer, and he is depicted—7 feet tall and weighing more than ten tons—wearing trunks and boxing gloves. When World War II came along, Joe gave up boxing to enlist in the Army, adding to his reputation as the ultimate American hero.

Several years ago, the Bedford Industrial Development Foundation, a nonprofit financial arm of the chamber of commerce, opened a twenty-acre limestone demonstration center overlooking the two largest quarries. A museum was built, displays of machinery and tools were set up, and construction was begun on the two main attractions—a one-fifth scale limestone reproduction of the Great Pyramid of Cheops and a 650-foot duplication of a segment from the Great Wall of China. The project was eventually abandoned due to lack of funds, but every once in a while someone decides to have a go at reviving it—thus far to no avail. Known locally as "the pyramid," the park-to-be now consists of a rusting Quonset hut that was meant to serve as the museum and a jumble of limestone boulders. For current information on the on-again, off-again tourist attraction, which occupies a fifteen-acre lot about 9 miles north of Bedford via State Road 37, write or call the Lawrence County Visitors Center, 533 West Main Street, Mitchell 47446; (812) 849–1090 or (800) 798–0769.

Bedford stone, another name for local limestone, is sometimes used for gravestones, and many fine examples can be seen in **Green Hill Cemetery** at 1202 Eighteenth Street in **Bedford;** (812) 275–5110. The monument for Louis Baker, a twenty-three-year-old apprentice stonecutter who died suddenly in 1917, was carved by his grieving fellow workers; they reproduced his workbench, fully detailed and to actual size, exactly as he had left it. The statue of Michael F. Wallner preserves his doughboy uniform down to the most minute crease. Also seen in the cemetery are some of the tree-trunk carvings that were popular around the turn of the twentieth century, including one adorned with high-button shoes and a straw hat that memorializes a seven-year-old girl who died in 1894. These and other Green Hill monuments have been featured on several national television shows. Free walking-tour maps of the cemetery are available from the Lawrence County Tourism Commission (see the preceding paragraph for the address and phone numbers). The cemetery is open from 9:00 A.M. to 5:00 P.M.

Visitors can explore the history of the area's limestone industry at the ***Land of Limestone Museum,*** housed in a historic limestone building at the Bedford campus of Oakland City University. Archival and architectural photographs, historical news accounts, and official records document the area's role in building the nation. Outside, visitors can see twenty-five different styles of limestone surfaces on a wall that surrounds the parking lot. It's located at 405 North I Street in Bedford; admission is free. Open 9:00 A.M. to 4:00 P.M. Monday through Friday. For further information writie or call the Lawrence County Visitors Center, 533 West Main Street, Mitchell 47446; (812) 849–1090 or (800) 798–0769.

At Purdue University's ***Feldun Purdue Agricultural Center,*** you can roam the 449 acres of the Moses Fell Farm. Mr. Fell donated the farm to Purdue in 1914, and it has been used ever since for experimental purposes. The center is located on State Road 458, which runs north off State Road 158, 3 miles west of Bedford; signs point the way. Open daily year-round, 6:30 A.M. to 5:30 P.M. Monday through Saturday and 6:30 A.M. to 4:00 P.M. Sunday; admission is free. Write or call Feldun Purdue Agricultural Center, 923 State Road 458, Bedford 47421; (812) 275–6327.

Southwest of Bedford, the longest "lost river" in the United States flows through a startling subterranean world. More than 20 miles of passageways have been explored at ***Bluespring Caverns,*** one of the world's ten longest, and most of those miles are wet ones—inundated by a system of underground streams. Visitors descend a stairway into a sinkhole entrance room, then venture 4,000 feet into the yawning depths aboard flat-bottomed boats that glide silently through a world of total darkness. The rare white fish and crayfish that live in these waters are blind, having adapted themselves over the years to a habitat where sight is of no use. Lights mounted on the bottom of the tour boat create shifting shadows on fluted walls and provide unique glimpses of water-sculpted formations on the mirrorlike surface of the stream. By prior arrangement you can also participate in a "wild tour," which includes exploring some of the dry portions of the cave, crawling, climbing, and viewing an underground slide show. Overnight stays in the caverns are offered from October through April.

To reach Bluespring Caverns Park from Bedford, go south on U.S. Highway 50 for about 6 miles, then turn west on County Road 4505 for about ½ mile; signs point the way. Open 9:00 A.M. to 5:00 P.M. daily, Memorial Day through Labor Day, and on Saturday and Sunday only from April 1 through the day before Memorial Day; an admission fee is charged. Campsites with water and electricity are available in the park. Bluespring Caverns Park is located at 1459 Bluespring Caverns Road; (812) 279–9471; www.bluespringcaverns.com.

The many attractions at **Spring Mill State Park** span a time period from the early 1800s to the threshold of the space age. As a boy growing up in nearby Mitchell, Virgil I. "Gus" Grissom loved this park. Grissom grew up to become one of the seven original astronauts and, in 1965, the second American in space. Two years later he was dead—one of three astronauts killed in a tragic spacecraft fire at Cape Kennedy. A *Gemini III* capsule like the one he once piloted now rests, along with his spacesuit and other items related to space travel, in the **Grissom Memorial Visitor Center,** P.O. Box 376, Mitchell 47446; (812) 849–4129. Open daily 8:30 A.M. to 4:00 P.M. year-round.

Nestled in a small valley among Spring Mill State Park's wooded hills is a **pioneer village** that was founded in 1814. Its sawmill, meetinghouse, apothecary, hatmaker's and weaver's shops, water-powered gristmill, general store, tavern, distillery, post office, and log cabin homes have all been restored, and from April through October the village is alive with inhabitants who go about their daily routine just as their long-ago counterparts did. You can purchase cornmeal ground at the old gristmill and products from the weaver's looms, and, on occasion, you can participate in candlelight tours of the tiny settlement.

Plants in the **Hamer Pioneer Gardens** are the same as those grown by the village's original occupants; some were used for medicine, some for cooking, and some simply to add beauty to a life that was often harsh. Uphill from the village is a pioneer cemetery that dates back to 1832. The stone markers provide a genealogical history of the town below.

During the spring and summer, nearly every variety of wildflower and bird indigenous to Indiana is found here, and to protect some of the 1,300-acre park's finest natural features the state has set aside two areas as nature preserves. A 2½-mile-loop hiking trail, the most beautiful in the park, winds through **Donaldson's Woods State Nature Preserve,** an outstanding seventy-six-acre virgin forest dominated by giant tulip trees and white oaks. Six acres surrounding the mouth of **Donaldson Cave,** reached by another trail, have also been designated a state nature preserve. The scene that meets your eye here—a small stream flowing from the cave's entrance and through a gorge whose slopes are thick with hardwood trees—is one of the loveliest in the state.

Park naturalists conduct walking tours into Donaldson Cave and into **Bronson Cave.** At **Twin Caves** you can take a short ride on the underground river while a naturalist tells you about the tiny blind cavefish swimming beneath you. To reach the park, go east on State Road 60 from Mitchell for about 3 miles; the park is on the north side of State Road 60—signs point the way. Write or call Spring Mill State Park, 3333 State Road 60 East, Mitchell 47446; (812) 849–4129.

Spring Mill Inn is a combination of rustic charm and modern conveniences. Constructed in 1939 of native limestone and remodeled in 1976, the buff-colored building is located in the heart of the park. Guest rooms are decorated with colonial furniture, and the dining room serves three meals a day. Dinner usually features cornsticks made from meal ground in the park. Swimming is a year-round activity in the unique indoor-outdoor pool. Rooms cost from $49 to $109 per night year-round, and rollaway cots are available for $5.00 each. Write or call Spring Mill Inn, P.O. Box 68, Mitchell 47446; (812) 849–4081 or (877) 977–7464.

The greatest concentration of Indiana's several earthquake faults is located in Posey County in the southwestern corner of the state, but the longest fault occurs in south central Indiana. Known as the **Mt. Carmel Fault,** it extends 50 miles southeastward from the Morgan-Monroe county line into Washington County. One of the few places in the state where a fault can actually be seen on the surface of the land is alongside State Road 446, 2½ miles south of the Monroe-Lawrence county line, where ancient movements along the Mt. Carmel Fault have uplifted the land. (It may be reassuring for visitors—and nearby residents—to know that no movement of this fault has been recorded in modern history.) For additional information visit the **Indiana Geological Survey** (IGS) at 611 North Walnut Grove Avenue in Bloomington, where detailed maps showing the location of the Mt. Carmel Fault are on open file. The IGS also can provide information about other faults in Indiana; it's open from 8:00 A.M. to 4:30 P.M. Monday through Friday; (812) 855–7636.

Nearby **Heltonville** is the home of the **Turner Doll Factory,** where Virginia and Boyce Turner began producing porcelain dolls in the mid-1980s. Because the dolls are collectibles, each doll is made in limited numbers ranging from 20 to 500. The Turner factory added vinyl dolls to its output in 1993, limiting each model to 2,500 or fewer dolls. Visitors may watch the production process free of charge from 10:00 A.M. to 3:00 P.M. Monday through Friday; call (812) 834–6692 or (800) 887–6372 for directions and, if you're bringing more than one carload, to make an appointment. The factory and a retail shop (open 10:00 A.M. to 5:00 P.M. Monday through Friday and 10:00 A.M. to 4:00 P.M. Saturday) are located at 3522 Pleasant Run Road.

Martin County

There's silver in them thar hills, if legend be truth! Since the first Europeans came to these parts, tales have abounded about the lost Indian treasure cave of **McBride's Bluffs.** For nearly one hundred years the Choctaw Indians lived in the bluffs area north of Shoals, taking shelter in one particular cave during severe weather. Absalom Shields, one of the first white settlers, told of the time when the natives blindfolded him and took him to this cave, where he was shown a fabulous amount of silver crudely molded into bricks. Shortly after their disclosure to Shields, the natives were forced to flee the area so hastily that they could not take the silver with them. They did, however, seal the entrance to the cave. When one of their tribe was later sent to claim the treasure, the trees he was to use as landmarks to guide him to the cave had been cleared away, and he was never able to find the silver. Since then a few isolated bars of silver have been found above ground, but the whereabouts of the cave remains a secret to this day. It's not for lack of trying, though—people still search for the silver.

The precipitous cliffs known as McBride's Bluffs, which soar 175 feet above the East Fork of White River, are riddled with small caves. Because country roads may be unmarked, it's best to ask locally for exact directions to the bluffs, which lie approximately 5 miles north of Shoals and are shown on the official state highway map. Start out from Shoals going northwest on U.S. Highway 50/150, then turn north onto State Road 450. Continue north to a side road about 1½ miles north of Dover Village and turn east toward the White River; a single-lane gravel road winds along the riverbank at the base of the bluffs.

Martin County is one of the best places in the state for shunpiking (driving the back roads). Meandering country lanes lead past little-known havens of beauty—rugged hills, dense woodlands, sheer sandstone cliffs—that are even more beautiful when wildflowers color the spring landscape and trees don their autumn hues.

Jug Rock, a striking sandstone monolith that is the focal point of a state nature preserve, is a product of centuries of erosion. Although it stretches to a height of 60 feet and is more than 15 feet in diameter, it is difficult to see when the surrounding trees are heavy with foliage. The bottle-shaped rock stands on the north side of US 50/150 a little to the northwest of Shoals, about a mile beyond the White River bridge and some 200 yards downhill from the Shoals Overlook Rest Park. Stop at a small roadside pull-off on a high point along the highway and look for a large, flat slab that tops this unusual formation. To gain a better perspective of Jug Rock's dimensions, walk to its base along a 60-yard-long woodland path. For additional information write or call the Division of Nature Preserves, Indiana Department of Natural Resources, 402 West Washington Street, Room W267, Indianapolis 46204; (317) 232–4052.

Directly west of Shoals you can see the bluffs of ***Beaver Bend,*** noted for the rare species of ferns that cling to the cliff and grow nearby. Beaver Bend is a sharp curve in the East Fork of White River where Beaver Creek flows into it. These cliffs reach their loftiest height at Spout Spring, where water emerges from a pipe driven into the solid rock wall. The honeycombed cliff that overhangs the spring is layered with ocher and yellow rocks that soar 400 feet into the air. Bald eagles are sometimes seen in the trees that line the riverbank. Ask for directions locally; an old country road passes near the base of the bluffs.

A few miles downriver from Beaver Bend you can explore the picturesque **Hindostan Falls** area. In the early 1800s the thriving community of Hindostan stood on the banks of White River. It was abandoned in 1828, at the height of its prosperity, when a mysterious disease began killing its citizens. Only 6 feet high but nevertheless impressive, Hindostan Falls extends from one bank of the river to the other, creating scallops of white foam along the uneven path it follows. The power produced by the tremendous volume of water that passes over it each day was harnessed by the people of Hindostan to power their mills, while a large sandstone ledge below the falls provided the rock for the mill's foundations. Still evident today are the large square holes from which the rock was hewn, but the ledge is now used primarily by picnickers and anglers looking for solitude. The pools below the falls teem with catfish, drum, crappie, white and smallmouth bass, buffalo, shad, and suckers. Officially designated a state fishing area, the site also offers a free concrete boat-launching ramp and some free primitive campsites. Do use caution here, though—the current is both strong and dangerous at times. To reach Hindostan Falls, go south from Shoals on US 50/150 to State Road 550, turn west, and follow the signs to the falls area on the south side of State Road 550. The area is open at all times; admission is free. Write or call the Regional Access Manager, Public Access South, Hindostan Falls State Public Fishing Area, RR 2, Box 300, Montgomery 47558; (812) 644–7731.

Hoosier National Forest, just east of Hindostan Falls, occupies the southeast corner of Martin County. A drive along forest roads reveals a seemingly endless panorama of some of nature's most stunning handiwork: huge rock bluffs, woods, waterfalls, streams, and box canyons. For additional information write or call Hoosier National Forest Headquarters, 811 Constitution Avenue, Bedford 47421; (812) 275–5987.

Northeast of Shoals, bordering the north side of US 50, is **Martin State Forest,** one of the nicest surprises in the state forest system. Within its 6,132 acres you can climb a fire tower, visit an arboretum, or tour one of five demonstration areas to learn about forest management practices. The most spectacular hike in the forest takes you over a rugged 3-mile trail that leads to Tank Spring, where water tumbles down 150 feet over moss-covered sandstone; come here in the spring when the greens are newborn and lustrous. Shady campsites atop a breezy ridge make this a great place to spend warm-weather days. The forest is open at all times; admission is free. Write or call Martin State Forest, P.O. Box 599, Shoals 47581; (812) 247–3491.

Monroe County

Indiana University, which sits in the heart of *Bloomington,* enrolls nearly 33,000 students from around the world. The diverse cultures they represent have given rise to a cuisine that is international in scope and truly extraordinary for a town this size (60,000 people, sans students). Eateries specialize in such ethnic cuisines as Irish, French, Greek, Mexican, German, Italian, Ethiopian, Middle Eastern, Malaysian, Indonesian, Afghan, African, Thai, Tibetan, Japanese, and all styles of Chinese foods. Of course, American dishes and that staple of every college town in the country—pizza—are also available.

Located in a quaint old home at 412 East Sixth Street is a small cafe/restaurant known as *The Runcible Spoon,* where patrons can sit upstairs, downstairs, or outside in a Japanese garden. A 300-gallon aquarium occupies a dominant position on the main floor; more fish reside in a bathtub in the restroom. Matt O'Neal, the owner, likes to think that this relaxing atmosphere brings out the philosopher in everyone. Freshly roasted gourmet coffee is the lifeblood of the cafe, luring a mix of customers that's as varied as the cuisine, and the homemade bagels produced in the in-house bakery are an exclusive in Bloomington. The restaurant is open 8:00 A.M. to 7:00 P.M. daily, and breakfast can be ordered all day. The cafe is open 8:00 A.M. to midnight daily; (812) 334–3997.

For gyros unsurpassed anywhere, stop in at *The Trojan Horse* on the southeast corner of Kirkwood and Walnut Streets. Paper-thin slices of beef and lamb are garnished with tomato slices, onion rings, and tzatziki sauce, then served on pita bread. Have a Greek salad on the side, and top it all off with a Greek pastry. Open 11:00 A.M. to 11:00 P.M. Monday through Thursday, 11:00 A.M. to midnight Friday and Saturday, and 11:30 A.M. to 10:00 P.M. Sunday; (812) 332–1101.

Bloomington also boasts the *Snow Lion,* one of only a few Tibetan restaurants in the country. The Bloomington restaurant, however, has a connection with Tibet that is one of a kind. Jigme K. Norbu, who owns the Snow Lion, is the nephew of the Dalai Lama, the Buddhist priest-king who is Tibet's political and spiritual leader. Although Norbu adjusts his recipes somewhat to appeal to the

trivia

The late James "Doc" Counsilman of Bloomington was the third-oldest person to swim the English Channel. He accomplished his feat at age fifty-eight in September 1979. During an illustrious thirty-three year career as the varsity swim coach at Indiana University (1957–1990), he coached fifty-nine Olympians. One of them was Mark Spitz, who won an unprecedented seven gold medals at the 1972 Summer Olympics in Munich.

American palate (Tibetan food features plenty of liver, mutton, barley, and fat), he achieves an authentic flavor by using traditional spices and herbs from Tibet. The menu includes such offerings as Phingtsel (bean thread sautéed with mixed vegetables), Thukpa Shamic (fried egg noodles sautéed with shrimp and vegetables), and Tasha Ngopa (Indian chicken curry with Tibetan seasonings served on a bed of rice). All entrees are served with a cup of Tibetan tea and a salad with a house dressing that's so popular many people come here just to eat the salad. The only dessert offered is Deyse, a dish of steamed sweet rice with raisins that's topped with cold yogurt.

In addition to serving food, the restaurant introduces diners to the culture of Tibet. The Tibetan national flag, which features two snow lions grasping an iridescent jewel, hangs near the door. Tibetan music is interwoven with the classical selections that play softly in the background, and several Tibetan hand paintings representing good luck adorn the walls. The Snow Lion, located at 113 South Grant Street, also offers cuisine from other parts of Asia; prices are moderate. Open for lunch from 11:00 A.M. to 3:00 P.M. Monday through Friday and for dinner from 5:00 to 10:00 P.M. daily; carryout is available all day. Call (812) 336–0835.

Tibet is a small nation that lies in a remote mountainous area along the southwestern border of China proper. The region has been intermittently governed by China through the centuries, last achieving independence in 1911. That status endured until 1950, when China once again asserted its rule. Since then some 1.2 million Tibetans have died in the struggle to regain their country's freedom, and the Dalai Lama has set up a government in exile in India. Thubten J. Norbu, a retired Indiana University professor who is the father of Jigme Norbu and the older brother of the Dalai Lama, was motivated by the plight of his homeland to found the **Tibetan Cultural Center** (TCC) in Bloomington. In 1987 the Dalai Lama came to Bloomington to consecrate the then-new **Jangchub Chorten,** the only Tibetan chorten in the United States and the cornerstone of the TCC. Rising 35 feet above its pastoral surroundings, the copper-topped, white, concrete monument to peace memorializes Tibetans who have died under Chinese rule. Sealed within the chorten are such religious artifacts as Buddhist scriptures, bits of clothing worn by ancient monks and saints, and hair clippings from thirteen Dalai Lamas (the current Dalai Lama is the fourteenth). Just prior to another visit by the Dalai Lama in 1999, a second monument was added to the center. Known as the **Kalachakra Stupa,** it is dedicated to world peace and harmony. The Dalai Lama returned again in September 2003 to bless the **Chamtse Ling Temple,** a new interdenominational peace temple. The chorten, stupa, and temple, located on the TCC's ninety-acre property at 3655 South Snoddy Road, can be seen free of charge during daylight hours. A nearby building houses a museum, library, and work-shop. Four retreat cottages deep in the center's woodlands, built to resemble Mongolian yurts, are available for rental. For further information and a sched-ule of special cultural events sponsored by the TCC, write or call the center at P.O. Box 2581, Bloomington 47402; (812) 334–7046 or (812) 336–6807.

Bloomington is also home to the **Dagom Geden Tensun Ling.** Established in 1998, it is the first Tibetan Buddist monastery to be founded in this country. The public is welcome to visit and to attend the many classes and meditation sessions led by the monks who live there. Located at 102 Club House Drive in Lower Cascades Park; call (812) 339–0857 for additional information.

Among the more unusual facilities on the Indiana University campus is the **Lilly Library of Rare Books and Manuscripts,** a repository of more than 400,000 books, including one of the world's largest collections of miniature books, and nearly seven million manuscripts. Among its acquisitions are the original scripts from the popular television shows *Star Trek* and *Star Trek: The*

The Puzzlemeister from Indiana

In 1974 Indiana University in Bloomington awarded what was believed to be the world's first degree in enigmatology. The young man upon whom it was conferred, a native of Crawfordsville, Indiana, designed the degree himself through IU's Individual-ized Major Program. When he first approached his adviser with the idea for such a degree, she was lukewarm, but the young man persisted and was eventually given the go-ahead to pursue the degree of his dreams. In 1993, at the age of forty-one, that man became the youngest puzzle editor ever at *The New York Times,* a job he still holds today. His passion also led to a second job as star of the puzzle-master segment that airs Sunday morning on National Public Radio (NPR).

Although Will Shortz went on to earn a law degree from the University of Virginia, he never practiced law. Instead, he went straight to an editing job at a puzzle magazine and by 1989 was editor of *Games* magazine. Then it was on to the *Times* and NPR.

Shortz has also authored or edited more than twenty books of puzzles, founded and served as director of the American Crossword Tournament, and founded the World Puzzle Championship. He lives in New York City and collects—what else?—puzzles and puzzle magazines. Among his prized possessions is the first "word-cross" puzzle ever invented; it was published in the December 21, 1913, *New York World,* a Christmas gift for the ages.

In 2006, Shortz was featured in a documentary film entitled *Wordplay.* He shared screen time with such puzzle aficionados as former President Bill Clinton and television personality Jon Stewart. Those folks at IU who allowed Shortz to pursue his dream now have an alumnus to be proud of.

Next Generation. One recent donation of note is the personal collection of more than 30,000 comic books from Michael Uslan, a former college professor who taught the world's first college course on comic books at Indiana University in the 1970s and later produced Batman films. Another donation of more than 30,000 mechanical puzzles was made in 2006; puzzle enthusiast Jerry Slocum chose the Lilly Library over the Smithsonian as the repository for his collection. The library draws on its vast holdings to set up a series of changing exhibits throughout the year, but such treasures as a Gutenberg Bible, George Washington's letter accepting the presidency of the United States, Thomas Jefferson's copy of the Bill of Rights, four Shakespeare folios, and a major Lincoln collection are on permanent display. Admission is free; hours vary with the seasons. Located at 1200 East Seventh Street. Free public tours are offered every Friday at 2:00 P.M.; call (812) 855–2452 or visit www.indiana.edu/~liblilly.

Although Indiana University's School of Music is world renowned, Bloomington-born songwriter **Hoagy Carmichael** earned a law degree here. Music was always his passion, however, and passion would eventually have its way. One night in 1926, while sitting alone on a spooning wall at the edge of campus thinking of the two girls in his life, Carmichael looked up at the starry sky and began whistling a tune. Unable to get the song out of his mind, he dashed over to use the piano at a local hangout. A few minutes later the proprietor closed up and tossed Hoagy out. Fortunately for the world, the song remained on Hoagy's mind—it ultimately became "Stardust," the most recorded American pop song ever. More than 2,000 versions have been performed by hundreds of artists. A visible tribute to the song can be seen in a westside Bloomington neighborhood. The notes from a line of "Stardust" are painted on a railroad overpass on Adams Street near its junction with Eighth Street and Vernal Pike.

Hoagy died in 1981 at age eighty-two and is buried in Rose Hill Cemetery on Bloomington's west side. In 1986 Hoagy's family donated a large collection of the composer's memorabilia to Indiana University, and the school established a **Hoagy Carmichael Room** in which to display it. The composer's piano, a jukebox, photographs of Carmichael with numerous Hollywood stars, and both of the original manuscripts of "Stardust" (one without orchestration and the other with scores for each instrument), both signed and dated by the composer, are just a few of the mementos visitors will see. Located in Room 006 of the **Archives of Traditional Music** in Morrison Hall, the Hoagy Carmichael Room is open free of charge by appointment. Other rooms of the archives—the largest university-based ethnographic sound archives in the country—house such varied holdings as tapes of 350 spoken languages from around the world, the music of the Tupi Indians of Brazil, and recordings of blues artists of the 1940s. The public is welcome to visit the archives and listen to its collections from 9:00 A.M. to 5:00 P.M. Monday through Friday; admission is free. Call the Hoagy Carmichael Room at (812) 855–4679 or the archives librarian at (812) 855–8631.

If you visit the archives, you might also want to take a tour of another of Morrison Hall's famous occupants—the world-famous **Kinsey Institute.** The late Alfred Kinsey established the institute in 1947 to conduct his ground-breaking studies of human sexuality. Its collection of art, photographs, and various artifacts in the art gallery, closed to the public until recently, can be seen free of charge during designated hours. Because hours vary, call the institute at (812) 855–7686 or visit www.kinseyinstitute.org before you go. Guided one-hour tours of the institute, library, and exhibition room can be arranged by advance reservation. You'll find the institute on the third floor.

Actor Liam Neeson visited here to research Kinsey's work in preparation for his portrayal of Kinsey in the acclaimed movie of the same name, released in 2004.

You can obtain more information about the facilities of Indiana University by contacting the Indiana University Visitor Information Center in the Carmichael Center on the corner of Indiana and Kirkwood Avenues in Bloomington; (812) 856–GOIU. Open 9:30 A.M. to 5:30 P.M. Monday through Friday, 10:00 A.M. to 4:00 P.M. Saturday, and noon to 3:00 P.M. Sunday.

If the IU campus looks familiar, it may be because you saw the award-winning movie *Breaking Away.* It was filmed in Bloomington and featured the university's **Little 500 Bicycle Race,** held here each spring. It's not open to the public, but you can drive by the house featured in the film; it's located at 756 South Lincoln Street. The swimming hole seen in the movie was an abandoned water-filled limestone quarry south of Bloomington known as the Empire Quarry; it provided the stone for the exterior of New York City's Empire State Building.

On the western edge of Bloomington lies beautiful **Rose Hill Cemetery**— as much a sculpture garden as a graveyard. Many of the memorials that mark its graves are works of art. In the oldest part of the cemetery are stones adorned with carvings of weeping willows, a symbol of grief that was popular when these markers were carved in the period from 1830 to 1865. These earlier tombstones are made primarily of marble, brought here from Vermont before the growth of the Indiana limestone industry. The image of willows and the use of marble to create them appear to have lost favor about the time the Civil War ended, replaced by the striking tree trunk memorials carved from the more enduring limestone. Other materials have gained favor in later years, but the limestone markers of Rose Hill still stand today as visible reminders of a unique

trivia

David V. Buskirk of Monroe County, whose height has been estimated from 6 feet, 10 inches, to 8 feet, was the tallest man to serve in the Union Army during the Civil War. The company he served in had 101 soldiers, sixty-seven of whom were more than 6 feet tall.

art that once brought worldwide fame to this part of Indiana.

The cemetery also serves as the final resting place for some of Bloomington's most renowned citizens, including Hoagy Carmichael and Alfred Kinsey. The university's first president also lies here, along with a former governor of the state and a Civil War general. Near the Elm Street entrance to the cemetery is a monument that honors the memory of a former resident who isn't even buried here. John B. Crafton was on a trip to Europe in the early 1900s when, overwhelmed by homesickness for his family in Bloomington, he decided to return home early. The wealthy businessman canceled his reservation on a German liner and booked an earlier passage on another ship. His decision cost him his life. The year was 1912; the ship was the RMS *Titanic.*

Rose Hill Cemetery extends westward from the corner of Fourth and Elm Streets; call (812) 349–3498.

Seven miles north of Bloomington on State Road 37, **Oliver Winery,** Indiana's oldest and largest, offers free weekend tours, free wine tasting, and, on Saturday evenings in June and July, outdoor concerts (most of which are free) on the parklike grounds. Owner Bill Oliver, a law professor at Indiana University, started his vineyards in 1971 and now produces 40,000 gallons of wine a year. His is also the only winery in the state to make ice wine. Several of the fifteen or so varieties have won gold and silver medals in competitions throughout the country. If you're in the mood for lunch, you can have "a jug of wine, a loaf of bread," and your own "thou" beside you at a picnic table outside or at a table in the cozy tasting room inside. You can also stroll through the winery's lovely gardens. Cheeses, summer sausage, fruits, popcorn, maple syrup, and unique limestone gifts are also available. Open 10:00 A.M. to 6:00 P.M. Monday through Saturday and noon to 6:00 P.M. Sunday; closes at 8:00 P.M. Friday and Saturday in June and July and at 5:00 P.M. daily January through March; free tours available every half hour from noon to 4:30 P.M. Friday and Saturday and from 1:00 to 4:30 P.M. Sunday. Write or call Oliver Winery, 8024 North State Road 37, Bloomington 47404; (812) 876–5800 or (800) 258–2783.

Morgan-Monroe State Forest wanders over 23,916 acres, most of which occupy northeastern Monroe County. Nestled in a clearing in the midst of the woods is a rustic log cabin where a true get-away-from-it-all experience awaits you. **Draper's Cabin** is described by the state as primitive, and the description is apt. There's no electricity, all water has to be carried in, heat is provided by a stone fireplace, and you make your bed on the floor. The forest provides plenty of wood for the fireplace, but it's up to you to gather it and carry it in. Only dead material can be used, and no saws are allowed. You can cook in the fireplace or, if you bring your own grill, on a concrete slab outdoors. The cabin contains nary a stick of furniture, but two picnic tables are just outside the door. A few yards away a small stream sometimes trickles by and sometimes doesn't—it depends on the rainfall.

Draper's Cabin is the only such cabin on any state-owned land, and you can rent it for $26.50 a night, including tax. The maximum stay is fourteen days. Available by advance reservation from April to mid-November and on a first-come, first-served basis the rest of the year. Write or call the Property Manager, Morgan-Monroe State Forest, 6220 Forest Road, Martinsville 46151; (765) 342–4026.

To reach the forest, go north from Bloomington on State Road 37 to Forest Road, the main entrance road, which runs east off State Road 37 into the forest just before you reach the Morgan-Monroe county line. If you go in the spring or fall, you probably won't be able to resist a hike through the woods. Brochures for the trails—which include two 10-mile loops, a ½-mile pathway through the **Scout Ridge State Nature Preserve,** and a ½-mile-square orienteering course called the Pathfinder Trail—are available at the office building. If you do your walking during hunting season, it's best to wear bright colors.

Orange County

When Larry Bird first burst on the professional basketball scene in 1979, he was promptly dubbed "the hick from French Lick" by many sportswriters across the nation. Larry went on to establish himself as the very heart of the Boston Celtics, and the sports world learned two things: He sure could play basketball, and, shyness and Hoosier dialect aside, he was no hick. What's more, Bird's hometown of **French Lick,** although small, is also the home of one of the most luxurious all-season resorts in the nation.

French Lick came into being because of some rich mineral springs that flowed from the hillsides. In 1837, to accommodate the hordes of people who flocked here to "take the waters," the French Lick Springs Hotel opened. Around the turn of the twentieth century, the hotel was purchased by Thomas Taggart, a nationally known political figure who served as mayor of Indianapolis and as U.S. senator from Indiana. Taggart, who juggled his two careers, was named chairman of the National Democratic Party in 1904. His national prominence came at a time when spas were at the height of their popularity, and the elite of society and politics from all over the country descended on French Lick to drink the waters from its springs and to partake of the mineral baths.

Gambling was added, luring even more visitors, including both celebrities and gangsters. In 1932 several state governors met here and decided to back Franklin Delano Roosevelt for president. The Vanderbilts, Morgans, and Whitneys came here to play, followed later by such stars as Lana Turner, Roy Rogers, Dale Evans, and Gene Autry.

Although the gambling had been discontinued for many years, the hotel continued to operate as the ***French Lick Springs Resort*** until 2005, when it closed down for a major restoration. Gambling returned in November 2006, when the hotel reopened along with a new casino that floats on a small lake on hotel property. Currently, the casino is open 9:00 A.M. to 4:00 P.M. Monday through Friday and 9:00 A.M. to 6:00 P.M. Saturday and Sunday; admission is free. The springs are still there, and guests can relax in the peaceful setting and enjoy such activities as golf, swimming, bicycling, and a health and fitness center. From approximately December to March, you can go skiing on six nearby slopes. Eight on-site restaurants provide food for every taste. For additional information, write or call the French Lick Springs Resort, 8670 West State Road 56, French Lick 47432; (812) 936–9300 or (800) 457–4042.

Railroad buffs will be intrigued by the ***Indiana Railway Museum,*** located just north of French Lick Springs Resort's parking lot on State Road 56. Operated as a nonprofit corporation, the museum has its headquarters in the old Monon Railroad station, where several steam locomotives, a rare railway post office car, and a 1951 dining car are among the memorabilia on display. Visitors can also buy a ticket and board the ***French Lick Scenic Railway*** for a one-and-three-quarter-hour, 20-mile, round-trip ride between French Lick and Cuzco, Indiana. A diesel locomotive pulls 1920s-era passenger cars away from the station and plunges into the wooded terrain of Hoosier National Forest, offering its passengers views of rugged Orange County backcountry where no roads penetrate. Along the way the train passes through the 2,200-foot-long Burton Tunnel, one of Indiana's longest. Children are especially delighted by the train robberies staged on special weekends. Trains depart at 10:00 A.M. and 1:00 and 4:00 P.M. each Saturday, Sunday, and holiday April through October; also at 1:00 P.M. on Tuesday June through October and on Saturday and Sunday in November. For additional information write the Indiana Railway Museum, P.O. Box 347, French Lick 47432; call (812) 936–2405 or (800) 748–7246; or visit www.indianarailwaymuseum.org.

Approximately 1 mile north of French Lick on State Road 56, visitors can see the magnificent ***West Baden Springs Hotel.*** The architectural masterpiece, once known as the "most unique hotel on Earth" and the "Carlsbad of America," was world famous in the early 1900s, but through the years it did not fare as well as French Lick's resort.

Begun in October 1901, construction on the West Baden Springs Hotel was completed eight and a half months later—an astonishing accomplishment in any day but truly extraordinary given the technology of the time. Its imaginative owner, Col. Lee Sinclair, had conjured up visions of a sumptuous hotel that established architects of the day said was impossible to build. Urged on by his daughter Lillian, Colonel Sinclair finally found an enterprising young architect who accepted the challenge not only to build the hotel but to do so for $414,000—with a $100-a-day penalty clause if construction took longer than the agreed-on 200 working days.

When finished, the dome above the immense central atrium, larger than the dome at St. Peter's Cathedral in Rome, was regarded as the "eighth wonder of the world." Two hundred feet in diameter, 130 feet above the floor, ribbed with twenty-four steel girders mounted on rollers to accommodate expansion and contraction, it remained the world's largest self-supporting dome until the Houston Astrodome was completed in 1965. The atrium floor was covered with twelve million Italian marble tiles, and the elaborate sunken gardens were planted with rare flowers from Europe and the Orient. Circling the atrium and its gardens were 708 guest rooms on six floors.

West Baden Springs Hotel thrived for thirty years, attracting an illustrious clientele that included Gen. John J. Pershing, J. M. Studebaker, and Diamond Jim Brady, as well as the likes of Al Capone. In 1932, however, it became a casualty of the Great Depression.

Subsequently it served as winter headquarters for the old Hagenbeck-Wallace Circus, as a Jesuit school, and as the home of Northwood Institute, a college that trained its students for employment in the hotel restaurant field. During the Jesuits' tenancy the face of the old hotel was altered forever. The Jesuits felt that some of the grander touches were unseemly for their austere lifestyle. And so the Roman-style baths were wrecked and hauled away, the gardens were left untended, the lavish furniture was sold, the beautiful Moorish towers were removed from the roof, and the arabesque brickwork atop the building was straightened.

The hotel was allowed to deteriorate for years until funds were acquired to begin its restoration. A gorgeous garden features fountains and brick pathways, and the Moorish towers have been replaced. Restoration of the one-of-a-kind building, which has been designated a National Historic Landmark, will be completed in June 2007, when it will once again operate as a hotel. Until then, visitors can view the building and gardens on special tours that are conducted at 10:00 A.M., noon, and 2:00 and 4:00 P.M. on Sunday. Admission fees are applied to renovation costs. For up-to-date information write the French Lick–West Baden Chamber of Commerce, 1 Monon Street, P.O. Box 347, French Lick 47432, or call (812) 936–4034 or (800) 450–4534.

Body Reflections, a beauty salon in French Lick, is home to the only museum of its kind in the world. Owner Tony Kendall has collected antiques related to hair styling for several years, and you can view them in his *Wild Hair Museum.*

Tony's collection includes vintage combs, hairbrushes, permanent-wave machines, razors, shears, and hair tonics. Relics heated by kerosene and gaslight share a shelf with more modern instruments heated by electricity. Tony's most prized possessions are a lock of hair that has been authenticated

Birthplace of the Slider

Most people who travel to and through Orleans know it as the small Orange County town that's the self-proclaimed Dogwood Capital of Indiana. Very few know that it is also the birthplace of the White Castle hamburger, affectionately called the slider by its legions of aficionados. (It's known by a few other names, too, mostly descriptive of the way in which the little burger affects the digestive system.)

Until 1992 a downtown factory was the only supplier of White Castle burgers in the United States. Approximately three million of the square, five-holed patties were produced here each week. Because of increasing demand, the company has since built a new Orleans facility with twice the production capacity and added a second facility in Lebanon, Indiana. There are currently more than 300 White Castle restaurants, and ten to fifteen new outlets are added each year. Unfortunately for the part of the nation that's excluded, White Castle shops are found only in a limited area, bound by New York on the east, Kansas on the west, Minnesota on the north, and Tennessee on the south.

The burger's reputation, though, has no boundaries. Visitors from White Castle–less parts of the country scorn other more expensive and certainly more luxurious restaurants to dash to the nearest White Castle outlet. A few years ago, a couple of transplanted midwesterners were married in Arizona. The food of choice for the wedding reception was the White Castle burger, several thousand of which were transported across the country in a refrigerated semi rented for the occasion by the bride and groom.

White Castle restaurants also have a reputation for cleanliness. An inspection of all Indiana restaurants, from the most to least expensive, chains and nonchains, revealed that White Castle kitchens tied with one other restaurant chain (Bob Evans) as the cleanest in the state. Apparently, when they're not cooking at White Castle, they're cleaning.

as belonging to Elvis Presley and a rare antique hair wreath. The wreath dates from Civil War times, when locks from generations of the same family were woven into an open-ended wreath of perfectly shaped flowers, with each flower representing an individual. Only a few survived because so many of them were burned during a plague scare in the early 1900s. People believed the hair could pass on the disease.

Since Tony was featured in an A&E documentary about hair a few years back, he's become a very popular guy in the industry. He's had to expand a bit because people keep bringing him things for his collection. The aforementioned lock of the King's hair now occupies a place of honor in Tony's new Elvis room.

Tony's latest project, which he hopes will earn him a place in the *Guinness Book of World Records*, is the construction of the world's largest hairball.

You can view Tony's collection free of charge at his salon at 448 South Maple Street during his normal business hours of 9:00 A.M. to 7:00 P.M. Tuesday through Friday and 9:00 A.M. to 2:00 P.M. Saturday; call (812) 936–7008 for additional information.

Orleans has called itself the **Dogwood Capital of Indiana** since 1970, a few years after Mr. and Mrs. C. E. Wheeler started planting dogwood trees along State Road 37, one of the town's main thoroughfares. It was a labor of love for the Wheelers, who believed that the dogwood's pink and white blooms had no equal for beauty. Today the trees cover a 12-mile stretch between Mitchell on the north and Paoli on the south, and more trees are added each year in what is now a communitywide project. They're usually in full bloom in late April and early May.

Orange County is also the site of two of the Hoosier State's most unusual natural landmarks. On the southern edge of **Orangeville,** which lies about 7 miles southwest of Orleans via country roads, you can view the **Orangeville Rise of the Lost River.** An underground river surfaces here as an artesian spring, flowing from a cave into a 220-foot-wide rock-walled pit at the base of a limestone bluff. The three-acre preserve is well marked, and there's a pull-off for parking. For additional information write or call The Nature Conservancy, Indiana Field Office, 1505 North Delaware Street, Suite 200, Indianapolis 46202; (317) 951–8818.

Not far from Paoli, on the edge of Hoosier National Forest, is an eighty-acre tract of virgin woodland known as **Pioneer Mothers Memorial Forest,** whose magnificent trees range from 150 to 600 years old. Its crown jewel is the Walnut Cathedral, a moist cove that, according to the U.S. Department of the Interior, contains the finest stand of black walnut trees in the entire country. From Paoli go south on State Road 37 for about 1¼ miles to the Pioneer Mothers State Wayside on the east side of the road. From this picnic area you can follow marked trails for a short distance into the memorial forest. Write or call the Forest Supervisor, Hoosier National Forest, 811 Constitution Avenue, Bedford 47421; (812) 275–5987.

Parke County

All of Parke County is a museum of *covered bridges.* Within its boundaries are more covered bridges than you'll find in any other county in the United States—more, in fact, than you'll find in most states. At last count, thirty of them were intact. What's more, they're all authentic, with the two oldest dating back to 1856 and the youngster of the bunch to 1920. All thirty were placed on the National Register of Historic Places in 1978.

Joe Sturm, a retired farmer and carpenter, has served as official bridge inspector for more than twelve years and can relate all kinds of interesting facts about them. He can tell you, for instance, that so many bridges were built because of the numerous zigzagging streams in the county, that the only metal used in constructing them is the bolts, and that the bridge at Mecca was built on dry ground and a nearby stream rerouted to pass under it.

Most of the bridges still support traffic, and the folks in Parke County have mapped out four automobile routes that provide access to most of them. A free map outlining each route is available at the Parke County Tourist Information Center, located at 127 South Jefferson Street in Rockville. It's open 9:00 A.M. to 4:00 P.M. daily Memorial Day weekend to the first weekend of November, and Monday through Saturday the rest of the year; (765) 569–5226.

The northwest route leads you to *West Union Bridge,* at 315 feet the longest in the county. The community of *Bridgeton,* with its many unusual shops, is a highlight of the southernmost route. Standing on the bank of Big Raccoon Creek, next to the *Bridgeton Bridge,* is the *Weise Mill.* It's been grinding meal since it was built in 1823, making it the oldest known gristmill west of the Allegheny Mountains that's still in service. Directly west of Rockville is the *Sim Smith Bridge,* which claims the distinction of being the county's only haunted bridge.

Parke County originally had more than fifty covered bridges, but several were lost to fire, flood, and natural deterioration before a preservation effort had begun. Each October since 1957, the county has celebrated its heritage with a ten-day *Covered Bridge Festival.* The nationally recognized event regularly lures some 500,000 visitors.

Another popular festival is the late-winter *Maple Fair,* which takes place when local sugar camps are producing maple syrup. For more information write or call the Parke County Convention and Visitors Bureau, P.O. Box 165, Rockville 47872; (765) 569–5226.

If you head northeast from Rockville, you'll come to **Turkey Run State Park,** noted for its steep ravines, its sandstone formations, and the **Rocky Hollow–Falls Canyon State Nature Preserve,** which protects a lush primeval forest. The **Narrows Bridge,** one of the most photographed in the county, crosses Sugar Creek in the park. A tree-shaded inn in the park offers overnight accommodations in fifty-two rooms and twenty-one nearby cabins, and it has two swimming pools and four tennis courts; call (765) 597–2211 or (877) 500–6151. Write Turkey Run State Park, 8121 East Park Road, P.O. Box 37, Marshall 47859, or phone (765) 597–2635.

On U.S. Highway 41 north of Rockville, just before you reach the state park, stands **Gobbler's Knob Country Store,** where you can purchase nostalgic wares that revive memories of grandmother—penny candies in jars, pickles from a barrel, sassafras bark, country hams, sunbonnets, corncob jelly, and carnival glass; call (765) 597–2558.

Follow U.S. Highway 36 east from Rockville for 1 mile, and cross Billie Creek Bridge into an early-twentieth-century village and farmstead where the crafts and skills of yesteryear are on vivid display. One of the finest living museums in the state, **Billie Creek Village** is open daily from mid-January to late December; hours vary. An admission fee is charged when craftspeople are in residence; admission is free at other times. Write or call Billie Creek Village, 1659 East US 36, Rockville 47872; (765) 569–3430.

Although many Hoosiers have never heard of **Mordecai "Three Fingers" Brown,** he has never been forgotten by his hometown of **Nyesville** and by diehard baseball fans. Brown, who was born in 1876, earned his nickname at age seven when his right hand was mangled in a corn-grinding machine.

Covered bridge in Parke County

Undaunted, he started throwing baseballs at a barn wall and developed a unique curve ball that made him one of the greatest pitchers ever to play the game.

During his fourteen years in the major leagues, Mordecai won 239 games and had a lifetime 2.06 earned-run average that remains to this day the third best in baseball history. His greatest fame came during his 1905–1916 tenure with the Chicago Cubs. While in Chicago he won twenty or more games six years in a row. He won twenty-nine games in 1908 and that same year became the first pitcher ever to record four consecutive shutouts. As the team's star pitcher, Mordecai helped the Cubs earn four National League pennants and two World Series championships.

When the arrival of the year 2000 prompted the compilation of lists of the greatest athletes of the twentieth century, *USA Today* listed Mordecai as one of the five greatest from Indiana, and *Sports Illustrated* listed him in the state's top ten. The great Ty Cobb once called Mordecai's curve ball "the most devastating pitch I have ever faced." When asked how he could achieve so much with only three fingers, Mordecai replied, "All I know is I had all the fingers I needed." In 1949, one year after his death, Mordecai Brown became the first Indiana native to be inducted into the Baseball Hall of Fame in Cooperstown, New York.

Today his memory is honored with a monument in a cornfield near Nyesville, where his boyhood home once stood. Engravings on the 3-foot-high, black-and-gray-granite marker depict the image of Mordecai launching his famous curve ball and relate the remarkable achievements of a man who turned adversity into achievement. To see the ***Mordecai Brown monument,*** go east from Billie Creek Village on US 36 a short distance to County Road 160 East (also known as the Nyesville-Judson Road); turn north and proceed to Nyesville. The monument can be seen near Nyesville, about 100 yards off the road. Ask locally for exact directions.

Perry County

Besides its bountiful natural beauty, this Ohio River county is worth visiting for its array of unusual monuments.

If ***Tell City*** has a landmark, it is the life-size ***statue of William Tell*** and his son that serves as the centerpiece for the fountain in front of city hall. The statue is a reflection of the town's Swiss heritage and a tribute to the legendary Swiss hero from whom Tell City took its name. Town residents were delighted when, in 1974, plans were announced for the construction of the fountain that would honor the town's namesake, but they never dreamed it would cause such a fuss.

After the statue had been formed by Evansville sculptor Don Ingle, it was sent to a New York foundry to be cast in bronze. Ingle and his wife then personally picked up the 500-pound statue in New York, placed it in a rented U-Haul van, and headed home for the formal dedication. Imagine their horror when, after spending the night in an Ohio motel, they discovered that the van—statue and all—had been stolen as they slept. Everyone got into the act, with local police and the FBI cooperating in a frantic search and news media throughout the country warning everyone to be on the lookout for the kidnapped William Tell. The nationwide furor was such that the thief eventually abandoned his ill-gotten gain on a side street in Cleveland, and the statue was escorted the rest of the way home without further ado. You can see William Tell today in his place of honor atop the fountain—one arm holding his crossbow, the other arm around his son's shoulder, and not an apple in sight.

trivia

The model for the image of Uncle Sam that appeared on the famous World War II "I want you!" recruitment poster was the late Walter Botts of Sullivan.

Poised above State Road 66 near Troy, a towering 19-foot statue of Christ overlooks the Ohio River, arms extended in an eternal blessing of all who gaze on it. Herbert Jogerst, a German artist, sculpted the statue when he was a prisoner of war in Indiana during World War II. It stands on a bluff once owned by Robert Fulton, of steamboat fame, and is now part of a summer camp for physically challenged children. Illuminated at night, the all-white *Christ of the Ohio* is always visible to travelers on land or water.

At St. Augustine's Church in *Leopold* stands the *Shrine of Our Lady of Consolation,* whose strange history dates back to the Civil War. Three young Union Army soldiers from Perry County, members of the church, were confined in the infamous prison at Andersonville, Georgia. They vowed to one another that if they lived through the horror of that experience they would donate a shrine to their church as a token of their gratitude. Miraculously they all survived, and one of them personally made a trip to Belgium to oversee the making of an exact reproduction of a shrine he remembered seeing in a small village church there.

Some historians claim that, unable to obtain the reproduction he desired, the young man stole the original and transported it back to Indiana, sparking an international incident between the governments of the two countries. It happened, however, that Leopold had been named for the Leopold who was then king of Belgium. The Belgian leader was so pleased to learn of his namesake that he allowed the shrine to remain there. It can be seen today, a statue of Mary and the infant Jesus, each wearing a white gown, a blue robe, and a crown of jewels. The church is located at 18020 Lafayette Street. Call (812) 843–5143 for information.

One of the Hoosier State's finest historical landmarks, the huge, castlelike **Cannelton Cotton Mill,** was a beehive of activity from 1849 to 1965. Once the busiest industry in Indiana, it contained the most modern textile machinery, rivaling the better-known mills of New England. Some 400 laborers operating 372 looms spun raw cotton into thread and cloth; a good worker in the old days could sometimes earn as much as $4.50 a day. Union Army uniforms were made here during the Civil War.

Often honored for its architecture and described as one of the most outstanding engineering feats of its time in the Midwest, the mammoth stone structure is 60 feet wide by 280 feet long and has 5-foot-thick interior walls. Two copper-roofed towers, each more than 100 feet tall, serve as landmarks for Ohio River traffic. One of the towers held water that could be used to flood each of the five floors in case of fire, a constant threat in a cotton mill. The second tower, besides serving as a fire escape, was designed to reduce the risk of fire; it contained five trapdoors that were opened twice each working day so that air could be drawn down through a chimney to remove accumulated lint.

Despite its magnificence and its status as a National Historic Landmark, the mill remained a gaunt gray ghost until 2001. That was when government grants provided the wherewithal to renovate the mill and convert it into an innovative apartment complex. The first tenants moved in in January 2002, and the townsfolk celebrated the mill's rebirth at a special festival in June 2002. For information about the mill, located on the southwest corner of Fourth and Washington Streets in **Cannelton,** write or call the Perry County Convention and Visitors Bureau, 645 Main Street, Suite 200, Tell City 47586; (812) 547–7933 or (888) 343–6262.

Rising from a soybean field not far east of Cannelton is a grim reminder of one of Indiana's worst air tragedies. The **Air Crash Memorial Monument,** 9 feet tall and 12 feet wide, recalls a March day in 1960 when a Northwest Airlines flight from Minneapolis to Miami plummeted to the ground at this spot. According to a witness, the plane's wings simply broke off in midair. The plane fell

Gone, but Not Forgotten

On August 21, 1865, the steamboat USS *Argosy III* was transporting a group of mustered-out Civil War veterans up the Ohio River to Cincinnati. A sudden storm hurled the boat against some rocks near the Perry County town of Magnet (then known as Rono) and caused its boiler to explode. Ten Union soldiers, on their way home after surviving years of brutal warfare, either drowned or were scalded to death. The survivors and local farmers pulled the dead from the waters and buried them in a mass grave.

The history of that accident and the mass burial site did not come to light until 1962. To commemorate the dead, the federal government supplied ten white stone markers that were anchored in a concrete base, and the Indiana Civil War Centennial Commission supplied a "Civil War Memorial Grave" marker. The names of the victims are carved into nine of the stones; the tenth bears the poignant message UNKNOWN U.S. SOLDIER. One day before the centennial of the riverboat tragedy, a gathering of Perry County citizens and interested visitors officially dedicated the site.

The late Clyde E. Benner became the small cemetery's self-appointed caretaker, clearing and weeding the gravesite until his death in 1985. Today, his four daughters carry on the tradition. One, Pat Irwin, is the primary caretaker. She says it's hard to believe how many people ask for directions to "that Civil War place around here."

There are no road signs to direct you there, but you can reach it by taking U.S. Highway 66 to the turnoff road for Magnet. Go east through Magnet and continue for about ½ mile to the cemetery, nestled in a grove of maples, poplars, laurels, and cottonwood on the right.

18,000 feet straight down, literally burying itself in the ground. The impact killed all sixty-three people on board and created a crater 20 feet deep and 30 feet wide. It took two weeks to complete the recovery operation. Investigators later blamed the crash on structural faults in the engine, which caused a flutter in the wings that caused them to snap off.

The Cannelton Kiwanis Club raised funds to erect the monument seen today at the crash site. Topped by a "torch of life," the granite memorial is inscribed with the names of all of the victims.

To reach the monument, head east from Cannelton on State Road 66 to State Road 166 and turn right. Follow 166 southeast about 1½ miles to Millstone Road. Turn left onto Millstone Road and proceed approximately 1 mile to the monument on the left side of the road.

Another monument, a tall obelisk in Tell City's ***Greenwood Cemetery,*** memorializes the same tragedy. Here an 1,800-square-foot plot was set aside in which to bury fifty-five of the crash victims, of whom only seventeen could be identified. The obelisk, inscribed with the names of the dead, was placed here by Northwest Airlines.

While in Tell City, tour the **Tell City Pretzel Company,** which may be the only company in the United States and one of the few in the world that still produces pretzels the original way—by hand-twisting them. A Swiss baker brought the recipe with him from Europe when he settled here more than one hundred years ago. Although the recipe is still a secret, passed down from owner to owner, visitors are welcome to watch the twisters at work each Monday through Friday from 7:00 A.M. until about 3:00 P.M. The 12,000 pretzels produced daily are sold on the premises and by mail order. Tell City Pretzels is located at 432 Main Street, Tell City; (812) 547–4631.

Posey County

In 1814 a group of German Lutheran separatists migrated westward from Pennsylvania to the verdant valley of the Wabash River. There they purchased some 30,000 acres of land along the riverbank and carved from the dense woodlands the personification of a dream—a tiny communal settlement they named Harmony. An industrious people, the Harmonists established a variety of successful industries that included the manufacture of fine silks and whiskey distilling, and their products were much in demand throughout the eastern United States. They developed prefabricated houses, dug tunnels beneath them, and used the cool air therein to air-condition their dwellings. Oranges were grown year-round in their greenhouses. Eventually they found themselves with enough leisure time to start bickering among themselves, and in 1825 their leader, Father George Rapp, sold the entire town to Robert Owen, a wealthy industrialist from Scotland.

Owen envisioned a utopia of a different sort, a commune that focused on innovative education and intellectual pursuits. His **New Harmony** lured scientists, social reformers, writers, and artists whose ideas and creations made a lasting impact on our country's history. America's first free public school system, kindergarten, day care center, free library, trade school, women's club, and civic dramatic club came to fruition here. One of Owen's sons, David Dale Owen, became an eminent geologist and was commissioned to make the first survey of new government lands in the West. After David Owen was appointed U.S. Geologist in 1838, he ran the U.S. Geological Survey from New Harmony for seventeen years. Another of Owen's sons, Richard, entered Congress, became an early crusader for the rights of women, and drafted the legislation that established the Smithsonian Institution. Yet another son became president of Indiana's Purdue University.

Although many of the concepts developed at Owen's New Harmony have survived, the commune foundered quickly in 1827. One reason for this was that its inhabitants did not possess the husbandry skills needed to feed its populace. While lofty ideas and ideals were being discussed inside, the hogs were invading the vegetables outside.

New Harmony was never deserted, however. Its reputation as an intellectual center gradually faded, but many residents stayed on, putting down roots that have kept the community alive to this day.

In the 1940s Jane Owen, wife of a direct descendant of Robert Owen, visited here and became so enamored of the settlement she initiated a restoration project. Today New Harmony is a state historical site, and people come from all over the country to take a twelve-point tour that traces the history of the settlement from its original log cabins to some striking structures added in recent years.

Enclosed within the brick walls of the Harmonist cemetery at the west end of Granary Street are more than 200 unmarked graves—symbolic of continued equality in death—and several Native American burial mounds. The Labyrinth, a fascinating maze of paths and hedges on the south edge of town, represents the twists and turns and choices that confront each of us in our passage through life.

Completed in 1979, the stark white **Atheneum** that rises from a meadow near the riverbank has garnered many honors for its architectural design. The visitor center within periodically shows a film entitled *The New Harmony Experience* and exhibits a scale model of the original town. Located at 401 North Arthur Street; (812) 682–4474 or (800) 231–2168.

Serving as the altar for the **Roofless Church,** a paved courtyard that's open to the sky, is a unique dome that's shaped like an inverted rosebud but casts the shadow of a full-blown rose. Its design was inspired by writer George Sand, who remarked that the sky was the only roof vast enough to embrace all of worshiping humanity. When Paul Tillich, the world-renowned philosopher and theologian, visited here in 1963, he was so impressed by the Roofless Church that he said it alone justified our century. When Tillich died not long afterward, his ashes were buried in **Tillich Park** opposite the church.

One of the most beautiful sights at New Harmony, however, is a seasonal event orchestrated by nature. The first golden raintree in the nation was planted at New Harmony, and today there is scarcely a lawn or street anywhere in town that does not boast at least one of these lovely trees. An ornamental tree that originated in Asia, the golden raintree is unusually beautiful throughout the year but is most glorious around the third week in June when it bursts into full bloom, then sheds its petals in a virtual shower of brilliant

The Thousand-Year Storm

Tornadoes, nature's most destructive storms, occur more frequently in the United States than in any other country on earth. Seventy-five percent of the world's tornadoes take place in the United States, and the vast majority of those strike our country's midsection. As residents of a tornado-prone heartland, Hoosiers are well acquainted with these violent whirlwinds (Indiana experiences an average of twenty-three tornadoes each year). Few people today, however, remember that Indiana was one of three states devastated by the single most destructive tornado in recorded history.

The weather forecast for much of the Midwest on March 18, 1925, called for "rains and strong shifting winds." It was a common forecast for a spring day in this part of the world. Midwesterners went about their business as usual but kept a wary eye on the sky, aware at all times how violent a spring storm could suddenly become.

No one, however, expected the unprecedented fury of the tornado that dropped from the skies that day. The Tri-State Tornado, as it is known in the record books, is the one tornado that stands apart from all others—before and since.

The tornado was born at 1:01 P.M. in the Missouri Ozarks. From there it raced northeastward across the Mississippi, through Illinois, and into Indiana, hugging the ground with a vengeance for three and a half hours. It did not lift, skip, or, until the last few miles of its life, veer from its straightforward path. When it finally dissipated, it had traveled 219 miles at forward speeds of more than 70 miles per hour. Its winds at times were in excess of 300 miles per hour. Its width varied from ½ mile to more than 1 mile wide. (By way of comparison, the average tornado lasts a few minutes, travels 5 miles at a forward speed of 30 miles per hour, produces winds of 150 miles per hour or less, and averages 220 yards in width.)

When the storm crossed the Wabash River and entered Indiana at about 4:00 P.M., it headed straight for Griffin, a small village located approximately 3 miles from the river in northwestern Posey County. It took less than three minutes for the twister to obliterate the entire town. Not a single structure was left standing. Stunned survivors could only guess where they had once lived.

gold. There's no place in the United States where this tree grows in greater quantity.

New Harmony is easily explored on foot. Historic New Harmony, Inc., has its headquarters at 506½ Main Street and offers general information as well as guided tours for nominal fees; Write or call the organization at 506½ Main Street, P.O. Box 579, New Harmony 47631; (812) 682–4488 or (800) 231–2168.

Even the town's commercial district has a revitalized early-twentieth-century aura, and although it's not historic, the redbrick *New Harmony Inn* is a charming mix of traditional and modern design that blends well with its surroundings.

Still the twister raced on, turning slightly northward toward Owensville and Princeton. Although narrowing in width, it increased its forward speed to nearly 75 miles per hour—faster than its top speed in either Missouri or Illinois. It created havoc in Owensville and swept away half of Princeton before finally exhausting itself about 3 miles southwest of Petersburg.

As survivors came together in the aftermath of the storm, tales of bizarre phenomena surfaced. The river mud that had been sucked up into the tornado by the time it reached Griffin left people there with mud so thoroughly embedded in their skin that they were unrecognizable. A baby, completely covered with mud, was dug from a ditch after its cries were heard; no one in the area had a baby, and its rescuers never learned if its parents had been found. At the site of one house, only a carton of eggs and a remnant of the floor on which it was sitting were found intact. A cow was found standing and chewing her cud, seemingly unperturbed, although the barn around her had been lifted up and carried away. An office in Princeton was razed to the ground, but a bundle of paychecks that had been stored in an office cabinet was found undamaged 55 miles away.

Property damage wrought by the storm was estimated at $16.5 million in 1925 dollars (equal to $159 million today). The storm had completely annihilated four towns and 15,000 homes, severely damaged six more towns, and injured 2,027 people. Most significant of all, there were 695 confirmed deaths, still a record for a single tornado.

On average, 800 to 1,000 tornadoes occur in the United States each year. Some 1,800 tornadoes were reported in 2004. But to this day, the 1925 Tri-State Tornado remains the deadliest tornado in history, a rare storm that some weather historians say comes along once in a thousand years.

In April 2004 ten survivors of that storm were among the onlookers as a black memorial marker was unveiled in the town of Griffin. The Indiana Historical Bureau marker relates the horror of that day. Plans also call for a brass plaque containing the names of those killed to be placed alongside the marker.

Wood-burning fireplaces, rush-seated rockers, kitchenettes, living rooms, and spiral staircases that lead to sleeping lofts are all available. Trees march right up to glass walls that enclose a heated pool, and the sky is always visible through a sliding glass roof. The beautifully landscaped grounds share the shoreline of a placid lake with open fields and patches of forest laced with biking and hiking paths. Rates vary seasonally. Write or call the New Harmony Inn, 504 North Street, P.O. Box 581, New Harmony 47631; (812) 682–4431 or (800) 782–8605.

Next door, a gourmet restaurant, the ***Red Geranium,*** serves lunch and dinner six days a week. The spinach salad with house dressing, warm homemade bread, and Shaker lemon pie are really special. Children's menus are available. Hours are 11:00 A.M. to 9:00 P.M. Tuesday through Thursday, 11:00 A.M. to 10:00 P.M. Friday and Saturday, and 11:00 A.M. to 8:00 P.M. Sunday; closed Monday and some major holidays. Call (812) 682–4431.

By driving south from New Harmony on State Road 69 for about 24 miles, almost to the Ohio River, you are suddenly confronted with a scene that might have been transported here from the Deep South. *Hovey Lake* resembles a southern swamp, particularly in the slough areas to the east of the lake. Its waters are studded with huge bald cypress trees—one noteworthy old patriarch has lived to about 250 years of age. Along the lakeshore are southern red oak, wild pecans, mistletoe, holly, and swamp privet.

trivia

Controversial labor leader James "Jimmy" Hoffa was born on February 14, 1913, in Brazil, Indiana. His disappearance on July 30, 1975, remains an unsolved mystery to this day, despite one of the largest FBI manhunts in history. Hoffa's middle name, ironically, was Riddle.

Bird-watchers spot great blue herons, American egrets, double-breasted cormorants, and pileated woodpeckers. Osprey have been known to nest here, and white ibis, bald eagles, hawks, and owls frequent the area. In the autumn, usually beginning in the first week in October, some 500,000 ducks and geese arrive for the winter.

Hovey Lake, formed about 500 years ago, is an oxbow lake that occupies an old channel of the nearby Ohio River. It's now part of a 4,300-acre state fish and wildlife area, but even if you don't like to fish, you can rent a rowboat, glide among the majestic trees that rise from the surface of the water, and enjoy the serenity and seclusion of this lovely place. When seen through the mists of early morning, Hovey Lake takes on a dreamlike aura.

Close to the launching ramp, you'll find an oak-shaded picnic area and forty-eight primitive campsites. Write or call Hovey Lake State Fish and Wildlife Area, 15010 State Road 69 South, Mt. Vernon 47620; (812) 838–2927.

Putnam County

In the valley of Big Walnut Creek lies one of the most beautiful and unusual natural areas in Indiana. The clear waters of the creek calmly meander southward through steep ravines studded with limestone outcroppings. A great blue heron rookery that has been continuously occupied for more than sixty years shares the forest with the great horned owl and more than 120 other species of birds. What is thought to be the largest sugar maple in the world, as well as the two largest sassafras trees, and the second biggest hemlock in Indiana, thrive within the preserve's confines.

Located about 1½ miles northeast of Bainbridge, the **Big Walnut State Nature Preserve** lies primarily along that part of the creek between Pine Bluff Covered Bridge and Rolling Stone Covered Bridge. It's open daily, free of charge, during daylight hours. For additional information and exact directions, write or call the Indiana Department of Natural Resources, Division of Nature Preserves, 402 West Washington Street, Room W267, Indianapolis 46204; (317) 232–4052.

It took an act of Congress to get it there, but one of only two buzz bombs in the country is displayed on the courthouse lawn in **Greencastle** (the other is in the Smithsonian Institution in Washington, D.C.). Perched atop a giant limestone *V*, the German-built bomb is one of the first guided missiles. It was among some captured military ordnance brought to the United States at the end of World War II, and a local Veterans of Foreign Wars post was given permission by Congress to bring the bomb to Indiana for use as part of a memorial. The **buzz bomb monument** can be seen at the corner of Washington and Jackson Streets. For additional information write or call the Putnam County Convention and Visitors Bureau, 12 West Washington Street, Greencastle 46135; (765) 653–8743 or (800) 829–4639.

Spencer County

Poised majestically atop a hill, the **St. Meinrad Archabbey** emerges unexpectedly from the trees and hills of northeastern Spencer County. Your eyes are first drawn to the soaring twin spires of the Abbey Church, then to the entire complex of beautiful buildings that house a theological school, a college, a monastery, and such income-producing enterprises as a publishing company, a winery, and a meat-packing plant.

When the abbey was founded by immigrant missionaries from Switzerland in 1854, the monks themselves transported the sandstone from a quarry 1 mile distant, hand-chipped it into the desired shape, and erected buildings patterned after the European medieval style so vivid in their memories. Newer, more modern buildings appear among the old ones these days, but all interiors remain starkly simple in keeping with the order's dedication to a spiritual rather than materialistic lifestyle.

trivia

As a child growing up in southern Indiana, Florence Henderson was inspired to become a singer when she heard the Gregorian chants sung by the Benedictine monks at the St. Meinrad Archabbey. The Dale native is best known today for her portrayal of Carol Brady, mother to television's *The Brady Bunch.*

Visitors who roam the well-maintained grounds find themselves in the company of priests and brothers in simple black gowns—teachers, lay employees, and some 400 students who are training for the priesthood. Although silence is part of the Benedictine life, it is expected only from 9:00 P.M. through breakfast the following day and at all times in the halls of the monastery. Otherwise, the monks and brothers are fun-loving, hospitable people who enjoy conversing with visitors. There's even a campus bar and pizzeria called the Unstable that's open two hours each weekday night and three hours on weekends. Overnight accommodations are also available by reservation.

You're welcome to join the monks for a worship service; Mass is in English. Brochures for self-guided tours can be picked up at the Guest House Office; hours vary. Free guided tours are available by advance appointment at 1:30 P.M. Saturday February through November; write or call St. Meinrad Archabbey, 200 Hill Drive, St. Meinrad 47577; (812) 357–6501. The abbey is located on State Road 62, just south of Interstate 64, near the Perry-Spencer county line; follow the signs.

One of the happiest places in Indiana can be found near Dale. Just follow the giggles to *Dr. Ted's Musical Marvels,* and join in the toe-tapping, swing-

St. Meinrad Archabbey

ing, swaying, and stomping to the delightful sounds that emanate from this extraordinary collection of mechanical musical machines.

Among the more than thirty music makers you'll see here is the Decap Belgian Dance Organ, one of the few in existence. Measuring 12 feet tall by 24 feet long and weighing 4,000 pounds, it is similar in operation to a player piano. With 535 pieces, two accordions, two saxophones, a snare drum, a bass drum, a wood block, a tempo block, and cymbals, all playing at the same time, it can very nearly substitute for an entire orchestra.

A Wurlitzer organ that dates from the early 1900s originally provided the music for merry-go-rounds. The KT Special is a nickelodeon with colored lights that flash on and off in time to the tunes it plays. There's also an air-drive calliope to evoke memories of the circus. And then there are the street organs, music boxes, player pianos, phonographs, and gramophones.

Dr. Ted's eclectic collection is open from 10:00 A.M. to 6:00 P.M. Monday through Saturday and 1:00 to 6:00 P.M. Sunday, Memorial Day through Labor Day; open 10:00 A.M. to 6:00 P.M. Saturday and 1:00 to 6:00 P.M. Sunday in May and September. Group tours are given year-round by advance appointment. Located on U.S. Highway 231, about ½ mile north of I–64; nominal admission fee. For additional information write Dr. Ted's at Route 4, Box 3017, Dale 47523; call (812) 937–4250; or visit www.drteds.com.

Two notable residents have made their homes in this county, and it would be tough to decide who is more famous—unless you are six years old or younger.

The U.S. Postal Service receives several million pieces of mail each Christmas addressed to Santa Claus, and it's all forwarded to Santa Claus's true domicile—a small town in southern Indiana. A few million more letters and packages are sent to the local postmaster with the request that they be stamped with the **Santa Claus, Indiana,** postmark before being sent on to their final destinations. Pretty heady stuff for a town with a population of about 500, give or take a few elves.

Although the town has borne its unusual name since 1852, it became world-famous only after Robert Ripley featured it in his *Believe It or Not* column in 1929. Such a hullabaloo followed that the annual Town Christmas Party had to be rescheduled for early October, when there was time to deal with such things. Today the **Santa Claus Post Office,** whose stone front resembles a castle, probably gets more visitors than any other post office in the country. Folks can't believe the stacks of mail they see there each year just before Christmas.

Elsewhere there's a city park where a 22-foot-tall statue of the jolly old man gazes down on the "little people of the world" to whom he is dedicated. Another Santa image sits atop a candy-striped water tower. The names of just about everything contribute to the aura of fantasy—Silver Bell Terrace, Donner Lane, Sled Run, Lake Rudolph, Lake Holly, Lake Noel, the Snowflake Drive-in, the Christmas Lake Village housing development, and a newspaper called *Santa's Country*. Some town shops carry out the Christmas theme in their architecture, and Santa Claus Land opened in 1946 as the first theme park in the nation.

Santa Claus Land has since been renamed **Holiday World,** but it still has all the attractions that endeared it to countless children—and adults—in the past. Santa's headquarters are there, of course, as are lots of toys; the animal farm where Santa's reindeer rest up for their arduous Christmas Eve journey; a variety of live musical, magical, and trained animal shows; a wax museum (the Hall of Famous Americans); antique toy and doll museums; a country music show; and a bevy of rides. Among them are the Raven, selected in 2003 as the best wooden roller coaster in the world, and the Legend, voted the fifth-best. The park's newest coaster, the Voyage, opened in 2006; some sixty people from the Roller Coaster Club of Great Britain arrived at the gate at 6:00 A.M. on the day the park opened for the season so they could be among the first to try it out. The 1.2-mile-long coaster, the third longest in the world, is part of a park expansion that features a Thanksgiving theme. ***Splashin' Safari,*** the park's seventeen-acre water park, was named the world's second-best water park, and the Zinga was named the world's best water-park ride. Additionally, as of 2006, visitors have named Holiday World number one in friendliness for eight consecutive years and in cleanliness for six consecutive years. The park generally adds one new ride a year to its water park. In 2006 it was the Bahari River, a 1,100-foot-long action river that includes a canyon with a waterfall and spray tunnels. A seven-story water slide with four-passenger tubes and tight turns will debut in 2007, along with a new cafeteria-style restaurant in the Thanksgiving section that will offer turkey dinners.

The one-price admission, extremely reasonable by today's standards, includes all rides, all shows and attractions, an unlimited amount of free soft drinks and coffee, free sunscreen, free inner tubes in the water park, and free parking. In general, Holiday World is open from 10:00 A.M. to dusk daily mid-May to mid-August, on weekends from mid-August through Labor Day weekend, and on most Saturdays the rest of September. Splashin' Safari usually opens at 11:00 A.M. and closes at 7:00 P.M. Holiday World may also be open on weekends from late November through the last weekend before Christmas. Because hours vary from year to year, it is best to request a schedule in advance. Write Holiday World, P.O. Box 179, Santa Claus 47579; call (812) 937–4401 or (877) 463–2645; or visit www.holidayworld.com. Santa Claus, the village, is located at the junction of State Roads 162 and 245 in the north central part of the county.

Spencer County's second famous resident is immortalized in the pages of history books. When people think of Abraham Lincoln, they usually think of the state of Illinois, but it was in Indiana that young Abe went to school, worked the land, and grew to manhood. Abe's father, Thomas Lincoln, brought his small family here in 1816 and homesteaded 160 acres along the banks of Little Pigeon Creek. Indiana was a wilderness then, a forest of giant oaks, maples, and hickories where open views of even 200 yards were rare. Lincoln himself described it thus, in a poem he wrote many years after leaving the state.

> *When first my father settled here*
> *'Twas then the frontier line.*
> *The panther's scream filled the night with fear,*
> *And bears preyed on the swine.*

In 1818, when Abe was nine and his sister Sarah was eleven, their beloved mother died, and little more than a year later a lonely Thomas married Sara Bush Johnston. A widow with three children, she raised Abe and Sarah as though they were her own, lavishing love and affection on them. She recognized the intimations of future greatness in young Abe and encouraged him to study, and Abe, on his part, loved her as few children love even their natural parents. When an adult Abe said, "All that I am, or hope to be, I owe to my angel Mother," he was speaking of his stepmother.

Lincoln left Indiana when he was twenty-one and moved to Illinois with his family, but his tenure in Spencer County is honored in a series of memorials. The **Lincoln Boyhood National Memorial** is next door to Lincoln State Park on State Road 162, just south of Lincoln City. Abe's biological mother, Nancy Hanks Lincoln, is buried at the memorial, and her grave and the reconstructed Lincoln cabin can be visited in this 200-acre park. A living-history farm that covers eighty acres of the Lincolns' original homestead is worked as Abe and his father once worked it and provides a fascinating, accurate insight into a way of life that shaped one of our nation's greatest men.

At the handsome visitor center, you can view exhibits related to Lincoln's fourteen years in Indiana and see a twenty-seven-minute film about his life. You can also learn much about the human side of Lincoln, little-known facts that breathe life into the saintly image. Young Abe, for instance, loved to wrestle and was recognized as one of the area's best tusslers. His great physical strength earned him the nickname "young Hercules of Pigeon Creek," and he could hoist more weight and drive an ax deeper than any other man around. In 1828 his horizons widened greatly when he accompanied the son of the richest man in the community on a flatboat journey down the Ohio and Mississippi Rivers to New Orleans. And one can only speculate how the course of history might have differed had Abe grown up in Kentucky, where slavery was legal. The national memorial is open 8:00 A.M. to 5:00 P.M. daily year-round, except major winter holidays; there's a nominal admission fee. Costumed interpreters work the farm from mid-April through September. Write the Lincoln Boyhood National Memorial, National Park Service, P.O. Box 1816, Lincoln City 47552; call (812) 937–4541; or visit www.nps.gov/libo.

The adjacent *Lincoln State Park,* which covers nearly 1,800 acres, includes the grave of Lincoln's sister, who died in childbirth; the site of the Little Pigeon River Primitive Baptist Church, where the Lincoln family worshiped; and the site of the first school attended by Abe, who was eleven years old at the time. You'll find many opportunities here for outdoor recreation, as well as campsites and housekeeping cabins. Open daily year-round, during daylight hours; nominal vehicle admission fee is charged from spring through fall. Write or call Lincoln State Park, State Road 162, P.O. Box 216, Lincoln City 47552; (812) 937–4710.

If you visit here in April through October, you may want to include a visit to the nearby *Colonel William Jones State Historic Site,* where you'll see the restored 1830s home of a merchant and Civil War soldier who was a friend of Lincoln's. Situated on one hundred acres of forest, it also offers a self-guided nature trail, a picnic area, and a restored log barn. It's located at 620 East County Road 1575 North in *Gentryville.* Open free of charge (donations are appreciated) from 9:00 A.M. to 5:00 P.M. Wednesday through Saturday and 1:00 to 5:00 P.M. Sunday, mid-March through mid-December. Additional information is available at Lincoln State Park or by writing Jones House State Historic Site, Route #1, Box 60D, Gentryville 47537; call (812) 937–2802.

On the banks of the Ohio River just west of Troy, the *Lincoln Ferry Landing State Wayside Park* on State Road 66 preserves another historical segment of Abe's life. Here, as an employee of a local farmer, sixteen-year-old Abe operated a ferry across the mouth of Anderson Creek, a tributary of the Ohio now called Anderson River. To increase his income, Abe built himself a scow to carry passengers to Ohio River steamboats in midstream. His first experience with the legal profession came when he was hauled into a Kentucky court for ferrying passengers on the Ohio without a license (the Ohio River was considered part of Kentucky). Lincoln pleaded his own case, stating that he didn't believe the law applied to a ferryman who went only halfway across the river. Agreeing with him, the judge dismissed the case. Abe's fascination with the law began with that encounter.

Following State Road 66 west along the banks of the Ohio, you come to *Rockport,* where the *Rockport Inn* offers one of the most unusual lodging experiences in southern Indiana. This tiny hostelry, originally built as a private residence around 1855, contains just six bedrooms. No two bedrooms are alike, but each has air-conditioning and a private bath. Thoroughly renovated with painstaking care, the building retains as much of the original aura and design as the owners could achieve. Early-twentieth-century furnishings throughout contribute to the overall effect. Open year-round, the moderately priced inn serves meals in its full-service restaurant. A continental breakfast is included in the room rates. Lunch is offered Tuesday through Saturday and dinner Wednesday through Saturday. There's also a Saturday brunch, but no meals are served on Sunday or Monday. Write or call the Rockport Inn, 130 South Third Street, Rockport 47635; (812) 649–2664.

Also in Rockport is *Lincoln Pioneer Village and Museum.* Although the fourteen log cabins are reconstructions, they reflect the lifestyle of Lincoln's boyhood years, and you can learn more interesting facts about our sixteenth president in the adjacent museum. Located at 222 South Third Street in Rockport City Park, the village is open by appointment. Write or call the Friends of Lincoln Pioneer Village, 317 Main Street, Rockport 47635; (812) 649–9147.

Sullivan County

The town of *Dugger* was built because of coal, laid out in 1879 in conjunction with the construction of the adjacent Dugger Coal Mine. To celebrate their heritage, the townsfolk established the *Dugger Coal Museum* in 1980. Visitors to the small but informative museum will see working mining equipment and learn how it has evolved through the years. Such artifacts as battered and scarred miners' hats bear mute testimony to the hardships endured by men who work at what has been described by many as the most dangerous job on earth. The history of the region has been further documented in the hundreds of photos, newspaper clippings, and scrapbooks on display. Each September the town hosts a weeklong *Dugger Coal Festival.* The museum is located next to the post office at 8178 East Main Street. Hours vary according to the availability of volunteers. If the museum should be closed when you arrive, you may call (812) 648–2381 or one of the phone numbers posted on the door, and a volunteer will be happy to come and let you in. For additional information write or call Cinda May at the Cunningham Memorial Library, Indiana State University, Terre Haute 47809; (812) 237–2534. Ms. May has been awarded a grant to document coal mining activities in west central Indiana.

Vanderburgh County

If architecture is your cup of tea, you'll want to tour two aesthetic treats in *Evansville.* The *John Augustus Reitz Home* at 224 Southeast First Street was erected in 1872 when Evansville was the hardwood capital of the country and Reitz was the "pioneer lumber king." Encircled by a black wrought-iron fence, the French Imperial house boasts three stories, seventeen rooms, ten fireplaces, and a display of Victorian-era opulence in the parquet floors, gilded bronze chandeliers, stained-glass windows, pier mirrors, gold-leaf cornices, and rare carved woods. Some of the first-floor ceilings are canvas, hand-painted in oil to match the original rugs. All heating units were turned on their sides and placed under the floor so that the radiators wouldn't show. The fireplaces were apparently for ornamentation only—they were never used. In the basement is a huge clothes dryer where clothes were hung on movable racks and dried by a gas heater beneath them.

The Reitz home sits in a 17-block historic district amid other massive homes built by wealthy owners who spent a considerable part of their fortunes trying to outdo the next fellow, but the home of the pioneer lumber king is the most impressive showplace of them all. Now a museum, it's open to the public from 11:00 A.M. to 3:30 P.M. Tuesday through Saturday and 1:00 to 3:30 P.M. Sunday; there's a nominal admission fee. Special tours can be arranged by calling (812) 426–1871.

The **Old Courthouse** that dominates the Evansville cityscape, built between 1888 and 1891, is one of the grandest in the country. During its construction special excursion trains brought visitors from Louisville, St. Louis, and many other midwestern towns to admire what was then regarded as one of the most elegant buildings ever erected in the Midwest.

Its Indiana limestone face is encrusted with an unbelievable number of sculptures and stone carvings, some of heroic proportions, each intricately detailed—fourteen statues, national emblems, ornamental friezes, cherubs, innumerable garlands of flora indigenous to the area, and Indiana's state seal. Inside are marble floors and wainscots, oak woodwork, brass handrails, silver-plated hardware, domes, and an awesome rotunda.

Abandoned by the county government in 1969, the Old Courthouse now contains boutiques, art galleries, import shops, clothing stores, and a community repertory company. You'll find the magnificent old building at the corner of Fourth and Vine; it's open 8:00 A.M. to 5:00 P.M. Monday through Friday and 1:00 to 5:00 P.M. Saturday and Sunday. Guided tours are available by appointment. For additional information write or call the Evansville Convention and Visitors Bureau, 401 Southeast Riverside Drive, Evansville 47713; (812) 421–2200 or (800) 433–3025.

At **Wesselman Park** you'll find 210 acres of primeval woodland. A virgin forest is extremely rare, but this one is particularly unusual because it lies entirely within the limits of a city and is of such high quality (most stands of woodland in or near cities have been adversely affected by pollution). A melting pot of northern and southern botanical species, **Wesselman Woods** is dominated by sweet gum trees. Spring here is bright with the blossoms of dogwood and redbud trees and with the wildflowers that are at their feet; autumn is a blaze of color. At the edge of the woods is a nature center where one-way glass provides a unique view of wildlife activity and a microphone brings sound and song indoors.

The woods, designated both a state nature preserve and a National Natural Landmark, make up approximately half of Wesselman Park; the remaining 200 acres offer typical recreational facilities, including a swimming pool. Along the park's northern boundary is a remnant stretch of the old **Wabash and Erie Canal,** the longest ever built in this country. Only two boats ever traveled its entire 468-mile length from Evansville to Toledo, Ohio.

The park lies on the east side of Evansville at 551 North Boeke Road. Admission is free. The grounds are open daily year-round, from early morning until sunset. The nature center is open 8:00 A.M. to 4:00 P.M. Tuesday through Sunday, April through September; reduced hours October through March. Call (812) 479–0771.

Mound builder Indians, too, found this part of the country to their liking. Sometime around 1300, they built a village on the banks of the Ohio River southeast of Evansville and stayed there for about 200 years before moving on. The eleven mounds they abandoned in this spot constitute the largest and best-preserved group in the state. One, the central mound, covers more than four acres in area and measures 44 feet in height, making it one of the largest such structures in the eastern United States.

After years of archaeological excavations here, the 430-acre site was opened to the public as **Angel Mounds State Historic Site.** Visitors can view a life-size replica of an ancient Mississippian Indian village, a simulated excavation site, and many artifacts from the digs in a state-of-the-art interpretive center, then walk the trails that lead among the mounds and reconstructed buildings of the Indian village. The site is located at 8215 Pollack Avenue, 7 miles southeast of downtown Evansville. Admission is free. The site is open 9:00 A.M. to 5:00 P.M. Tuesday through Saturday and 1:00 to 5:00 P.M. Sunday, mid-March through mid-December; closed Easter and Thanksgiving. Call (812) 853–3956.

Vermillion County

Journalist Ernie Pyle wrote about World War II as experienced by the common foot soldier. His newspaper columns were read by millions, and his writings were compiled in several books. When his life was ended by a Japanese sniper in 1945, he was mourned by millions and eulogized by the President of the United States. Today veterans of that war are among the more than 16,000 visitors who come to Indiana each year to pay homage to the beloved correspondent at the *Ernie Pyle State Historic Site* in *Dana.*

A focal point of the site is the house in which Ernie was born in 1900, moved here in 1975 from its original location about 2 miles away. It is adjoined by an interpretive center that occupies two World War II military Quonset huts. They are filled to overflowing with memorabilia from every part of Pyle's life, from the cradle he slept in as a baby to his high-school report cards to the tattered wool jacket he wore when he had tea with Eleanor Roosevelt. Exhibits include re-created scenes from the war that Pyle wrote about so eloquently—Omaha Beach after D-Day, a Marine campsite in Okinawa that features a restored 1944 Willy's Jeep, and a soldier saying his last good-bye to his fallen captain, Henry T. Waskow. Pyle won a Pulitzer prize in 1944 for a column he wrote about Captain Waskow's death; a mannequin of the journalist sitting at his typewriter can be prompted by the touch of a button to read that famous column.

A 1945 movie, *The Story of G.I. Joe,* told Ernie Pyle's story. Pyle was played by Burgess Meredith, and Robert Mitchum, in the role that made him a star, played Captain Waskow. Years later, Pyle was also an inspiration for Charles Kuralt. Kuralt wrote that "Ernie Pyle was there first. He showed everybody else the way."

A sense of what Ernie Pyle meant to the soldiers of World War II can be gleaned from the fact that he is the only civilian who was allowed a burial plot in the National Memorial Cemetery of the Pacific in Honolulu, Hawaii. More than 33,000 veterans are buried there, but to this day more people request directions to Pyle's gravesite than to any other.

trivia

The world's largest and our country's first manufacturer of compact discs is Digital Audio Disc Corporation in Terre Haute. When it opened in 1984, it produced 300,000 discs per month; in 2003, the company produced more than three billion CDs and DVDs.

The homestead and interpretive center are located at 120 West Briarwood Avenue in Dana; (765) 665–3633. Open 9:00 A.M. to 5:00 P.M. Wednesday through Saturday and 1:00 to 5:00 P.M. Sunday, April through November; closed Easter and Thanksgiving. Hours may vary. A nominal admission fee is charged.

Not far north of Dana, the *Colonial Brick Company* in *Cayuga* makes bricks the old-fashioned way. It is the only firm in the country producing bricks in coal-fired beehive kilns. Because the antique process it employs allows Colonial to manufacture bricks in small runs and different shapes and colors that match historical brick, the company is in great demand for restoration projects. Visitors who take a free tour will see a fascinating and unique manufacturing process. Located at 817 West Park Street; call (765) 492–3355 to make a tour reservation.

Vigo County

The ocean came to the Hoosier State in 1993. That was when Morgan Lidster, with the help of his father, Richard, opened the doors to *Inland Aquatics* in *Terre Haute.* Begun as a part-time business in a 400-square-foot facility, it has grown into a full-time enterprise that now occupies 13,000 square feet.

Inland Aquatics breeds fish and corals in a 40,000-gallon hatchery that is the world's largest. What makes its products unique is a patented scrubber system developed at the Smithsonian Institution's Marine Systems Laboratory that emulates what the ocean does—it cleans itself. The self-sustaining aquariums sold by Inland Aquatics allow customers to enjoy a little piece of the ocean

The Bottle Known 'Round the World

Until 1915 Coca-Cola was sold in flat-sided bottles. That was the year the Coca-Cola Company began bottling its product in the curvy bottle now recognized around the world.

It all started with the soft drink company's desire to market a product unique in taste in a container unique in shape. A nationwide campaign was launched for a design that would let customers know instantly what they were holding, even in the dark.

The company that came up with the winning design was the Root Glass Company of Terre Haute, whose answer to Coke's quest was a bottle shaped like an encyclopedia drawing of a cocoa bean pod.

In 1950 a bottle of Coke became the first consumer product to be featured on the cover of *Time* magazine, elevating it to national icon status. In 1994 the state of Indiana placed a marker alongside U.S. Highway 41 in Terre Haute that officially recognizes the historic event. The marker reads in part: BIRTHPLACE OF THE COCA-COLA BOTTLE, THE WORLD-FAMOUS TRADEMARK CREATED IN 1915 ON THIS SITE AT ROOT GLASS COMPANY.

In 1994 the Coca-Cola Company returned to Terre Haute to test market a new container for its soft drink—a twenty-ounce plastic bottle contoured like its original glass bottle. In 1997 the company once again came to Terre Haute to market another new container—a twelve-ounce can with curves. A spokesperson for the company said it chose Terre Haute because it was the place in which Coke's curves were born.

Pay as You Go

When restrooms were installed at the Terre Haute railroad station in 1910, they became an attraction for curious tourists and townspeople. Indoor restrooms were a novelty at the time. So many people came to see them that passengers on incoming trains, for whom the restrooms were intended, couldn't get in to use them.

The stationmaster came up with an ingenious solution. He installed nickel-operated locks on the toilets to discourage their use by nonpassengers. When a train arrived, he would temporarily remove the locks because toilet privileges were included in the price of a train ticket.

Thus Terre Haute gained the unique distinction of having the first pay toilets in the country.

in their homes without a need for water changes, artificial filters, or chemical treatments. Visitors to the retail showroom will see a 225-gallon tank with a miniature reef and corals and fish living in water that hasn't been changed in more than five years.

trivia

The real creator of the expression "Go West, young man!" was John B. L. Soule, who coined the phrase in an 1854 editorial in the *Terre Haute Wabash Express*. Horace Greeley denied authorship but is still generally credited with the quote.

Inland Aquatics is a multifaceted business that includes a retail store filled with forty-gallon saltwater tanks, a gift shop, custom-designed aquariums, a classroom for educational programs, and the aquariums and production tanks of the hatchery.

Lidster describes a visit to his facility as being like "dry snorkeling." Visitors can view unusual marine animals and rare corals just as they would see them in the ocean—without ever getting wet. His business draws customers from around the globe, including aquarium hobbyists and representatives from museums and zoos.

Inland Aquatics is located at 10 Ohio Street; hours are noon to 7:00 P.M. Tuesday through Saturday and noon to 6:00 P.M. Sunday. Guided tours are available; call (812) 232–9000 or visit www.inlandaquatics.com for additional information.

Bibliophiles and intellectuals will find the ***Cunningham Memorial Library*** on the campus of Indiana State University in Terre Haute of special interest. It houses what is said to be the world's largest collection of old and rare dictionaries—more than 12,000 volumes dating back to 1475 that represent the entire history of Western lexicography. Among them are more than 200 editions and issues of Samuel Johnson's *A Dictionary of the English Language.* Known as the **Cordell Collection,** it grew from an initial donation of 500 dictionaries by Warren Cordell, an ISU alumnus and executive with Nielsen's television-rating firm. The collection, located in the library's Rare Books and Special Collections section on the third floor, is open free of charge throughout the year. Hours vary; call (812) 237–2580.

trivia

The largest U.S. flag ever made was produced at Anchor Industries in Evansville and was donated to the federal government in 1983. Comparable in size to one and a half football fields, the polyester flag weighed seven tons and measured 210 feet by 411 feet. Each star stretched 13 feet from tip to tip, and each stripe was 16 feet wide.

Warrick County

First settled in 1803, **Newburgh** perches picturesquely on the banks of the Ohio River. Footpaths lead along the riverbank, with views that include the Newburgh Locks and Dam. River traffic passing through these locks carries more tonnage than passes through the Panama Canal. The town contains some lovely restored homes, and a 4-square-block section in the downtown area is on the National Register of Historic Places. For additional information write or call Historic Newburgh, Inc., 9 West Jennings Street, Newburgh 47630; (812) 853–2815 or (800) 636–9489. Historic Newburgh's office is open 10:00 A.M. to 4:00 P.M. Monday through Friday and noon to 4:00 P.M. Saturday.

Places to Stay in Southwest Indiana

BLOOMINGTON

The Grant Street Inn
310 North Grant Street
(812) 334–2353 or
(800) 328–4350
Moderate

**Indiana Memorial
Union Hotel at
Indiana University**
900 East Seventh Street
(812) 856–6381 or
(800) 209–8145
Moderate

Scholars Inn
801 North College Avenue
(812) 332–1892 or
(800) 765–3466
Moderate

The Wampler House B&B
4905 South Rogers Street
(812) 824–2446 or
(877) 407–0969
Moderate

BRISTOW

**Mary Rose Herb Farm
and Retreat**
23112 Cattail Road
(812) 357–2699
Moderate

CLINTON
Pentreath House
424 Blackman Street
(765) 832–2762
Moderate

DERBY
Ohio River Cabins
13445 North State Road 66
(812) 836–2289
Moderate

EVANSVILLE
Starkey Inn Bed and Breakfast
214 Southeast First Street
(812) 425–7264 or
(800) 580–0305
Moderate

FRENCH LICK
Lane's Motel
8483 West State Road 56
(812) 936–9919
Inexpensive

Patoka Lake Village
Log Cabin Rentals
7900 West County Road
1025 South
(812) 936–9854 or
(888) 324–5350
Moderate

GREENCASTLE
College Inn
315 South Bloomington
Street
(765) 653–4167
Inexpensive

The Walden Inn
2 Seminary Square
P.O. Box 490
(765) 653–2761
Moderate

JASPER
Powers Inn B&B
325 West Sixth Street
(812) 482–3018
Inexpensive

LEAVENWORTH
Leavenworth Inn
930 West State Road 62
(812) 739–2120 or
(888) 739–2120
Moderate

MARSHALL
Turkey Run Inn at Turkey Run State Park
8102 East Park Road
(765) 597–2211 or
(877) 500–6151
Moderate

MONTGOMERY
Gasthof Village Inn
County Road 650 East
P.O. Box 60
(812) 486–2600
Moderate

NASHVILLE
Abe Martin Lodge and Cabins at Brown County State Park
1810 State Road 46 East
P.O. Box 547
(812) 988–4418 or
(877) 265–6343
Moderate

Allison House Inn
90 South Jefferson Street
P.O. Box 1625
(812) 988–0814
Expensive

Always Inn Bed and Breakfast
8072 State Road 46 East
(812) 988–2233 or
(888) 457–2233
Moderate

Artists Colony Inn
Franklin and
Van Buren Streets
P.O. Box 1099
(812) 988–0600 or
(800) 370–5168
Moderate

Green Valley Lodge
692 State Road 46 West
(812) 988–0231 or
(800) 205–8369
Moderate

Hickory Shades Motel
5714 State Road 46 West
(812) 988–4694
Inexpensive

McGinley's Vacation Cabins
P.O. Box 386
(812) 988–7337 or
(877) 229–6637
Moderate

Olde Magnolia House
213 South Jefferson Street
(812) 988–2434 or
(877) 477–5144
Moderate

Rawhide Ranch
1292 State Road 135 South
(812) 988–0085 or
(888) 947–2624
Moderate

The Seasons Lodge
560 State Road 46 East
(812) 988–2284 or
(800) 365–7327
Moderate

PAOLI
Big Locust Farm B&B
3295 West County Road
25 South
(812) 723–4856 or
(877) 875–7150
Moderate

Underwood Inn B&B
405 North Gospel Street
(812) 723–4639
Moderate

ROCKVILLE

Billie Creek Inn
U.S. Highway 36 East
(765) 569–3430
Moderate

Knoll Inn B&B
317 West High Street
P.O. Box 56
(765) 569–6345 or
(888) 569–6345
Moderate

Miss Anna's Bed and Breakfast
514 North College Street
(765) 569–5660
Moderate

SPENCER

Canyon Inn at McCormick's Creek State Park
State Road 46 East
(812) 829–4881 or
(877) 922–6966
Moderate

TASWELL (PATOKA LAKE)

White Oak Cabins and B&B
2140 North Morgan Road
(812) 338–3120
Moderate

TERRE HAUTE

Farrington Bed and Breakfast
931 South Seventh Street
(812) 238–0524
Moderate

UNIONVILLE

Red Rabbit Inn
9200 East State Road 45
(812) 330–1216
Expensive

VINCENNES

The Harrison Inn Bed and Breakfast
902 Buntin Street
(812) 882–3243
Moderate

Places to Eat in Southwest Indiana

BLOOMINGTON

The Bakehouse
125 North College Avenue
(812) 331–6029
Inexpensive
Deli/pizza

Bear's Place
1316 East Third Street
(812) 339–3460
Inexpensive
American/pizza

Grazie!
106 West Sixth Street
(812) 323–0303
Inexpensive
Italian

The Irish Lion
212 West Kirkwood Avenue
(812) 336–9076
Moderate
Irish

La Torre
1155 South College
Mall Road
(812) 336–5339
Inexpensive
American

The Laughing Planet Cafe
322 East Kirkwood Avenue
(812) 323–2233
Inexpensive
Healthy fast food/vegan

Lennie's Restaurant
1795 East Tenth Street
(812) 323–2112
Moderate
Italian/American

Le Petit Cafe
308 West Sixth Street
(812) 334–9747
Moderate
French country

Limestone Grille
2920 East Covenanter Drive
(812) 335–8110
Moderate
Upscale American

Macri's Deli
1221 South College
Mall Road
(812) 333–0606
Inexpensive
American

Malibu Grill
106 North Walnut Street
(812) 332–4334
Moderate
American

Mother Bear's
1428 East Third Street
(812) 332–4495
Moderate
Pizza/Italian

Opie Taylor's Burger Works
110 North Walnut Street
(812) 333–7287
Inexpensive
American

The Peach Garden
536 South College Avenue
(812) 332–3437
Inexpensive
Chinese buffet

Puccini's
420 East Fourth Street
(812) 333–5522
Moderate
Italian/tapas

Samira's Restaurant
100 West Sixth Street, #1
(812) 331–3761
Moderate
Afghan/Mediterranean

BOONVILLE

Lee's Garden
966 West Main Street
(812) 897–5420
Inexpensive
Chinese

Locust Street Cafe
118 West Locust Street
(812) 897–4724
Inexpensive
American

DALE

Windell's Cafe
6 West Medcalf Street
(812) 937–4253
Inexpensive
Home cooking

SOURCES FOR ADDITIONAL INFORMATION ABOUT SOUTHWEST INDIANA

**Clinton/Vermillion County
Chamber of Commerce**
1302 North Ninth Street
Clinton 47842
(765) 832–3844

Crawford County Tourism Center
6225 East Industrial Lane
Suite A
Leavenworth 47137
(812) 739–2246 or (888) 846–5397

Daviess County Visitors Bureau
1 Train Depot Street
Washington 47501
(812) 254–5262 or (800) 449–5262

**Evansville/Vanderburgh County
Convention and Visitors Bureau**
401 Southeast Riverside Drive
Evansville 47713
(812) 421–2200 or (800) 433–3025

**Historic Newburgh, Inc.
(Warrick County)**
9 West Jennings Street
Newburgh 47630
(812) 853–2815 or (800) 636–9489

Lawrence County Visitors Center
533 West Main Street
Mitchell 47446
(812) 849–1090 or (800) 798–0769

**Lincoln Hills/Patoka
Lake Recreation Region**
125 South Eighth Avenue
Cannelton 47520
(812) 547–7028

**Linton-Stockton Chamber of
Commerce (Greene County)**
159 First Street Northwest
P.O. Box 208
Linton 47441
(812) 847–4846

**Martin County Chamber of
Commerce/Tourism Commission**
Route 3, Box 37a
Loogootee 47553
(812) 295–4093

**Monroe County Convention and
Visitors Bureau**
2855 North Walnut Street
Bloomington 47404
(812) 334–8900 or (800) 800–0037

**Mount Vernon/Posey County
Chamber of Commerce**
915 East Fourth Street
Mount Vernon 47620–0633
(812) 838–3639

EVANSVILLE

Canton Inn Restaurant
947 North Park Drive
(812) 428–6611
Moderate
Chinese

Dogtown Tavern
6201 Old Henderson Road
(812) 423–0808
Moderate
American

Hacienda Restaurant
990 South Green River Road
(812) 474–1635
Inexpensive
Mexican

Hilltop Inn
1100 Harmony Way
(812) 422–1757
Inexpensive
American

Jacob's Pub and Restaurant
4428 North First Avenue
(812) 423–0050
Moderate
American

Nashville-Brown County Convention and Visitors Bureau
10 North Van Buren Street
P.O. Box 840
Nashville 47448
(812) 988–7303 or (800) 753–3255

Orange County Convention and Visitor Bureau
8291 West Beechwood Avenue
French Lick 47432
(812) 936–3418 or (877) 422–9925

Parke County Convention and Visitors Bureau
127 South Jefferson Street
P.O. Box 165
Rockville 47872
(765) 569–5226

Perry County Convention and Visitors Bureau
645 Main Street
Suite 200
Tell City 47586
(812) 547–7933 or (888) 343–6262

Putnam County Convention and Visitor Bureau
12 West Washington Street
Greencastle 46135
(765) 653–8743 or (800) 829–4639

Seymour/Jackson County Visitor Bureau
Tanger Outlet Center
357 Tanger Boulevard
Suite 231
Seymour 47274
(812) 524–1914 or (888) 524–1914

Spencer County Visitors Bureau
356 East Christmas Boulevard
Santa Claus 41579
(812) 937–4199 or (888) 444–9252

Spencer-Owen County Chamber of Commerce
205 East Morgan Street
Spencer 47460
(812) 829–3245

Terre Haute/Vigo County Convention and Visitors Bureau
643 Wabash Avenue
Terre Haute 47807
(812) 234–5555 or (800) 366–3043

Vincennes/Knox County Convention and Visitors Bureau
102 North Third Street
Vincennes 47591
(812) 886–0400 or (800) 886–6443

Jojo's Family Restaurant
3901 U.S. Highway 41 North
(812) 425–1486
Moderate
American

Old Mill Restaurant
5031 New Harmony Road
(812) 963–6000
Moderate
American

Shyler's Bar-B-Q
405 South Green River Road
(812) 476–4599
Moderate
Barbecue

Turonis Forget-Me-Not Inn
4 North Weinbach Avenue
(812) 477–7500
Moderate
American

Wolf's Bar-B-Que
6600 North First Avenue
(812) 424–8891
Moderate
Regional American

FERDINAND

Ferdy Flyer
133 West Tenth Street
(812) 367–2222
Inexpensive
American

Fleig's Cafe
905 Main Street
(812) 367–1310
Inexpensive
American

Homestead Pizza
1510 Main Street
(812) 367–1808
Inexpensive
Pizza

Oasis Restaurant
935 Main Street
(812) 367–1250
Moderate
American

GREENCASTLE

Almost Home
17 West Franklin Street
(765) 653–5788
Inexpensive
American

**A Different Drummer
(The Walden Inn)**
2 Seminary Square
(765) 653–2761 or
(800) 225–8655
Expensive
American

HAUBSTADT

Haub's House
Main and Haub Streets
(812) 768–6462 or
(800) 654–1158
Expensive
American

Nisbet Inn
6701 Nisbet Road
(812) 963–9305
Moderate
American

JASPER

Schnitzelbank Restaurant
393 Third Avenue
(812) 482–2640
Moderate
Traditional German

LINCOLN CITY

Buffalo Run Grill
3804 State Road 162
(812) 937–2799
Moderate
American

LINTON

The Grill
60 Northeast A Street
(812) 847–9010
Inexpensive
American

The Happy Greek Cafe
269 Northwest A Street
(812) 847–3444
Inexpensive
Greek/American

Stoll's Country Inn
State Road 54 West
(812) 847–2477
Moderate
American

LOOGOOTEE

**Stoll's Lakeview
Restaurant**
U.S. Highway 231 North
(812) 295–3299
Inexpensive
American/Amish

MILLTOWN

Blue River Cafe
128 West Main Street
(812) 633–7510
Moderate
American/vegetarian

NASHVILLE

Abe Martin Lodge
Brown County State Park
State Road 46 East
P.O. Box 547
(812) 988–4418 or
(877) 265–6343
Moderate
Country cooking

**Accent Dining Room at
The Seasons Lodge**
560 State Road 46 East
(812) 988–2284 or
(800) 365–7327
Moderate
American/home cooking

The Artists Colony Restaurant
Franklin and Van Buren Streets
P.O. Box 1099
(812) 988–0600 or
(800) 370–5168
Moderate
American

Gourmet Grille
Family Fun Center
216 South Van Buren Street
(812) 988–9490
Inexpensive
Sandwiches/salads/pizza

Hobnob Corner
17 West Main Street
(812) 988–4114
Inexpensive
American

Maldonado's
51 South Parkview
(812) 988–4535
Inexpensive
Mexican

The Ordinary
61 South Van Buren Street
(812) 988–6166
Moderate
American

Story Inn
6404 South State Road 135
(812) 988–2273 or
(800) 881–1183
Expensive
American/innovative

NEW HARMONY

The Main Cafe
508 Main Street
(812) 682–3370
Inexpensive
American

NEWBURGH

Edgewater Grille
7 East Water Street
(812) 858–2443
Moderate
American

The Homestead Restaurant
10233 West State Road 662
(812) 853–3631
Moderate

ROCKPORT

The Rockport Inn
130 South Third Street
(812) 649–2664
Moderate
American

SOLSBERRY

Rose's Diner
Route 1, Box 188
(812) 876–3181
Inexpensive
American

SPENCER

Chambers Restaurant
72 West Market Street
(812) 829–3022
Inexpensive
American

TELL CITY

Capers Restaurant
701 Main Street
(812) 547–3333
Moderate
American

TERRE HAUTE

Runyon's Black Angus
502 South Third Street
(812) 235–5549
Moderate
American

VINCENNES

Bill Bobe's Pizzeria
1651 North Sixth Street
(812) 882–2992
Moderate
Pizza

Charlie's Smorgasbord
630 Kimmel Road
(812) 882–5115
Inexpensive
American/buffet

WARRENTON

The Log Inn
Warrenton Road at
Old State Road
(812) 867–3216
Moderate
Country cooking

WASHINGTON

Black Buggy Restaurant
910 State Road 57 South
(812) 254–8966
Inexpensive
Amish

Knepp's Country Cafe
U.S. Highway 50 East
(812) 486–3545
Inexpensive
Amish

The New White Steamer
21 East Main Street
(812) 254–9973
Inexpensive

WORTHINGTON

Front Porch Steak House
118 North Canal Street
(812) 875–2306
Inexpensive
American

Index